Tourism in Frontier Areas

T0326513

Tourism in Frontier Areas

Edited by
Shaul Krakover and
Yehuda Gradus

LEXINGTON BOOKS
Lanham • Boulder • New York • Oxford

LEXINGTON BOOKS

Published in the United States of America
by Lexington Books
An Imprint of the Rowman & Littlefield Publishing Group
4720 Boston Way, Lanham, Maryland 20706

12 Hid's Copse Road
Cumnor Hill, Oxford OX2 9JJ, England

Published in cooperation with the
Negev Center for Regional Development
Ben-Gurion University of the Negev
Beer Sheva, Israel

British Library Cataloguing in Publication Information Available

Library of Congress Cataloging-in-Publication Data

Tourism in frontier areas / edited by Shaul Krakover and Yehuda Gradus.
    p. cm.
  Includes bibliographical references and index.
      ISBN: 978-0-7391-0287-9

    1. Tourism. 2. Regional planning. 3. Rural development. I. Krakover, Shaul, 1947- II.
Gradus, Y., 1942-

Printed in the United States of America

♾™ The paper used in this publication meets the minimum requirements of American
National Standard for Information Sciences—Permanence of Paper for Printed Library
Materials, ANSI/NISO Z39.48–1992.

Contents

Tables

Figures

Preface

This book contains a collection of articles, most of which have never before been published, dealing with a wide spectrum of issues related to tourism development in frontier areas. The term "frontier" is defined by Johnston (1981) as "an area at the margins of the integrated territory of a state, or any political unit, into which expansion may take place." In this respect "frontiers" is interchangeable with another frequently used term, "peripheries." Although these two terms may suggest different connotations—the former represents a situation while the latter refers to a state (Gradus, 1996)—authors in this volume were given discretionary freedom to entertain both issues and apply both terms according to the context of their particular research area. The term "frontier" was selected for the book's title to convey two meanings. It emphasizes the instrumental role of tourism as a vehicle for the development of frontier areas and peripheries. In addition, it implies that papers included in this volume represent the frontier of our knowledge on tourism in peripheral areas.

The conception of this book goes back to 1998, when a conference on the role of urban development as a challenge for frontier regions was held in Beer Sheva, Israel, organized by the Negev Center for Regional Development. Two sessions of this conference were devoted to the impact of tourism on the development of frontier areas. The contributions to the book, however, represent nine papers based on presentations made at the conference and another six papers recruited to embrace the breadth of tourism development in frontier areas.

Prior to the conference date, there were only a few authors who dealt directly with the development of tourism in frontier areas. In the early tourism literature, peripheral areas were considered as prime locations for tourism development (Christaller, 1963). Later it was realized (e.g., Diamond, 1977) that the road to peripheral area development through tourism is as yet unpaved. It was understood that tourists tend to flow to rather central destinations (Mansfeld, 1990). Although several authors have pointed out the long evolutionary process required for tourism to mature in remote areas (e.g., Miossec 1977; Krakover, 1985), it was only since the mid-1990s that exploration into the difficulties of the development of peripheral areas via tourism has gained weight (e.g., Hohl and C. A. Tisdell, 1995; Wanhill and Buhalis, 1999; for more bibliographical items see chapter 2 in this volume).

The fifteen chapters of this book are arranged in five parts, representing several frontiers in tourism development. "Part 1: Issues and Approaches," named after the first chapter, authored by Richard W. Butler, exposes the reader to various issues and approaches involved in the development of tourism in frontier areas. On the one hand, the tourism industry is potentially an easy branch to develop in peripheral regions due to low investment requirements, as well as myth and geographical appeal involved. On the other hand, the limited access to peripheral areas, their remoteness, and the time it takes to get there make it hard to attract the mass tourism necessary for service providers to stay in business. Krakover's chapter highlights the consequences associated with the partition of personal time budgets to time on site devoted for self-enjoyment vis-à-vis time en route required for reaching the peripheral tourist attraction. A simple model is constructed to show that the historical development of tourism resort areas in peripheral regions is related to changes in the ratio of personal time allocation. Kruger-Cloete raises the issue of the gap that persists between policy formulation and the actual delivery of tourism services. South African examples are used to demonstrate that appropriate policies are but a first step toward sustainable tourism development in frontier areas.

Parts 2 and 3 bring together several articles contemplating the economic feasibility of tourism development in frontier areas. While part 2 concentrates on economic activities, part 3 treats tourism attributes pertaining to rural peripheries. The chapter by Freeman and Sultan presents the results obtained in a Multiregional Input-Output (MRIO) model, wherein the economic contribution of the tourism sector to peripheral areas' development was estimated. The authors applied the model to the six regions of Israel and concluded that foreign tourists generate most of the derived output in the central regions, while domestic tourists have a proportionately higher impact in the outlying northern and southern regions.

Two chapters analyze potential contributions of the gambling industry to frontier areas. Goodovitch provides an international overview of the development of the casino industry and shows that casinos have undergone a periphery-to-core diffusion process. The international evolution of the gaming industry provides the background for the analysis of the Israeli debate over the legalization of casino houses, and addresses the economic and social impacts of these establishments. This is precisely the dilemma taken up by Felsenstein and Freeman, examining the socioeconomic cost involved in licensing casino houses on either or both sides of borders separating international entities. The worse case situation occurs when the positive economic benefits are harnessed by one entity while the negative social impacts affect its neighbor across the border.

Part 3 hones in on tourism frontiers in rural areas. Pizam and Upchurch examine and outline the complexities involved in training farmers to deal with the economic and bureaucratic needs of tourism operations in rural frontier regions in the United States. A closely related issue is taken up by Haber and Lerner. They examine the hardships facing small tourism ventures in peripheral areas. Pizam and Upchurch conclude that unless training and advisory assistance is provided, the rate of failure is likely to be high; Haber and Lerner found such assistance to be of lesser predictive value for rates of success than environmental attractiveness. In a different vein, Fleischer attempts to assess the economic value of rural agricultural land and landscapes for tourism in peripheral areas. The economic surpluses generated at three regions in Israel are compared. Fleischer concludes that farmers who are encouraged to reap the economic benefits of their agricultural land in terms of both farm production and tourism entrepreneurship are more likely to resist urban sprawl.

Part 4 points out that tourism frontiers can be found even in urban areas. As a matter of fact, many urban areas located in frontier regions struggle for a piece of the tourism industry. The three articles in this section present but a sample of problems and opportunities tourism offers to urban places located in frontier areas. Problems in terms of environmental, as well as mental, impacts are outlined by R. B. Singh in the case study of Himachal Himalaya in northern India. Opportunities of applying postmodern concepts for tourism program planning in the desert town of Yeruham, Israel are presented by Reichel and Uriely. The third chapter in this section, authored by Moreno, reflects the bureaucratic complexities impinging upon tourism development programs in the peripherally located central town of Beer Sheva. The intertwined power relationships of actors from local and central government agencies are highlighted.

Part 5 concentrates on the unique frontier features offered by borderlands. In our new age of diminishing boundary barriers between nations, borderlands—that used to be remote frontiers—pose new opportunities of cooperation, especially for the tourism industry. Timothy, for instance, argues that the traditional approach to regional economics is inadequate for some types of borderland tourism. Instead, the nature of the attraction base and the level of cooperation between sides determine whether or not a specific border region is complementary or competitive. Lew and Kennedy claim that the social and cultural differences that exist on the two sides of an Indian reservation's boundary, as reflected in the tourism sector, are as diverse as that found on any international border, and probably, in some instances, even greater. Hall's contribution, closing this section and the book, is an antithesis work. It reminds the reader that national parks and wilderness areas in Western societies symbolize remnants of constantly eroding frontiers. National parks may be interpreted as a physical boundary between invasive civilization and wild nature. Therefore, any clues as to the future direction of frontier tourism development need to be related to ideas of cultural change, as much as they are to notions of the economic periphery.

Most chapters in this collection are innovative and thought-provocative rather than having a modeling and quantitative orientation. The editors of the book believe that the breadth of views presented by the contributors and wealth of information compiled in the book will no doubt enrich the knowledge base of scholars in the fields of tourism studies, economic geography, and regional development.

Finally, the editors would like to thank the financial assistance of the Negev Center for Regional Development, as well as the Faculty of Humanities and Social Sciences at Ben-Gurion University of the Negev, Beer Sheva, Israel; the tedious assistance of our dedicated cartographer, Mr. Pieter Loupen; and our industrious typesetter, Ms. Margo Tepper-Schotz from the WordByte enterprise. Our thanks are also extended to Rowman & Littlefield Publishing Group for its permission to reproduce Butler's chapter from the book *Frontiers in Regional Development* (1996), edited by Y. Gradus and H. Lithwick. The current volume, *Tourism in Frontier Areas*, joins four previous books on frontier development prepared at the Center of Regional Development in Beer Sheva, Israel. Besides the aforementioned *Frontiers in Regional Development*, the three other books, published by Kluwer Academic Publishers, are *Developing Frontier Cities: Global Perspectives, Regional Contexts* (1999), edited by H. Lithwick and Y. Gradus; *Ethnic Frontiers and Peripheries* (1998), edited by O. Yiftachel and A. Meir (1998); and *The Arid Frontier*, edited by H. Bruins and H. Lithwick (1998).

Shaul Krakover & Yehuda Gradus
Beer Sheva, Israel

References

Christaller, W. 1963. Some considerations of tourism location in Europe: The peripheral regions—underdeveloped countries—recreation areas. *Papers, Regional Science Association*, 6:95–105.

Diamond, J. 1977. Tourism's role in economic development: The case re-examined. *Economic Development and Cultural Change*, 25:539–553.

Hohl, A. E., and C. A. Tisdell, 1995. Peripheral tourism: Development and management. *Annals of Tourism Research*, 22:517–534.

Krakover, S. 1985. Development of tourism resort areas in arid regions. In Y. Gradus ed., *Desert Development: Man and Technology in Sparselands*. Reidel: Dordrecht, pp. 271–284.

Mansfeld, Y. 1990. Spatial patterns of international tourist flows: Towards a theoretical framework. *Progress in Human Geography*, 14:372–390.

Miossec, J. M. 1977. Un modele de l'espace touristique. *Espace Geogrphique*, 6:41–48.

Gradus, Y. 1996. The Negev desert: The transformation of a frontier to a periphery. In Y. Gradus and G. Lipshitz eds., *The Mosaic of Israeli Geography*. Beer Sheva: Ben-Gurion University of the Negev Press, pp. 321–334.

Johnston, R. J. 1981. *The Dictionary of Human Geography*. Blackwell: Oxford, UK.

Wanhill, S., and D. Buhalis, 1999. Introduction: Challenges for tourism in peripheral areas. *International Journal of Tourism Research*, 1:295–297.

Part 1

Issues and Approaches

Chapter 1

The Development of Tourism in Frontier Regions: Issues and Approaches

Richard W. Butler

As tourism has grown throughout the world (WTO, 1993), one of the most noticeable characteristics of that growth has been the continuous thrust to the periphery, such that most, if not all, regions of the world are now touched by tourism and its effects. For many years, during the early period of mass tourism growth, development was focused in urban resorts primarily because of limitations of transportation, cost, and time (Peace, 1989; Shaw and Williams, 1994). In the last half century, increasing growth has taken place in rural or remote locations, as people, particularly in the developed Western nations from which the majority of tourists originate, have had the time and money to travel considerable distances for their vacations.

This freedom (in a spatial sense) has allowed them to overcome problems such as seasonality by traveling from their cold places of origin during the winter to warm destinations, and to escape the urban environments in which most of them live by visiting rural and remote areas and experiencing new physical and cultural environments. The results have not always been satisfactory for all concerned. Communities in destination regions are coming to appreciate that tourism brings with it problems as well as benefits (Mathieson and Wall, 1982), and tourists are becoming increasingly concerned that destination areas and their populations are not as untouched and welcoming as they may have been led to believe. An unfortunate but perhaps predictable response by the tourism industry and by many public-sector agencies has been to promote and develop new destinations even more remote than before. Thus, tourism development is now found in the Arctic (Keller, 1987), in remote Himalayan communities (Zurick, 1992), in the jungles of southeast Asia (Dearden and Harron, 1992), in the rain forests of the world (Wearing and Parsonon, 1991), in the Australian outback (Altman, 1988), and even in Antarctica (Boo, 1900; Lindberg, 1991).

Such trends have been fueled by tourists' increasing interest in natural environments, in traditional cultures, and in places that are truly different from their home situations (Cohen, 1994). The tourism industry has been quick to stimulate and encourage such trends—successfully—through the marketing of products such as ecotourism, adventure travel, and culturally sympathetic tourism (Farrell and Runyan, 1991; Wheeler, 1993). Partly as a result of these trends, remote and peripheral areas such as frontier regions have seen extensive development for tourism in recent decades. These regions, like islands, have a particular appeal to some types of people (Butler, 1993c), and for a long time have attracted visitors, albeit traditionally in small numbers, until recently. Their relative inaccessibility, the absence of much development, and the presence of few other tourists have all been additional attractions to many visitors. These characteristics inevitably mean that development of facilities for tourism on a large scale poses particular problems, one of the major ones being the potential loss of just those attributes of an area that made it attractive to tourism in the first place.

Frontier regions, again like islands, are often blessed with few natural resources, and may suffer the same problems of relative or absolute inaccessibility, a small or even nomadic population, and an insufficient market for successful conventional development, as well as weak political influence (Butler, 1993c; Wilkinson, 1994). Frontier regions also tend to suffer from being on the political periphery in absolute terms, which may be compounded by problems of security and also may be regarded as unimportant in anything but strategic terms. By definition, such regions are peripheral, at least to the mainstream of the countries to which they belong, and may very well be peripheral in terms of climate and environment, which increases the overall difficulty of development.

To tourists and other visitors, however, such characteristics may enhance the appeal of a region as a vacation destination. Attributes that emphasize the difference of a region to the origin of potential tourists are to be valued and maintained, despite the fact that they may pose difficulties and increase costs of development. It is of equal importance to maintain those attributes of a region that make it different from other tourist regions in order to maintain its competitiveness and appeal. This is much easier said than done, for as noted by many researchers, tourist destinations tend to evolve in common ways and often lose their distinctiveness as development takes place (Butler, 1980; Plog, 1973; Wolfe, 1966).

In order to achieve successful tourist development of a type and scale suitable for any frontier region, it is necessary to ensure that certain basic issues are resolved. First, local residents and decision makers must understand the nature and dimensions of tourism and of the development process that is likely to occur, and they must be willing to accept the changes that will inevitably take place. Second, the type and scale of tourism must be appropriate for the specific frontier region in which it is being developed, which requires that the limits of both the physical and socioeconomic environments be determined before any development option is selected and implemented. A third requirement is that control be maintained over the development of tourism with respect to both its dimensions and its nature, because tourism, perhaps to a greater extent than most economic activities, is capable of dominating marginal economics far more rapidly and comprehensively than is generally appreciated. Finally, integration with existing land uses and the resource base is essential for the long-term well-being of tourism and the other economic activities in the region (Butler, 1993a).

Frontiers and Tourism

Tourism is one form of economic activity found in many frontier regions, and indeed, it has often been one of the first forms of development in such areas. In many cases, however, tourism in frontier regions has often been characterized by the following qualities. It has existed on a very small scale, drawing in a consumptive form on the natural resources of the region, for example, wildlife for hunting. It has been elite in nature, at least as far as the participants were concerned, and has involved foreign rather than domestic travelers. It has left relatively few economic benefits, and it has not provided a very satisfactory base for employment or significant development (Butler, 1985; Kellan, 1993). In many cases also, such tourism has often been brief in duration, lasting only until the region has been permanently settled and could no longer be regarded as a frontier. Once industrial and agricultural development occurs, some, if not most, of the appeal of the region for tourism disappears, along with most of the tourists. They may be replaced with local residents in search of recreational and leisure opportunities, but in such a situation, of course, there is little new money coming into the region, and the primary economic appeal of tourism has therefore disappeared (Lundgren, 1989).

Myth

Frontiers, as noted above, have long held a fascination for travelers, a trait that may have its origins in past times when a tourist was an explorer, who sought out regions not previously visited (Cohen, 1994). The myth of the frontier has been a powerful one, and is still to be seen clearly today in advertisements relating to specific forms of tourism such as ecotourism and adventure travel (Dann, 1994). Here the traveler is made to feel that he or she is playing a role of the explorer, and a significant part of the marketing of the destination is that not every tourist can or would be able to get to the place. This is not a new phenomenon: at the end of the nineteenth century such advertising was common in North America for both the American West and the Canadian Rockies (Albers and James, 1988; Hart, 1983; Nash, 1994). The appeal of frontier regions has often been accentuated by the appeal of frontier individuals, in particular the cowboy in the American West and the canoe voyageur in the Canadian wilderness. In most recent times, this image has been revisited, as illustrated in the movie *City Slickers* (and before *Westworld*), while the frontier myth has also been apparent in other movies such as *Deliverance*, where the threatening nature of the hostile environment was mirrored in the local population. An area's image or myth as a frontier may, therefore, be an important aspect of its appeal as a potential tourist destination (Butler, 1990; Riley, 1994).

Geographical Appeal

The geographical reality of frontiers, that is, their peripheral location relative to the origin of most potential visitors, appears to have a similar appeal. While the friction effect of travel cost and travel time applies to tourist travel as well as other kinds of movement (Ball, 1991), there is considerable evidence that the effect of added travel costs (in terms of both time and money) is not as strong or as consistent in tourism, particularly in the cases of unique areas or destinations with unusual attributes or where the tourist has specific goals (Mark, 1981). To tourists who are "collecting" destinations, such regions represent attractions to be acquired almost regardless of location, difficulty or cost of access, and often even regardless of risk or hazard. Indeed, the more remote the location, the more valued it is as a collector's item. Where the destination also has features that are unique or rare, its potential value is considerably enhanced. Thus, for example, while Canadian Arctic regions are remote and relatively inaccessible, they also have the added appeal of a unique people (the Inuit) and several unique or rare animal species such as musk ox, narwhal, and polar bear. The tourist visitor to such a region not only has the satisfaction and prestige of being one of only a few people to visit a remote location, he or she also has the benefits of being a member of a similarly exclusive group to have seen rare or exotic wildlife or other special features (Wheeler, 1993).

Attitudes and Ethics

The unfortunate traditional attitude toward frontier development has given rise to the term "frontier ethic," implying the existence of a develop-at-any-cost mentality (Husbands, 1981) and a lack of concern for the ecological integrity of the region, and often for the well-being of its indigenous populations. There are many examples of this, including the "discovery" and subsequent development of the New World, and the North American attitude toward the western frontier (Nash, 1967) and then toward its northern frontier. Only in the last two or three decades has this attitude changed to some degree in North America, as witnessed by the appearance of the report of the Berger Commission on gas pipeline development in the Canadian Arctic, aptly titled *Northern Frontier Northern Homeland* (Berger, 1970).

The development ethic has ironically increased the appeal of frontier regions to many potential visitors, as they desire to see an area before it becomes transformed (Boo, 1990). Although the negative attitude toward the maintenance of the natural attributes and resources of frontiers may have changed in North America, it still exists in other parts of the world, for example Amazonia. Tourists interested in seeing such regions before they become developed are therefore responsive to tourist industry marketing, whether it be for ecotourism tours, culturally focused expeditions, or simply sightseeing excursions (Lindberg, 1991).

Political Aspects

The political nature of frontiers also adds an element of attraction for tourists in certain situation. While the possibility of actual danger to tourists resulting from a frontier region's political reality—its often unsettled state and the fact it may share a disputed border with another political unit— has little appeal to most tourists, the excitement of visiting a politically controversial area apparently does appeal to many tourists. "Checkpoint Charlie" and the Berlin Wall were major tourist attractions before the demise of communism, and the demilitarized zone between North and South Korea is still one of the heavily visited tourist sites in South Korea. A frontier region, especially where this may border on other states or disputed areas may, therefore, represent an attraction precisely because it is something that most people do not experience in their normal lives.

To governments, frontiers that are thinly populated or even unpopulated present a problem, since their emptiness could be viewed as reason enough for acquisition by unfriendly neighbors. One partial solution to this problem is to establish a regular pattern of tourist visitation from the host country and also from other friendly countries in such a manner that the host nation is able to demonstrate the occupation and development of the frontier region. The establishment of features such as national parks in remote or frontier areas is one way of encouraging tourism and establishing an internationally recognized presence. While the area of northern Ellesmere Island in the Canadian Arctic undoubtedly has sufficient attributes to justify the designation of a national park in this frontier region, there is little doubt that the region's unsettled aspect along with not entirely resolved territorial claim in the Arctic Ocean were factors in the Canadian government's decision to declare part of the area a national park in the 1980s. While tourist visitation is still extremely low and likely to remain so for the indefinite future, there is now both a physical presence in the area and evidence of development that did not exist before the establishment of the national park. While the post–1982 Falkland Islands may not be primarily politically inspired, such activity bolsters the British presence on the islands and marks them more strongly as part of the British realm of influence, if not possession.

Tourism Development Issues

Tourism has faced a number of difficulties: ignorance regarding the scope and complexity of tourism, divergent viewpoints and interests, and the evolutionary nature of tourist activity.

Knowledge

A major problem with the development of tourism in most locations is that public and private sector agencies alike are much better at promoting and developing tourism than they are at managing and controlling it. There are two main reasons this happens. One is the normal development focus of both types of agencies, neither of whom rarely look beyond the problem of attracting tourists and tourism development to a location. Most public sector tourism agencies have promotion, marketing, and development as their principle objectives, as Pearce (1993) notes in his book *Tourist Organizations.* The second is general ignorance of tourism. For many years the public sector in particular has ignored tourism, or if it did consider it at all, regarded it as an easy option for development that required little effort to start and less involvement once it had begun. Many Western governments relegate tourism to minor cabinet status if it is formally recognized at all. In reality, tourism is a very complex industry with many unusual characteristics compared to other forms of economic development, particularly with respect to its effects and its dynamics. One of the most characteristic features of tourism that makes it difficult to plan and manage is the high degree of fragmentation within the tourism industry, with elements operating at widely varying scales, often with very different, and even competitive goals. Within the same relatively small area, there may be representatives of multinational corporations targeting three very different markets: an elite international market that places a high premium on luxury and exclusivity; elements of mass tourism that cater to a large and relatively indiscriminate market to whom the location and its inherent attributes are relatively unimportant but price may be crucial; and elements of an elite national or international market that places primary emphasis on natural attributes, undisturbed environment, and a low level of development. Thus, internal disagreement within the tourism industry is potentially as high as disagreement between the tourism industry and other forms of economic activity.

There tends to be widespread ignorance over the dimension, the nature and the power of tourism, and difficulty over separating myths about tourism from reality (Butler, 1991). Few people seem aware that it is one of the largest, if not the largest, industries in the world (WTO, 1993), that it can exercise tremendous power and influence, and that it is far from homogeneous. There is a general inability to determine appropriate levels of development or the carrying capacity of destination areas (Saleem, 1994), and a similar inability to mange tourism and to control the scale and rate of development. Many of these problems may stem from an apparent ignorance or lack of appreciation of the fact that tourism does have impact (fig. 1.1), not only in positive economic terms but also in environmental and sociocultural terms, where the effects may not always be positive or easily reversible (Snaith and Haley, 1994; Whelan, 1991; Ziffer, 1989). There is insufficient appreciation of how extremely dynamic tourism is. It causes change and responds to change itself, and could well be regarded as part of the fashion industry, at least in the sense that it is subject to changes in fashion and taste. Finally, there is often a lack of unanimity—not only between the public and private sectors, but also between the different levels of the public-sector communities—over the nature, scale, and rate of development of tourism that is felt appropriate for a destination.

MYTHS	REALITIES
Tourism supplementary	Often dominant
Tourism complementary	Often competitive
Few demands	Specific demands
Low impacts	Scale/activity dependent
Local control key	May be inappropriate
Locals receptive	Locals may be unreceptive

Figure 1.1. Frontier Tourism: Myth and Realities

Viewpoints

It is important to recognize that there are a variety of viewpoints to consider when planning the promotion and development of tourism in a particular destination area (Brown and Giles, 1994). Tourism is not a homogenous phenomenon; it is composed of a wide variety of viewpoints about tourism that cannot be reconciled, it is highly unlikely that development will proceed smoothly, and it may well prove incompatible with one or more existing uses of the area.

One can note at least five sets of actors with potentially different preferences, desires, and goals with respect to tourism. In frontier regions such viewpoints may be much more obvious and problematic than in more developed areas. (1) The *economic and development* viewpoint is most commonly promoted by the private sector, by various levels of government, and by some local residents, mostly potential entrepreneurs. (2) A second common viewpoint is that of *environmental interests*, and those expressing such opinions are often nongovernmental organizations, perhaps specific branches of government, some local residents, and in some cases some tourists. (3) A third sector is related to *mental or spiritual beliefs*, and generally pertains to the attraction and qualities of a region as wilderness and a place for spiritual renewal. This viewpoint is particularly strongly held in North America, where the wilderness concept had its origins (Nash, 1967) and is commonly expressed by nongovernmental organizations, academics, and some locals. (4) A fourth viewpoint relates to *quality of life* in existing communities, normally in the context of anticipated undesirable changes resulting from tourism development. This is most often expressed by local residents and some local politicians; in a slightly different form it may be expressed by some tourists who feel the quality of the tourist experience is declining because of what they regard as over-development or inappropriate development. (5) Finally there is the *pleasure* viewpoint of the tourists themselves who are visiting a region, often at considerable expense, and who expect and demand an enjoyable experience and the ability to engage in specific activities in a preferred environment. Research has shown that the level of satisfaction of a tourist-recreational experience correlates strongly with the expectations of the visitors and their prior experience of that region (Manning and Ciali, 1980; Manning, 1985; Shelby and Heberlein, 1986).

In the case of small frontier areas such as Israel's Negev, additional viewpoints and requirements may be involved. For example, the issues of strategic importance for defense and training of military forces or of historical legacies may still influence policy formulation. In frontier and remote regions, where the permanent population may be thinly scattered or even nomadic and where government presence may not be strong, tourist-associated development may be highly visible and possibly controversial. For such development to be sustainable in the long term, it should be based on the natural resources of the area and compatible with the desires and preferences of local residents, while respecting the desires of the wider public. Because it is often extremely difficult to achieve such a goal, it is important that tourism be understood, and its effects anticipated and communicated, before development options are selected and alternatives foreclosed.

Dynamics of Tourism

Perhaps of prime importance among the other issues to be considered is that of change. Tourism is highly dynamic and evolves and changes constantly, according to the tastes of tourists, the whims of the market, political realities, foreign exchange rates, perceptions of destinations and appropriate activities, and a range of other social, cultural, and economic factors. Various theories and models have been proposed to illustrate the process of tourism development and change, some relating to the destination area itself (Butler, 1980; Miossec, 1977), some relating to the attitudes of locals toward tourists (Brown and Giles, 1994; Reisinger, 1994; Doxey, 1975). Models of tourism development do not normally focus on frontier or remote regions specifically, although a few refer to peripheral regions (Christaller, 1963) and to the pattern of tourist penetration into peripheral regions (Lundgren, 1989).

Almost all of the models, however, view tourism development as an evolutionary process (Butler, 1993b), although there is no unanimity of opinion about the nature or rate of such a process. This evolutionary nature of tourism means that tourism tends to take on a life of its own, particularly once development appears successful, and that it is difficult to manage and alter the process should this prove necessary, for example to redirect development or to alter the type of tourism in a destination. The images that tourists have of a destination tend to be based on impressions rather than hard information, and these appear to be difficult to change, at least in a positive manner (Gartner, 1993; Dann, 1994). Thus two things are important: that an appropriate image and development approach be selected before tourism is promoted and developed in a region, and that the image and nature of development remain compatible with the destination and its resources, environment, and population for a considerable period of time.

Policy Issues

Effective tourism development policy requires an ability to control the activity and to mediate among competing uses in the proposed region in order to achieve sustainability while meeting the needs of various communities.

Control

One of the most crucial issues with respect to policy for tourism development, in frontier regions in particular, is the issue of control and responsibility. For tourism to be successful in the long term, it is essential that there exist the ability to control tourism and that tourism development that does take place in a region be within the capability of the region to withstand change (fig. 1.2). Tourism, unlike many forms of economic activity, does not normally consume specific resources in the conventional sense. Most forms of tourism utilize the climate, the scenery, the ambiance, and the local population of a destination, and may also draw on the wildlife, vegetation, and water of the area, although normally in the case of the first two in a nonconsumptive manner. This is not to say that tourists have no impact on such resources, but rather that they do not consume them in the same manner, as for example, commercial fishing, forestry, or mining. This has often led governments to assume that tourism does not need specific controls on its development, except perhaps in protected areas such as national parks, and as a result has allowed the creation of what are generally regarded as poor examples of tourism development, for example, on the Costa Brava in Spain or in parts of Florida. In such areas, over-extensive or unsuitable development has threatened and in some cases ruined the natural attractions of the areas, reducing their general appeal for tourism (Pearce, 1989).

LONG-TERM OR SUSTAINABLE TOURISM IS DEPENDENT UPON A REGION'S	
Ability to Control Tourism	Ability to Withstand Tourism
Desire to control tourism	Environmental elements
Strategies/policies	Cultural elements
Institutional arrangements	Wildlife characteristics
Opportunity to implement	Geographical patterns

Figure 1.2. Long-Term or Sustainable Tourism Dependency Factors

It is essential that control be exercised over tourism since many of the re-sources on which it draws are common resources, often unvalued or under-valued in economic terms and often uncontrolled in the sense that no agency has responsibility for their overall well-being and continued existence. To achieve long-term sustainability, it is critical to have the ability and desire to control and manage tourism and to understand the capability of the area to withstand use and development. Without such control and responsibility, the common resources are liable to be overused, and the area will ultimately lose its inherent tourism appeal (Getz, 1983). Frontier regions are particularly vulnerable in this respect because they are generally physically further from government control, and they often suffer from what has been described above as a frontier mentality as far as development is concerned.

Balance

The allocation of resources to tourism requires a balance between the need to maintain the quality of the environment and other features on which tourism is based, the capability of the environment to sustain long-term tourist use, and the economic aspirations and needs of local and other levels of population. In most frontier regions, there are various forces acting to promote growth and other forces promoting or desiring limitations of development (fig. 1.3). Some of these are external influences and some internal, and it is the role of the policy to maintain a balance between these forces such that the region is able to fulfill the tourism role allocated to it without losing its appeal and without unnecessarily restricting other uses in the region.

Area attributes: Sensitive environment
                      Unique culture
                      Limited capacity for change

ELEMENTS EXERTING CONTROL		ELEMENTS ENCOURAGING GROWTH
Location		Frontier ethic
Climate		Government attitude
Lack of infrastructure		Absentee control
Short season	Policy	Uniqueness
Distance		Wildlife/scenery
Limited appeal		Fragmentation
Cost		Ecotourism/adventures
		Boom

Figure 1.3. Sustainability in Frontier Tourism

In terms of those forces influencing tourism growth in frontier regions, there are two primary sets. Internal influences include the inherent attributes of the region itself, such as its scenery, wildlife, and relative uniqueness. Other internal influences are the attitude toward development that is present in most frontier regions and the fragmentation of communities and interests of populations normally found in frontier regions. Among the external influences are the normal wish of the central government to see development in the frontier, and the probable heavily absentee or external nature of control over resources and development in such regions. Other factors include a global boom in the types of tourism likely to be attracted to frontier regions, such as ecotourism and adventure travel.

Of these influences acting as controls or restrictions upon tourism development, the most powerful factors appear to be the geographical location and physical characteristics of frontier regions themselves, which make such regions difficult to reach and travel in. Often in peripheral regions, the climate and environment may be hostile or unattractive to visitors, and the tourist season may be short. This works against economic development, because it is difficult in such a situation to obtain investment funds and an adequate rate of return on investment if tourists are few in number and only present for a short period. In addition, many frontier regions are characterized by limited infrastructure, such as transportation, accommodation, and other services.

---

1. Tourism is seen as desirable, but in dispersed form.
2. Tourism should only be developed in communities wishing and ready for it.
3. Primarily responsibility lies with the private sector, but incentives are needed for government
4. Free enterprise should rule and ventures should be allowed to succeed or fail.
5. An overall increase in tourism is desirable.
6. New forms of tourism in the area are desirable.
7. The goal is to establish tourism on a year-round basis.
8. Tourism numbers should be small in small communities.
9. Tourism should be built on unique resources and should minimize impacts on local society and environment.
10. Tourism should maximize involvement by and benefits to locals.

Figure 1.4. Policy Principles for Tourism Development

These forces and influences are illustrated in figure 1.3, with policy shown as the hinge or fulcrum on which critical issues such as the environment and the local culture are balanced. The translation of such issues into policy is illustrated in the policy directions taken by the government of the North West Territories of Canada with respect to the development of tourism in that frontier region (fig. 1.4).

Conclusions

On the one hand, frontier regions possess particular attributes that make them highly attractive to tourists and thus appropriate for tourism development; but on the other hand, much of the appeal of such regions to tourists is precisely because these regions are undeveloped, perhaps difficult to reach, and represent a challenge to the visitor in physical and/or cultural terms. Increasing general interest in the natural environment is reflected in the rapid growth of forms of nature tourism. Development has to be cognizant of this inconsistency or paradox and be sympathetic to the attributes of the frontier region if the type of tourism developed is to be compatible with the environment, the resources, the population, and other existing resource uses, and is to achieve long-term success (Butler, 1993a).

First, it must be recognized that it is essential not only to manage the supply side of tourism (i.e., the resources, infrastructure, and flow of capital) but also to manage and control the demand side of the equation (i.e., the number and type of tourists and the marketing of the region), which helps to shape that mix. Second, it must be recognized that tourism is not only part of the economic structure of a region but is also intimately involved with the area's ecological systems and the social-cultural framework of the region's population. This understanding needs to be incorporated into policy for the development of tourism and protection of those resources on which tourism depends. Finally, any long-term sustainable policy for tourism, whether in frontier regions or elsewhere, has to incorporate principals of equity and responsibility (Nelson, 1993).

Frontier regions are dynamic: few remain as frontiers forever, particularly in developed countries. Their appeal for tourism, therefore, may be transitory, but this is no justification to allow tourism development to be short-term and exploitive in nature. Sympathetic and appropriate planning before development can maintain and prolong the appeal of frontier regions and the values they embody for tourism and recreation without precluding other development options.

References

Albers, R., and W. James. 1988. Travel photography—A methodological approach. *Annals of Tourism Research,* 10:123–48.

Altman, J. C. 1988. *Aborigines, Tourism and Development: The Northern Territory Experience ANU.* Darwin: North Australian Research Unit.

Ball, A. 1991. *The Economics of Travel and Tourism.* London: Belhaven Press.

Berger, T. 1970. *Northern Frontier Northern Homeland.* Ottawa: Queens Printer.

Boo, E. 1990. *Ecotourism: The Potentials and the Pitfalls,* Vols. 1 and 2, Washington, D.C.: World Wildlife Fund.

Brown, G., and R. Giles. 1994. Coping with tourism: An examination of resident responses to the social impact of tourism. In A. V. Seaton ed., *Tourism: The State of the Art.* Chichester: Wiley.

Butler, R. W. 1980. The concept of a tourist area cycle of evolution and implications for management. *The Canadian Geographer,* 24:5–12.

———. 1985. The evolution of tourism in the Scottish Highlands in the 18th and 19th centuries. *Annals of Tourism Research,* 12:371–91.

———. 1990. The role of the media in influencing the choice of vacation destinations. *Tourism Recreation Research,* 15:45–53.

——. 1991. Tourism, environment and sustainable development. *Environmental Conservation,* 18:201–9.

——. 1993a. Integrating tourism and resource management: Problems of complementarity. In M. E. Johnston and W. Haider eds., *Communities, Resources, and Tourism in the North.* Thunder Bay: Lakehead University.

——. 1993b. Tourism—An evolutionary approach In J. G. Nelson, R. W. Butler, and G. Wall eds., *Tourism and Sustainable Development: Monitoring, Planning, Management.* Waterloo: University of Waterloo.

——. 1993c. Tourism development in small islands: Past influences and future directions. In D. G. Lockhart, D. Drakakis-Smith, and J. Schembri eds., *The Development Process in Small Island States,* London: Routledge.

Christaller, W. 1963. Some considerations of tourism location in Europe: The peripheral regions, underdeveloped countries, and recreation areas. *Papers of the Regional Science Association,* 12:95–105.

Cohen, E. 1994. Contemporary tourism, trends and challenges, sustainable authenticity or continued post modernity? In R. W. Butler and D. G. Pearce eds., *Change in Tourism: People, Places, Process.* London: Routledge.

——. 1979. Rethinking the sociology of tourism. *Annals of Tourism Research,* 6:18–35.

Dann, G. 1994. A socio-linguistic approach towards changing tourist imagery. In R. W. Butler and D. G. Pearce eds., *Change in Tourism: People, Places, Process.* London: Routledge.

Dearden, P., and S. Harron. 1992. Tourism and the hilltribes of Thailand. In B. Weiler and C. M. Hall eds., *Special Interest Tourism.* Toronto: Belhaven Press.

Doxey, G. 1975. A causation theory of visitor resident irritants: Methodology and research inferences. In *Impacts of Tourism* (Proceedings, 6th Travel and Tourism Research Association Conference, San Diego), Salt Lake City, Utah: Travel Research Association.

Farrell, B. H., and D. Runyan. 1991. Ecology and tourism. *Annals of Tourism Research,* 18:26–40.

Gartner, W. 1993. Image formation process. *Journal of Travel and Tourism Marketing,* 2:191–215.

Getz, D. 1983. Capacity to absorb tourism: Concepts and implications for strategic planning. *Annals of Tourism Research,* 10:239–63.

Government of the North West Territories. 1990. *Tourism: The Northern Lure.* Yellowknife: Ministry of Economic Development and Tourism.

Hart, E. J. 1983. *The Selling of Canada: The C.P.R. and the Beginnings of Canadian Tourism.* Banff, Alberta: Altitude Press.

Husbands, W. 1981. Centres, peripheries, tourism and socio-cultural development. *Ontario Geography,* 17:37–60.

Kellan, G. 1993. *Protected Places.* Toronto: Dundurn Press.

Keller, C. P. 1987. Stages of peripheral tourism development—Canada's northwest territories. *Tourism Management,* 8:20–32.

Lindberg, K. 1991. *Policies for Maximizing Nature: Tourism's Ecological and Economic Benefits.* Washington, D.C.: World Resources Institute.

Lundgren, J. 1989. Patterns. In G. Wall ed., *Outdoor Recreation in Canada.* Toronto: Wiley and Sons.

Manning, R. E. 1985. Crowding norms in backcountry settings: A review and synthesis. *Journal of Leisure Research,* 17:75–89.

Manning, R. E., and C. P. Ciali. 1980. Recreation density and user satisfaction: A further exploration of the satisfaction model. *Journal of Leisure Research,* 12:329–45.

Mark, D. 1981. On the positive relation between distance and attractivity in recreation travel: The example of birding. *Ontario Geography,* 17:83–90.

Mathieson, A., and G. Wall. 1982. *Tourism: Economic, Physical and Social Impacts.* London: Longman.

Miossec, J.-M. 1977. Un-modele de l'espace touristique. *L'espace Geographique,* 1:41–48.

Nash, D. 1994. An exploration of tourism as superstructure. In R.W. Butler and D. G. Pearce eds., *Change in Tourism: People, Places, Processes.* London: Routledge.

———. 1967. *Wilderness and the American Mind.* Baltimore: Johns Hopkins Press.

Nelson, J. G. 1993. An introduction to tourism and sustainable development with special reference to monitoring. In J. G. Nelson, R. W. Butler, and G. Wall eds., *Tourism and Sustainable Development: Monitoring, Planning, Management.* Waterloo: University of Waterloo Press.

Pearce, D. G. 1993. *Tourist Organizations.* London: Longman.

———. 1989. *Tourism Development.* London: Longman.

Plog, S. C. 1973. Why destination areas rise and fall in popularity. *Cornell Hotel and Restaurant Management Quarterly,* 13:13–16.

Reisinger, Y. 1994. Social contact between tourists and hosts of different cultural backgrounds. In A. V. Seaton ed., *Tourism: The State of the Art.* Chichester: Wiley.

Riley, R. W. 1994. Movie-induced tourism. In A. V. Seaton ed., *Tourism: The State of the Art.* Chichester: Wiley.

Saleem, N. 1994. The destination capacity index: A measure to determine the tourism carrying capacity. In A. V. Seaton ed., *Tourism: The State of the Art.* Chichester: Wiley.

Shaw, G., and A. M. Williams. 1994. *Critical Issues in Tourism.* Oxford: Blackwell.

Shelby, B., and T. A. Heberlein. 1986. A conceptual framework for carrying capacity determination. *Leisure Sciences,* 6:433–51.

Snaith, T., and A. J. Haley. 1994. Tourism's impact on host lifestyle realities. In A. V. Seaton ed., *Tourism: The State of the Art.* Chichester: Wiley.

Wearing, S., and R. Parsonon. 1991. Rainforest tourism. *Tourism Management,* 12:236–44.

Wheeler, B. 1993. Sustaining the ego. *Journal of Sustainable Tourism,* 1:21–29.

Whelan, T., ed., 1991. *Nature Tourism—Managing for the Environment.* Washington, D.C.: Island Press.

Wilkinson, P. F. 1994. Tourism and small island states: Problems of resource analysis, management and development. In A. V. Seaton ed., *Tourism: The State of the Art.* Chichester: Wiley.

Wolfe, R. I. 1966. Recreational travel: The new migration. *The Canadian Geographer,* 10:1–14.

World Tourism Organization (WTO). 1993. *WTO News.* Madrid: WTO, September–October.

Ziffer, K. A. 1989. *Ecotourism: The Uneasy Alliance.* Washington, D.C.: Conservation International.

Zurich, D. N. 1992. Adventure travel and sustainable tourism in the peripheral economy of Nepal. *Annals of the Association of American Geographers,* 82:608–28.

Reprinted by permission of author and publisher from *Frontiers in Regional Development,* edited by Yehuda Gradus and Harvey Lithwick, Rowman & Littlefield: Lanham, Maryland, pp. 213–229.

Chapter 2

Time Dimensions and Tourism Development in Peripheral Areas

Shaul Krakover

By definition, peripheries are separated from the populated cores both in terms of physical distance and the time required to travel to and from them. It is generally accepted that a major obstacle to the development of peripheral areas is their limited accessibility (Friedmann, 1966). However, while most studies and modeling of core-periphery relationships put a heavy stress on the distance dimension (Berry, 1972), very few, if any, give fair treatment to the time dimension. In this respect, not very much has changed since Carlstein, Parkes, and Thrift (1978:2) complained, "Time certainly did not evoke the same degree of enthusiasm as the other physical dimensions."

This work attempts to highlight the importance of the time dimensions in relation to tourism development in peripheral areas. It is argued in this chapter that tourists' personal considerations in relation to their own time budgets have a strong impact on the development of tourist resort areas. It will be pointed out that the options available for the allocation of personal time measured in hours are interrelated to peripheral resort area development through time measured in decades.

Thus, the major objective of this study is to substantiate the aforementioned argument concerning the crucial role of the utilization of personal time on the path to peripheral area tourism development. In order to achieve this objective, the study undertook a comprehensive review of time-related studies in geography in general and in tourism research in particular. Throughout this review, special attention was given to the specification of time in its two components: time *en route* on the one hand, and time *on site* devoted for self-enjoyment on the other. A summary of this review is provided in the following section. Against the background of this review, a model of temporal tourism resort area development in peripheral areas is then presented.

Summary of Literature Review: Time Dimension in Geography and Tourism Studies

Time has been studied in most, if not all, branches of knowledge. The philosophical meaning and peculiarities of time have constituted topics for debates among philosophers throughout history (for a brief summary see Parkes and Thrift, 1980:10–12). Since Einstein's (1922) work on "The Meaning of Relativity," time has been given a greater significance in the realm of physics, while in the 1960s, several sociologists treated time from sociological and behavioral perspectives (De Grazia, 1962; Moore, 1963; Orme, 1969).

However, this brief literature review concentrates on the progress in the treatment of the time variable, starting with "time-budget" analysis, proceeding to "space-time-budget" studies with special emphasis on the tourism sector, moving on to "time value" studies in economics, and finally, to the presentation of time in "resort area development" models. It will be shown that the two former areas of study concentrate on the utilization of time and/ or space in site, at the destination. The "economic value of time" studies are mainly concerned with the meaning of time en route, although some scholars also incorporate the time spent at destinations. The "resort area development" literature pays implicit attention to the relationships between both segments of time—on site and en route—and their impact on the development of the resort areas. The following subsections present the main contributions made in each of these fields of study.

Time-Budget Analysis

A common way of treating time in social studies is through the analysis of daily, or longer period, time-budget patterns. One of the best-known collection of such studies is Szalai et al. (1972), which provides a compendium of time-budget research in urban areas in twelve capitalist and socialist countries, while Zuzaneck (1980) offers an account of the citizens' time-budget utilization during the communist regime in the Soviet Union. However, time-budget studies, originating in the field of sociology, have largely ignored the spatial dimensions of the investigated activities (Carlstein and Thrift, 1978).

The spatial dimension was added to time-budget studies by the Lund school of geography led by the prominent Swedish geographer Torsten Hagerstrand and his disciples (1953; 1975). The Lund school emphasizes the spatial context as well as the limits and constraints attached to human space-time activities. Alongside the Lund school, several scholars researched the time-budget patterns of activities in cities and analyzed their impact on urban land use structures (e.g., Chapin, 1968; Anderson, 1971).

Space-Time-Budget Studies

The understanding that both space and time are restrictive in nature has led scholars to conceptualize substitutive space-time relationships (Ullman, 1974). This idea of substitutability between space and time was brilliantly captured in the title given to the three volumes edited by Carlstein, Parkes, and Thrift (1978): *Timing Space and Spacing Time (TSST).* Two years later, Parkes and Thrift (1980) summarized their perceptions of "Times, Spaces, and Places" under the subtitle of "chronogeographic perspectives." Interestingly, although the distinction between work time and leisure time had already been made in earlier sociological studies (De Grazia, 1962), none of the papers included in the three TSST volumes and no chapters or sections in the summary volume of Parkes and Thrift (1980) dealt with space-time chronogeography during times devoted to vacations.

The space-time behavior of people during periods of time devoted to tourism and recreational activities was not researched until fairly recently. Cooper (1981) is one of the earlier scholars analyzing the spatiotemporal behavior of tourists visiting the island of Jersey in the English Channel. His findings indicate that most visitors choosing the island as their holiday destination pay visits at their earliest convenience to the major and easily accessible tourism sites on the island. Those staying for longer periods, or those belonging to the upper and more educated social strata tend to venture to the more peripheral and less popular sites. Cooper's methodology, with various modifications, was applied to the tourism sector by other studies, such as Cosper and Shaw (1985), Pearce (1988), Debbage (1991), Hottola (1992), Dietvorst (1994; 1995), Montanari and Muscara (1995), Fennell (1996), Thornton et al. (1997a; 1997b), and Van der Knaap (1999). Each of these studies emphasizes a different aspect of the space-time behavior, with or without suggesting further advancement of the methodology involved. Common to all, however, is their concern with the intradestination travel behavior. On the other hand, they pay little attention, if any, to the relationships between the total time spent on enjoying the tourist attractions and the time required to reach the destination. This distinction between time on site and time en route has been implicitly incorporated in the treatment of the time variable in the field of economics and is presented in the next subsection.

Economic View on the Value of Time

Carlstein and Thrift (1978) provide a good summary on the subject "Time allocation in economics from Marx to Becker" (pp. 241–250). They quote Soule (1955), who, nearly half a century ago, complained that "economists have not regarded time as a scarce resource" and have not included time in their theories of resource allocation (p. 89). Ten years later, in a landmark paper, Becker (1965) attempted to develop a general theory of the allocation of time. He called for the incorporation of the "foregone value of the time used up" in any activity with the price directly paid for consuming that activity or commodity (p. 494).

One year later, two economists contemplated the issue of measuring the opportunity cost of leisure time. The better-known of these studies produced the Clawson technique (Clawson and Knetsch, 1966), which rests on the assumption that the cost of visiting a free admittance site is composed of the actual travel cost and the opportunity cost attributed to the forgone wages that could have been earned during the time spent en route to the site. Clawson, however, does not attach a price tag to the time spent at the recreation site itself. The other study, by Johnson (1966), refers explicitly to the "travel time and the price of leisure." He introduces leisure time as a separate variable and infers that "the value of leisure and value of travel time must be less than the [conventionally assumed] money wage rate" (p. 139).

DeSerpa (1971) formalized the previous two models of allocation of time and valuation of leisure or travel time into a more general "theory of the economics of time." Among the essential features of his theory there is the recognition that:

(1) "utility is a function not only of commodities but also of the time allocated to them;
(2) the individual's decision is subject to a money constraint and a time constraint; and
(3) the decision to consume any commodity requires that some minimum amount of time be allocated to it."

Later he adds, "pure time might be consumed independently" (p. 828), an assumption essential for understanding the consumption of leisure.

Consequent studies ventured into the quality and utility of the time en route. For instance, Troung and Hensher (1985) demonstrate how Becker's (1965) and DeSerpa's (1971) specifications of time lead to different solutions with respect to the selection of travel modes. In a different vein, Cheshire and Stabler (1976) question Clawson's assumptions by pointing out that some people utilize the journey itself as a source for enjoyment (Walsh, et al., 1990). Finally, Wennergren and Johnston (1979) incorporate the "decreasing marginal utility" concept into their decision-making model regarding the question of how much time a person spends in a recreation site before he or she decides to leave.

Time Dimensions in Resort Area Development Models

The reviewed literature on the economic value of time clearly points out that "time is money" both on site and en route. However, this literature seems to neglect the effects of the ratio of time spent for self-enjoyment and utility at the destination versus travel time. This relationship constitutes a cornerstone in the model to be presented in the next section. Before moving to the model, however, it should be pointed out that this relationship was implicitly embedded in the two best-known models of resort area development, those of Miossec (1977) and Butler (1980).

The Miossec (1977) model presents the development of a peripherally located resort area from its inception into a complex hierarchical tourism area in terms of historical time dimensions. Alongside the developmental stages, the model follows the reaction of potential and actual tourists and improvements in transportation as two separate variables. The model portrays the parallel development of the resort, transportation improvements, and the increasing number of visitors. Thus, Miossec's model implicitly assumes a relationship among the increasing number of attractions, improvements in transportation, and the increase in demand.

Butler's (1980) model predicts increased demand in parallel to increasing investments in the attractiveness of the resort area. Although the historical time dimension is theoretically justified as having the form of a logistic curve, the model does not incorporate the location of the resort and the travel time required to get there. The resort area development model, presented below, was suggested by Krakover (1985) but was then submerged in the literature of desert development. However, this resort development model explicitly takes into account the interrelationships among individual tourist behavior in terms of time spent on site, time spent en route, and the historical time dimension of resort area development.

Temporal Resort Area Development Model

The model presented in this section is designed to point out the significance of the interrelationships between personal time and historic time with respect to tourism development in peripheral areas. Being remote from the large centers of population, these kinds of area are characterized by low levels of investments and a slow pace of development. Most such peripheries are sparsely inhabited and suffer from low levels of public and private services. Furthermore, these areas are often characterized by poor transportation systems and low levels of connectivity to major urban centers (Friedmann, 1972; Husbands, 1981; Hohl and Tisdell, 1995; Blomgren and Sorensen, 1998; Wanhill and Buhalis, 1999).

Despite early observations indicating some tourist preference toward peripheral destinations (Christaller, 1963; Turner and Ash, 1975), it became obvious that the great majority of tourists follow the "beaten track." Accumulated evidence suggests that the masses refrain from venturing into the remote peripheries both on the international (Williams and Zelinsky, 1970; Turner, 1976; Husbands, 1983; Mansfeld, 1990; Weaver, 1998) and the intranational scales (Cooper, 1981; Zurick, 1992; Williams and Shaw, 1995; Fennell, 1996). An understanding of the reasons for this pattern of behavior is essential to further the main argument of this study.

Logic for Preferring the Beaten Track

The logic behind tourists preferring the beaten track over remote or less-known peripheries seems to lean on behavioral assumptions concerning the treatment of scarce time and money resources. As long as one has not reached retirement, most of one's time is allocated to production of income. The number of free paid days is quite limited, thus they are rare and scarce. As is the case with other scarce resources, vacation days are highly valued and thoughtfully treated. To paraphrase the economist's point of view (Becker, 1965; DeSerpa, 1971), time is a scarce resource but vacation time is even scarcer (Bull, 1991).

Moreover, when people leave home for vacation, they become spenders rather than earners of income. Thus, *homo economicus* aspires to the highest possible returns in terms of self-utility in order to justify spending hard-won resources. Since vacation days are scarce, and spending them away from home usually requires higher than normal expenditure, rational decision-making leads tourists to choose destinations that are likely to minimize the risk of failure and dissatisfaction in the allocation of the scarce time and money resources (Bull, 1991; Debbage, 1991).

This logic leads to the conclusion that ordinary working families or individuals will strive to maximize their utility and satisfaction from the time and money spent during their vacation days. The further one ventures from the beaten track, the higher are the time and money resources required to cover the expense and the higher is the risk of failure. As a result, most people reach a decision to follow the masses to the most popular destinations. Actually, these people are the masses.

The proven utility of popular destinations, combined with the low cost of transportation and guaranteed availability of conveniences, usually outweighs the adventurous spirit and extra novelty ascribed to less well-known destinations. In addition, if the remote destination has very little to offer the tourists in terms of self-enjoyment—as is the case with most peripheral locations in their early stages of development (Miossec, 1977)—only a few tourists with special patterns of demand will make a decision to go there.

The aforementioned logical considerations will be presented later in a more formal manner. Before doing so, there is a need to refine our understanding of the time resource allocated to visiting tourist destinations. Clearly, not all tourists are equal in terms of their objectives, personalities, taste, age, and many other variables. The best-known classifications of tourists are those of Cohen (1972) and Plog (1973). Less well-known is Walmsley and Jenkins' (1991) distinction between "space-searchers" and "space-sitters." Regardless of the way tourists define their self-utility preferences, all share several attributes in common. All have only twenty-four hours a day, all try to maximize their self-enjoyment utility functions (however defined) for each day, and all move from one attraction to another, following the law of decreasing marginal utility (dU) as a function of time (T) spent at any single attraction (Wennergren and Johnston, 1979).

The law of decreasing marginal utility as a function of time (dU/dT) provides the rationale for tourists changing activities and proceeding to see and experience other attractions. The time spent on any one attraction depends on the perceived utility assigned to other not-yet-visited ones. As the self-enjoyment utility at attraction A1 decreases below the perceived utility that is supposed to be obtained from visiting the next destination/attraction, A2, the visitor's urge to move on will increase. That is, if $(dU/dT)_{A1} <$ $(dU/dT)_{A2}$, then the tourist will be motivated to move from A1 to A2.

However, the radius search for the other attraction (A2) is constrained by the investment in terms of transportation cost and amount of time required for covering the distance. Thus, distance is a deterrent factor restricting tourists to search additional attractions within a limited radius. The higher the cost in terms of time and money required to reach a remote attraction A2, the lower the likelihood for such a visit to take place, unless the gap between the expected utility at A2 and the current utility from A1 makes it plausible. This relationship explains why tourists are attracted to places rich in high grade attractions concentrated in close proximity; why so many tourists remain within such areas; and why so few elect to go to poorly endowed peripheral destinations, even if they are blessed with certain unique attractions.

Partitioning of Tourists' Personal Time

The relationship between the tourists' aspirations to utilize as much of their personal time as possible on attractive activities, vis-à-vis the tyranny of the physical conditions, can be specified by classifying the total time of the day into three types. These are Ts, which denotes time spent *on sites* for *self-enjoyment* of attractions or other desired activities; Tr, which denotes time *en route* devoted for moving from one place to the other; and Tt, which denote the rest of the twenty-four hours of the day (Clawson and Knetsch, 1966; Bull, 1991).

Without doubt, when tourists consider allocating their personal time, they try to reduce Tt to the minimum needed for physical comfort (e.g., sleeping, eating, etc.). Also, Tr is surely perceived by most tourists as a necessary nuisance to overcome on their way to reach Ts destinations. True, under special conditions and for some tourist populations, the various types of time are not exclusively defined. Some utilize Tr for Tt, for example, by eating and sleeping in trains. Some others dine in fancy restaurants, converting Tt to Ts. For some, the act of travelling along a particularly scenic route can transform Tr into a first grade Ts experience (Cheshire and Stabler, 1976; Walsh, et al., 1990). However, under normal conditions and for most tourists, Tt always prevails, Ts is the trip's objective, and Tr is most often considered as an unavoidable necessity to be decreased to a minimum.

Given these conditions, it can be assumed that each traveler has an average constant Tt. Thus the sum of Ts+Tr is constant too. However, if Tr, or at least part of it, is defined as a nuisance, the objective of the ordinary tourist is to maximize Ts and, by the same token, minimize Tr. This objective may be written as maximization of the Ts to Tr ratio (Ts/Tr). As long as one does not consider time *en route* (Tr) to be equal to time for *on site self-enjoyment* (Ts), maximization of Ts/Tr may be achieved by traveling to tourism destinations located close to the point of origin and by visiting places closely knit to each other (Wennergren and Johnston, 1979). Achieving the highest ratio possible of Ts to Tr per day or per trip yields the highest utility for the ordinary traveler. These kinds of expeditions will be in high demand. By contrast, traveling to remote destinations and/or sightseeing-dispersed attractions results in lowering the Ts/Tr ratio, and, consequently, reducing the demand for these kinds of excursions. In short, it can be assumed that the higher the Ts/Tr ratio, the higher the demand. This relationship is portrayed in figure 2.1.

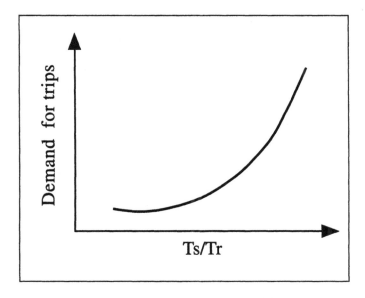

Figure 2.1. Demand for Vacation Trips with Relation to Ts/Tr Ratio

Linking Personal Time to Historical-Developmental Time

Now that the major elements in the definition of personal time have been delineated, I turn to linking personal time attributes to historic time considerations in the development of resort areas in general and those located in peripheral areas in particular. Most resort areas undergo evolutionary paths of development as outlined by Miossec (1977), Butler (1980), and others (Krakover, 1985; Haywood, 1986). The evolutionary phases start with the identification of an attraction, setting up some sort of accommodation and related services, opening up a road, and providing some sort of transportation.

Usually, in the initial stages, the time it takes to reach the attraction is long (high Tr), on site facilities are poor, and the self-enjoyment time offered at the attraction is short (low Ts). Thus, the personal time ratio Ts/Tr for the average tourist is very low. Such low personal Ts/Tr ratios may only appeal to rather special tourist populations such as adventurers, explorers, drifters, and the like. For these tourists, at least some of the time en route (Tr) is considered as part of the self-enjoyment (Ts), so their personal time ratio is considerably improved. In certain cases, such as touring sports cyclists, the journey itself is the main objective, in which case Tr is entirely converted to Ts.

A most extreme case that exemplifies these assertions is the climb to the peak of Mount Everest. The time en route—to and from—is measured in many days and weeks, while the time on the top is extremely short, measured in minutes. Unless the excitement, challenge, and self-enjoyment involved in the preparation and the ascending and descending stages are taken into account, the number of those electing to undertake this trip will decrease to near zero. Under normal conditions, however, almost every vacation trip involves making decisions wherein the Ts/Tr ratio is considered. This is usually the case when a long detour is required to include a specific attraction located off the beaten track. Ayers Rock in Australia, the Kyongju area in South Korea and Eilat in Israel used to be, and to a certain extent still are, examples of such places.

The growth and development of tourism resort areas are measured in terms of historic times—in decades. Resort area development may undergo periods of decline or stagnation before growth picks up again (Butler, 1980). Even the growth stage itself is rarely a smooth and continuous process, especially in the initial stages. In order for a resort area in the periphery to continue developing beyond its initial stage, there is a need for increased demand by visitors. Such demand can be increased in several ways, such as good public relations and intensive advertising. This may awaken some latent demand of more visitors of the same type for whom the current Ts/Tr ratio is appealing.

Another effective advertising strategy to increase demand is to intensify and glorify the perceived image of the resort area. This strategy may result in increased demand on the part of the romantic or imaginative visitor. For this group, the value of the current actual Ts may be intensified by an exponent α, to make it Ts^α. Thus, if $\alpha>1$, then Ts is either perceived longer than in real time and/or visitors extend the time they are willing to spend on site, since their perceived marginal utility following the promotion campaign is greater than before ($dU_{after} > dU_{before}$). If such a campaign fails and leads to disappointment on the part of the visitors, it will be reflected in the personal time ratio by Ts raised to exponents $\alpha<1$.

However, in order to attract more visitors who belong to the mainstream populations, there is a need for a real—not only an imaginary—change in the condition of the peripheral resort area. This kind of change may be brought about by following one or both of two development strategies: (1) the addition of attractions and/or (2) shortening time en route. The development and/or providing access to existing attractions, both man-made and nature-based, potentially enable visitors to increase their personal time on site devoted to self-enjoyment, Ts. This strategy was exemplified, for instance, by Pearce (1980). Improving roads or means of transportation acts to shorten time en route, Tr, a factor emphasized by Janelle (1969). If this two-pronged improvement process continues through historic time, then on-site personal time Ts increases, while personal Tr decreases, as depicted in figure 2.2.

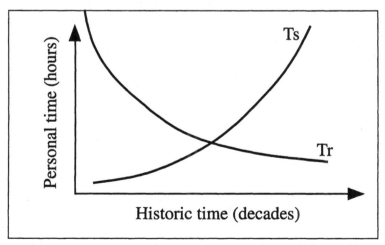

Figure 2.2. Expected Changes in the Path of Ts and Tr through Historic Time

This process results in a long-term decrease in the Ts/Tr ratio and makes a visit to the site more feasible to more visitors in terms of the allocation of the constrained scarce personal time and money resources. Ultimately, once the resort area is well developed, direct air transportation links are established. When this occurs, time en route is decreased to a minimum, Ts/Tr ratio becomes high, and demand for this site is expected to rise.

The operation of the temporal resort area development model was examined for the case of the Dead Sea resort area in Israel (Krakover, 1985). The construction of new transportation arteries leading to the Dead Sea area shortened driving time from the core areas of Tel Aviv and Jerusalem from seven to nine hours in the 1950s, to four hours in the 1960s, and to a mere one to two hours since the 1970s. During these decades, access to major attractions, such as Massada, the Dead Sea, and nearby hot springs, and good hotels with special facilities such as health spas, has dramatically improved. As a result, demand for tourist bed-nights has increased to over 1.5 million per annum with consistently high hotel occupancy rates.

Summary and Conclusions

This study concentrated on the impact that changes in the ability to utilize personal time may have on the development of peripherally located tourism resort areas. Time as well as money is considered a scarce resource. Thus, ordinary tourists are keen to utilize these resources to their utmost satisfaction and to minimize the risk of failure. Undoubtedly, reaching these goals requires obtaining information with respect to the nature of the available attractions, as well as the routes and means of transport available to reach them. The objective function of the ordinary traveler is assumed to include the following two qualities: one, maximization of time devoted for self-enjoyment at attractions, denoted as time *on site* (Ts), and two, minimization of time *en route*, denoted Tr. Exceptions are those tourists enjoying the route itself, thus converting Tr to Ts.

The study surveyed four bodies of literature related to time utilization: time-budget studies, space-time-budget studies, research on the economic value of time, and treatment of time in tourist resort development studies. Most of the surveyed literature dealt separately with either time *on site* or time *en route*. This study suggests considering the impact of the changes in both time components conjointly by applying the Ts to Tr ratio (Ts/Tr). Usually, through historic time, measured in decades, improvements in transportation make it possible to drastically reduce the time required to cover long distances (Janelle, 1969), thus shortening Tr. At the same time, internal and external entrepreneurs are engaged in efforts to expand the self-enjoyment facilities available for the tourist at the resort area under their jurisdiction, offering longer Ts. As a result, both time components change to generate a much more favorable and attractive Ts/Tr time ratio. The higher the Ts to Tr ratio, the larger will be the number of tourists likely to be attracted to visit this area.

Thus, personal time considerations, measured in hours, can be used to understand the path of development of a resort area through historic-developmental time. Under certain circumstances it can also be used to predict the number of visitors at a peripheral tourist location at any point in its development. Furthermore, the model provides a two-pronged strategy for the development of peripheral tourist resort areas—promoting both the development of more attractions on the one hand and improving transportation links on the other. Treating both components together increases Ts/Tr more rapidly and, hence, increases demand and speeds up the pace of development. In a previous study (Krakover, 1985), the model was examined in the Dead Sea resort area, Israel. More applications are required in order to calibrate the model for varying environments.

References

Anderson, J. 1971. Space-time budgets and activity studies in urban geography and planning. *Environment and Planning A*, 3:353–368.

Becker, G. S. 1965. A theory of the allocation of time. *The Economic Journal*, 75:493–517.

Berry, B. J. L. 1972. Hierarchical diffusion: The bases of developmental filtering and spread in a system of growth centers. In N. Hansen ed., *Growth Centers in Regional Economic Development*. New York: The Free Press.

Blomgren, K. B., and A. Sorensen. 1998. Peripherality—Factor or feature? Reflections on peripherality in tourism research. *Progress in Tourism and Hospitality Research*, 4:319–336.

Bull, A. 1991. *The Economics of Travel and Tourism*. Melbourne: Longman Cheshire.

Butler, R. W. 1980. The concept of a tourism area cycle of evolution: Implications for management of resources. *The Canadian Geographer*, 24:5–12.

Carlstein, T., D. Parkes, and N. J. Thrift, eds., 1978. *Timing Space and Spacing Time*, Vol. 2. London: Edward Arnold.

Carlstein, T., and N. J. Thrift. 1978. Afterwards: Towards a time-space structured approach to society and environment. In T. Carlstein, D. Parkes, and N. J. Thrift eds., *Timing Space and Spacing Time*, Vol. 2. London: Edward Arnold.

Chapin, F. S. Jr. 1968. Activity systems and urban structure: A working schema. *Journal of the American Institute of Planners*, 34:11–18.

Cheshire, P. C., and M. J. Stabler. 1976. Joint consumption benefits in recreational site "surplus": An empirical estimate. *Regional Studies*, 19:343–351.

Christaller, W. 1963. Some considerations of tourism location in Europe: The peripheral regions—underdeveloped countries—recreation areas. *Papers, Regional Science Association*, 6:95–105.

Clawson, M., and J. L. Knetsch. 1966. *Economics of Outdoor Recreation*. Baltimore: Johns Hopkins University Press.

Cohen, E. 1972. Towards a sociology of international tourism. *Social Research*, 39:164–182.

Cooper, C. P. 1981. Spatial and temporal patterns of tourist behaviour. *Regional Studies*, 15:359–371.

Cosper, R. L., and S. M. Shaw. 1985. The validity of time-budget studies: A comparison of frequency and diary data in Halifax, Canada. *Leisure Sciences*, 7:202–225.

Debbage, K. G. 1991. Spatial behavior in a Bahamian resort. *Annals of Tourism Research*, 18:251–268.

De Grazia, S. 1962. *On Time, Work, and Leisure*. New York: Twentieth Century Fund.

DeSerpa, A. G. 1971. A theory of the economics of time. *The Economic Journal*, 81:828–846.

Dietvorst, A. G. J. 1994. Cultural tourism and time-space behaviour. In G. J. Ashworth and P. J. Larkham eds., *Building a New Heritage: Tourism, Culture and Identity in a New Europe*. London: Routledge.

Dietvorst, A. G. J. 1995. Tourist behaviour and the importance of time-space analysis. In G. J. Ashworth and A. G. J. Dietvorst, *Tourism and Spatial Transformations*. Wallingford, U.K.: CAB International.

Einstein, A. 1922. *The Meaning of Relativity*. Princeton: Princeton University Press.

Fennell, D. A. 1996. A tourist space-time budget in the Shetland Islands. *Annals of Tourism Research*, 23:811–829.

Friedmann, J. 1966. *Regional Development Policy: A Case Study of Venezuela*. Cambridge, MA: MIT Press.

Friedmann, J. 1972. A general theory of polarized development. In N. Hansen ed., *Growth Centers in Regional Economic Development*. New York: The Free Press.

Hagerstrand, T. 1975. Space, time and human conditions. In A. Karlqvist, L. Lundqvist, and F. Snikcars eds., *Dynamic Allocation of Urban Space.* Farnborough: Saxon House.

Hagerstrand, T. 1953. *Innovation Diffusion as a Spatial Process.* Chicago: University of Chicago Press. (Translated from Swedish by A. Pred in 1967.)

Haywood, K. M. 1986. Can the tourist-area life cycle be made operational? *Tourism Management,* 7:154–167.

Hohl, A. E., and C. A. Tisdell. 1995. Peripheral tourism: Development and management. *Annals of Tourism Research,* 22:517–534.

Hottola, P. 1992. Tourist space-time budgets in Eilat, Israel. Unpublished M.Sc. thesis, University of Joensun, Finland.

Husbands, W. C. 1981. Centers, peripheries, tourism and socio-spatial development. *Ontario Geography,* 17:37–59.

Husbands, W. C. 1983. Tourist space and tourist attraction: An analysis of the destination choices of European travelers. *Leisure Sciences,* 5:289–307.

Janelle, D. G. 1969. Spatial reorganization: A model and concept. *Annals of the Association of American Geographers,* 59:348–364.

Johnson, M. B. 1966. Travel time and the price of leisure. *Western Economic Journal,* 4:135–145.

Krakover, S. 1985. Development of tourism resort areas in arid regions. In Gradus, Y. ed., *Desert Development: Man and Technology in Sparselands.* Reidel: Dordrecht.

Mansfeld, Y. 1990. Spatial patterns of international tourist flows: Towards a theoretical framework. *Progress in Human Geography,* 14:372–390.

Miossec, J. M. 1977. Un modele de l'espace touristique. *Espace Geographique,* 6:41–48.

Montanari, A., and C. Muscara. 1995. Evaluating tourist flows in historic cities: The case of Venice. *Tijdschrift voor Economische en Sociale Geografei,* 86:80–87.

Moore, W. E. 1963. *Man, Time, and Society.* New York: Wiley.

Orme, J. E. 1969. *Time, Experience, and Behaviour.* London: Iliffe Press.

Parkes, D. N., and N. J. Thrift, 1980. *Times, Spaces, and Places: A Chronogeographic Perspective.* Chichester: John Wiley.

Pearce, D. G. 1980. Tourism and regional development: A generic approach. *Annals of Tourism Research,* 7:69–82.

Pearce, D. G. 1988. Tourist time-budget. *Annals of Tourism Research,* 15:106–121.

Plog, S. C. 1973. Why destination areas rise and fall in popularity. *Cornell H.R.A. Quarterly*, November: 13–16.

Soule, G. 1955. *Time for Living*. New York: Viking Press.

Szalai, A. ed. 1972. *The Use of Time: Daily Activities of Urban and Suburban Population in Twelve Countries*. Mouton: The Hague.

Thornton, P., G. Shaw, and A. M. Williams. 1997a. Revisiting time-space diaries: An exploratory case study of tourist behaviour in Cornwall, England. *Environment and Planning A*, 29:1847–1867.

Thornton, P. R., G. Shaw, and A. M. Williams. 1997b. Tourist group holiday decision making and behaviour: The influence of children. *Tourism Management*, 18:287–297.

Troung, T. P., and D. A. Hensher, 1985. Measurement of travel time values and opportunity cost from a discrete choice model. *Economic Journal*, 95:438–451.

Turner, L., 1976. The international division of leisure: Tourism and the Third World. *World Development*, 4:253–260.

Turner, L., and J. Ash. 1975. *The Golden Hordes: International Tourism and the Pleasure Periphery*. London: Constable.

Ullman, E. L. 1974. Space and/or time: Opportunities for substitution and prediction. *Transaction: Institute of British Geographers*, 63:125–139.

Van der Knaap, W. G. M. 1999. Research report: GIS-oriented analysis of tourist time-space patterns to support sustainable tourism development. *Tourism Geographies*, 1:56–69.

Walmsley, D. J., and J. M. Jenkins. 1991. Mental maps, locus of control and activity: A study of business tourists in Coffs Harbour. *The Journal of Tourism Studies*, 2:36–42.

Walsh, R. G., L. D. Sanders, and J. R. McKean. 1990. The consumptive value of travel time on recreation trips. *Journal of Travel Research*, 29:17–24.

Wanhill, S., and D. Buhalis. 1999. Introduction: Challenges for tourism in peripheral areas. *International Journal of Tourism Research*, 1:295–297.

Weaver, D. B. 1998. Peripheries of the periphery: Tourism in Tobago and Barbuda. *Annals of Tourism Research*, 25:292–313.

Wennergren, E. B., and W. E. Johnston. 1979. Economic concepts relevant to the study of outdoor recreation. In C. S. Van Doren, G. B. Priddle, and J. E. Lewis eds., *Land and Leisure: Concepts and Methods in Outdoor Recreation* (2nd edition), Chicago: Maroufa Press.

Williams, A. M., and G. Shaw. 1995. Tourism and regional development: Polarization and new forms of production in the United Kingdom. *Tijdschrift voor Economische en Sociale Geografei*, 86:50–63.

Williams, A. V., and W. Zelinsky. 1970. On some patterns in international tourist flows. *Economic Geography,* 46:549–567.

Zurick, D. N. 1992. Adventure travel and sustainable tourism in the peripheral economy of Nepal. *Annals of the Association of American Geographers,* 82:608–628.

Zuzaneck, J. 1980. *Work and Leisure in the Soviet Union: A Time Budget Analysis.* New York: Praeger.

Chapter 3

Sustainable Tourism Development in South Africa: From Policy to Delivery

Elsa Kruger-Cloete

Tourism is a leading economic driver for the new millennium. The World Travel and Tourism Council (WTTC) estimates that tourism contributes 11 percent of global gross domestic product (GDP). The WTTC provides a general policy direction based on the *"Millennium Vision"* (WTTC, 1998). The World Tourism Organization (WTO) is likewise calling on governments around the world to unleash tourism's job creation potential by improving information networks, and exploiting tourism's human resource capital by incorporating innovation and investment know-how (WTO, 1998).

Travel and tourism are now the largest generator of jobs, accounting for about 11 percent of the global workforce. A vision of a globally competitive tourism industry is the focus of the WTTC report entitled *South Africa's Travel & Tourism-Economic Driver for the 21st Century* (1998). The report assesses the size and impact of travel and tourism in South Africa as it ripples through the economy and demonstrates the job creation potential of the industry. The analysis uses the modern statistical technique of satellite accounting to identify direct and indirect economic effects of travel and tourism. The concept evolved through international public and private sector collaboration.

Where tourism is well integrated into the economy, the job creation prospects are good. The WTTC estimates that where linkages with other industries and economic sectors are strong, the employment multiplier that generates a job in the tourism industry, generates a further 1.1 indirect job opportunities in the rest of the economy. South Africa's growing tourism and associated economy is estimated to be worth $ 8.8 billion or 8.2 percent of GDP in 1998 (WTTC/WEFA estimates).

Buoyant forecasts for tourism growth in the third millennium are contained in *Tourism: 2020 Vision* (WTO, 1999). The trends emerging are that tourists will be travelling further afield to long-haul destinations. The expected growth in demand to visit Africa—7.5 percent over the next two decades—is well above the average for the world as a whole.

Global forces of competitiveness, information technology, and social-cultural dynamics are significantly impacting and shaping tourism destinations. Global shifts in the economy are driven by new waves of technological, political, and social transformation. Places, culture, and identities seem to converge in the world of international travel. In all this, tourism is testimony to the power of place and the sustaining lure of local uniqueness.

The tourism industry in South Africa has experienced marked peaks and slumps in investment over the past five years. The emphasis has been mainly on property development, with a shift now needed toward sophisticated product differentiation to provide memorable experiences for tourists. The key challenge is whether South Africa can overcome delivery constraints as well as external perceptions of safety and security and capture a growing share of the world's future tourism market. Delivery is constrained because the ability to put policy into practice lags far behind the policy itself.

A New Paradigm in Sustainable Tourism

An evolution of policies in the context of globalization is evident. A key feature of globalization is the mobility of information, capital, and people, driven by the restructuring of economic relations and competition. The competitive advantage of local areas rests more within their own specific context. Dawe and Bryden (1998) argue that local communities are shaped by the interplay between what occurs on the local and global levels. With the reality of the global-local nexus, globalization has made the local angle of tourism development even more relevant. Meeting the global challenge calls for local initiative that is both innovative and flexible. The uniqueness of the local context provides opportunity to embark on innovative action.

The key policy interventions for sustainability now incorporate technology, territory, and lifestyles for long-term impact. Such policy interventions are oriented toward a structural change in activities and behaviors and incorporate the selection of more sustainability-oriented technologies and settlement patterns (Campagni, Capello, and Nijkamp, 1998). The rapid transformation in new technology, the evolution of more experienced and discerning travelers, global economic restructuring, and environmental limits to growth all auger for a new paradigm in sustainable tourism. Competitive strategies are setting the stage and are prerequisites to ensure that industry players and tourism destinations create competitive positions.

As the world's largest industry, tourism certainly provides an appropriate foray into conceptual debates on globalization and localization. Drawing on theoretical and conceptual insights from the broader domain of geographic analysis, Chang (1999) and Dawe and Bryden (1998) place tourism in the center of the local-global nexus debate.

Tourism development is incumbent on the outcomes of global and local forces as they impinge on the economy, where tourism caters to the needs and interests of global audiences but is also geared toward the cultural needs and leisure aspirations of local communities. The challenge is to integrate the local with the global in a relational context. The goal is to strike a balance, reconciling different market needs to create landscapes appealing to visitors and local residents alike. This approach demonstrates that it is crucial to place tourism development in the context of the localities and the local circumstances in which it is embedded.

Global-local forces are mutually reinforcing. The notion of collaboration, while competing at the same time, demonstrates the reflexive way in which the economy operates (Soros, 1998). The localization of culture and the concurrent globalization of localities are happening simultaneously. Together, the locality concept and the contingent debate provide the needed tools to analyze and appreciate global-local interactions. What transpires is the intertwined nature of social, cultural, and spatial processes.

There is growing evidence of a new paradigm in tourism policy to influence the competitive position of a destination under conditions of global competition. Current international practice indicates that tourism development is evolving institutionally, because of the complexity of the competitive macro environment. Institutions must be able to adapt quickly to the changing competitive situation. Applying the pioneering work of Porter's diamond cluster to the new tourism policies (Fayos-Solà, 1996) takes on the challenge of translating the cluster into effective demand and strengthening the tourism industry's strategic position within the value chain.

A new dimension has been added to the debate, in which staging experiences has emerged as the next step in the progression of economic value (figure 3.1). In moving up the value chain, tourism takes center stage in advancing from the service economy to the experience economy. Pine II and Gilmore (1998:105) argue that the "experience economy will grow through 'gales of creative destruction' as economist Joseph Schumpeter termed it— that is, business innovation which threatens to render irrelevant those who relegate themselves to the diminishing world of goods and services."

For a hospitable and sustainable tourism industry, a country needs all the major stakeholder groupings, that is, government, private business, and the community sector, to develop and act in harmony to give substance to tourism policy. Lessons from "tourism-smart" nations show that these countries rely on a *public-private partnership framework* for tourism. The *Malé Declaration* (WTO, 1997) has a similar core objective for tourism development policies.

Reliability of policy is crucial both to competitiveness and to attracting investment. In terms of securing a competitive position, the main obstacles to social and economic development relate to weak institutional structures. The roles become blurred and government will be hard put to contribute to competitiveness unless its powers and management processes are redefined.

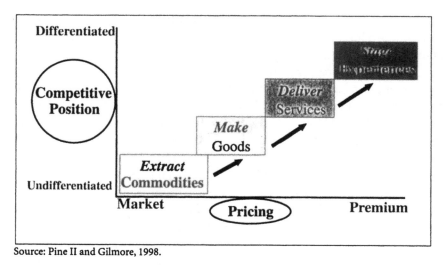

Source: Pine II and Gilmore, 1998.

Figure 3.1. Progression of Economic Value

The efficiency of public action is still at stake. Cooperation with the private and voluntary sectors is a prerequisite for the efficient implementation of policy programs.

Such a process needs to create an environment that enables the different role players to innovate in their own interests while serving the overall job creation purpose of the industry. This is also the outcome of the *Bali Declaration on Tourism* (WTO, 1996), which outlines guiding principles for sound tourism development and entails the active participation of all stakeholders, including the private sector and local communities. More importantly, an implementation mode is recommended that will improve the quality of life at the community level by expanding business opportunities, increasing employment, and capitalizing on scientific and technological progress.

Putting Tourism to Work

With job creation arguably the greatest challenge to the economy, growth and employment targets are indicated in *Tourism in GEAR: A Strategy to Implement the Tourism White Paper: 1998–2000* (South Africa, 1997). The potential for tourism to produce revenue and emerge as a major job creator is evident from the WTTC scenarios. Under the baseline scenario, it is estimated that travel and tourism could add more than *half a million jobs* across South Africa's economy over the next twelve years. Currently, tourism provides some 250,000 direct jobs and 300,000 indirect jobs in an environment where official unemployment in rural and urban areas is pegged at 27 percent and 22 percent, respectively. No breakdown is available as to how many jobs are provided in the various subsectors or what they contribute to GDP.

Finding Balance in Sustainable Environmental Management

Following the Rio Earth Summit, the WTO, WTTC and the Earth Council produced a draft *Agenda 21 for the Travel and Tourism Industry*. At the dawn of the third millennium, this agenda will be the essential reference to becoming environmentally responsible and thereby more sustainable. The environmental limits to growth hold several important lessons for tourism. In terms of the goals of Agenda 21, tourism is capable of providing a financial incentive for protecting the natural, cultural, and social environment. The intertwined nature of the coevolutionary process in an economic environmental system requires balance in the economic, ecological, and equity paradigms.

As part of a series of regional reviews in Agenda 21, delegates from ten countries examined the economic and environmental patterns in Africa. They concluded that the best potential for job creation, poverty eradication, and social development in the twenty-first century lies in sustainable tourism. In a consensus statement with Agenda 21 at its core, the delegates reiterated the challenge to create effective public-private partnerships that would also benefit local communities. Reviewing a number of successful programs for environmentally responsible tourism, it is evident that:

- Tourism can be a key element in poverty eradication and social development.
- Partnerships between all relevant stakeholders are crucial to scope, shape, and deliver tourist activities.
- Sustainability principles must be included in the vision, planning, and delivery of all tourism development programs.

The globalization of tourism has engendered concerns over its effects on destinations, particularly the impacts on local environments, cultures, and social systems. A Charter for Sustainable Tourism (WTO, 1995) incorporates the following criteria:

- balancing ecologically sound, economically viable, and socially equitable tourism development;
- the natural, cultural, and human environments must be integrated in assessing the impacts on cultural heritage and local communities;
- ensuring participation at all levels requires efficient cooperation mechanisms;
- incorporating innovation is the real challenge in creating integrated planning and management instruments;
- by using ecologically honest pricing, a more equitable distribution of the benefits of tourism can be achieved;
- in technical assistance grants, priority areas, such as environmental and cultural spaces, should be targeted; and
- the creation of open networks for information, research, dissemination, and transfer of appropriate tourism and environmental knowledge and technology are prerequisites.

The progress in addressing sustainable environmental practice is notable, but there are still many challenges to be addressed in finding balance in sustainable tourism practice. There is still a way to go in creating awareness, but the gradual incorporation of sustainable tourism development principles in a framework for development augers well for ensuring sustainable practices in the future. There are strong linkages with the issues emerging from the global network for biodiversity management.

Integrated Tourism Strategy

In the digital economy, there is an emerging infrastructure of networks that blurs the boundary between sectors. Therefore, in the drive toward sustainable tourism, development requires integrated strategies. It is well known that tourism's impacts and linkages pervade a number of industrial and services sectors. Private business is *essential* to drive the strategic positioning and implementation of competitive tourism and marketing strategies. Forging collaborative alliances is the pattern that can result in a dynamic interplay of capacity in strengthening strategic partnerships.

The WTTC scenarios and the policy recommendations give a powerful boost to the proposal for stronger regional integration. Of the cooperative ventures in the region, transfrontier conservation areas (TFCA) are among the more significant. The TFCA concept is in tune with interventions to achieve balanced sustainable development in terms of creating advantages by interlinking local/transfrontier/global challenges and actions. These new corridors, or tourism access routes, may enhance the tourism appeal of the region. The concept aims to unlock economic and tourism potential with the specific goals of creating environmentally sustainable nature reserves, sustainable jobs and growth in the economy of the area as well as contributing to restructuring the ownership base in the economy.

A recently signed *Memorandum of Understanding on Transfrontier Conservation Areas* supports the establishment of a TFCA that will bring together the parks of Gaza in Mozambique, the Kruger National Park in South Africa, and Gonarezhou in Zimbabwe under joint management, creating one of the biggest conservation areas in the world. The agreement recognizes that ecosystems transcend national boundaries and recognizes the need for transfrontier cooperation in the conservation and management of natural resources for the benefit of the people and tourism in the region. The purpose is to promote biodiversity management and socioeconomic development in the area.

The necessity of embarking on an integrated tourism strategy is now appreciated by most role players. The various initiatives need to be integrated with new insights. The myriad of opportunities in support of integrated tourism strategies, such as multimedia tourism technologies, virtual reality, and digital image technologies catering for ecotourism development, cultural heritage, and adventure tourism are all options for better delivery.

Infrastructure and Transport Systems

Good transport infrastructure is critical for the development of tourism in the region. With fierce competition prevalent in the tourism industry, a key issue is the provision of appropriate infrastructure to catalyze demand. The rapid increase in the number of trips into and out of South Africa has increased pressure on infrastructure. Globally, the airline transport market has continued to expand, and this trend is expected to continue. This growth demands improvements in airport and airline capacity as well as in the efficiency of the civil aviation industry. The international tourists' ability to reach their desired destination from their point of origin is dictated by international treaties and standards, particularly with regard to air travel, which affects safety over the long haul. Aviation safety is critical to successful competition in the emerging global economy. At the same time, it will be a catalyst to trade, investment, and growth of the tourism industry. The air traffic control infrastructure in airspace north of South Africa is acknowledged as deficient. Sufficient investment in navigational facilities (radar, VHF radio coverage, meteorological information), airports, and airways is needed.

Moving South Africa 2020 determined the country's land, sea, and air transport needs over the next twenty years. The project focuses on the structure, infrastructure, and functioning of the South African transport system and advances solutions for the short, medium, and long terms It also clarified responsibilities while foreseeing the creation of separate agencies to deal with issues such as the construction and maintenance of roads, and aviation safety.

With the purpose of developing a tourism infrastructure investment framework, KPMG (1999) was commissioned to identify tourism infrastructure development areas where future tourism potential was strong and the need for development clear. The priority tourism infrastructure investment areas identified the linkages between areas and focused attention on the tourist flows that take the visitor through a series of gateways, routes, staging posts, and distribution points to various destinations and attractions. Delivery of tourism services will take place at the local level.

The methodology for developing the framework incorporated Geographic Information Systems (GIS). A spatial pattern emerged through layering factors, such as existing infrastructure, product strengths and weaknesses, current demand and supply, potential growth of products, and demographic

Table 3.1. Type of Infrastructure Required

• **Transport infrastructure** such as passenger transport, service utility, and communications infrastructure required to transport the tourist safely and efficiently to tourism consumption points (TCP).
• **Delivery infrastructure** such as freight transport, service utility, and communications infrastructure needed to deliver goods and services to the TCP, thereby ensuring its functionality.
• **Location infrastructure** such as scenic and built environment, culture, history, trade, retail, and entertainment necessary to ensure that the TCP is able to attract tourists.

patterns. The advantage of the framework lies in incorporating socioeconomic issues and poverty indicators to identify priority tourism development areas. However, affordability of the required infrastructure was not factored into the equation, and the viability of an infrastructure requirement often stalls on this critical element (table 3.1).

The KPMG study concludes that the main potential pressure points, impacting directly on infrastructure, are road and air traffic facilities, and tourism growth could be constrained if the provision is inadequate. The types of infrastructure required, particularly in peripheral areas, include:

- Transport infrastructure that serves the traditional destinations but is lacking in emerging destinations and at border posts. Gaps emerged in internodal transport systems, capitalizing on the trend toward rail usage by international tourists and identifying areas for internodal connectivity. The overregulation of the coach industry also impacts negatively on competitiveness.

- Delivery infrastructure is not yet in place in all areas with tourism potential, but key stakeholders are confident that they can provide the required delivery elements once demand is proven.

- Location infrastructure is polarized around the traditional tourist areas and the economic hub of Gauteng. Likewise, accommodation is highly concentrated in the triangle of Cape Town, Durban, and Gauteng accounting for approximately 40 percent of total room stock. A general lack of tourist information centers is evident.

The direction provided by the tourism infrastructure investment framework (TIIF) focuses mainly on an integrated national spatial framework and identifies potential tourism investment opportunities in nineteen priority areas. Although the infrastructure base supporting tourism is good, it is highly polarized, resulting in limited dispersal of tourists to other areas with potential. To maximize the tourism potential, targeted investments in tourism infrastructure are predicated to leverage private sector investments into peripheral areas that have product strength and can satisfy future market needs. The TIIF provides direction for investing in all the major elements of tourism infrastructure and also recommends maximizing the use of sunken investment in a rail network, thereby providing opportunities for the emerging market to become an active participant in the tourism economy.

The need for tourism to expand along a continuum into rural and peripheral areas is clearly evident. Several opportunities can be explored, using emerging technologies to open up the provision of rural infrastructure, such as providing clean water and effluent treatment as well as renewable energy technologies in border areas.

Beyond Human Resources Development to Capacity Strengthening

In the human resources sphere, the development and nurturing of an attitude of friendliness, helpfulness, and service are as necessary for the private sector as for the public. Teaching people to appreciate the potential benefits and responsibilities associated with the industry is a prerequisite for creating a culture friendly to tourism. The opportunities forthcoming in support of human capacity building include multimedia options and computer-based instruction.

The hospitality industries training board (HITB) is in the process of getting its tourism learnership project underway. Skill needs are to be tackled by the new sector training authority and a South African tourism training institute. Both the HITB and the travel, education, and training authority of South Africa (TETASA) are training facilitators rather than training providers, promoting training as the key to improved services and quality levels. The business trust will fund tourism education facilitated by the HITB. The Reach & Teach organization's travel and tourism program assists aspirant entrants to the industry and has also been instrumental in spearheading the introduction of travel and tourism as a subject in sixty-five pilot high schools throughout South Africa.

Tourism is essentially a local demand-led activity, and because it is locally driven, capacity to manage and implement at the local level needs to be strengthened. The division of responsibilities between the various government levels is being more clearly defined. At least three provinces, namely the Western Cape, KwaZulu-Natal, and the North-West, have embarked on tourism implementation strategies. The remaining six provinces are all on a steep learning curve and will benefit from the knowledge of the provinces that already have experience. Sustainable tourism development requires active involvement to translate the principle of "learning by doing" into concrete actions. Active involvement also brings commitment to the lessons being learned.

African Renaissance

Global trends are adopted everywhere and are moving to the stage where tourists now unquestionably seek new experiences. Global tourism and local identity complement each other. Imaging strategies in the form of branding messages embody the overall vision of a place. South Africa's tourism office (Satour's) slogan of *"a world in one country"* not only offers the promise of value for tourists but also creates a desirable experience in the global-local nexus. Integration of experience into the larger social system can result in a renaissance of indigenous culture (Chang, 1999).

Global realities and the inevitable demands of a location shape marketing strategies. The branding theme of a tourism renaissance will drive the marketing strategies. The vision of an African renaissance serves the purpose of promoting a memorable African experience. To competitively market South Africa as a preferred tourist destination, it is not surprising to find Satour embracing the African experience in its mission statement: to make tourism the leading economic sector for sustainable development and social empowerment of the people. Images used for marketing also serve as guidelines in the development of plans and policies.

A focused marketing drive, capitalizing on the African renaissance theme, could draw far greater numbers of tourists. South Africa competes with many other destinations considered "long haul" by tourists. In 1997, the top ten tourism sending countries made up more than 60 percent of the international visitors. Europe is also the origin of most outbound travelers, with forty million travelers moving on long haul journeys to other parts of the globe. Long-haul tourists from Europe, America, and East Asia amount to almost 100 million per annum. In all regions of the world, most outbound tourists are intraregional or domestic. The high level of intraregional and domestic travel is largely due to geographical locations, continental size, and diversity of tourist attractions.

The country's unique heritage and rich culture together account for 46 percent of foreign tourist motivations; they are second only to scenic beauty. The real value of cultural attributes and artifacts—their role in creating jobs and cementing societies together—has not yet been properly recognized

(Dini and Wofensohn, 1999). The African renaissance poses the challenge of drawing on its traditions, values, and indigenous knowledge to make development more effective. African crafts and indigenous products using African lifestyle technologies could be used to brand the renaissance theme. The branding of products with this theme will go a long way to stimulate local economic activity. Niche operators, offering integrated products across all interest areas, can explore lifestyle technologies for this purpose. Several process technologies and branding of cosmetics and indigenous exotic foods and beverages can make the dream a reality! Unfortunately, marketing and investments in community-based tourism initiatives will matter little if soaring crime levels are not brought under control.

Drive toward Safety and Security

Sociopolitical stability and security are the necessary minimum, but not sufficient, conditions for tourism development. The safety aspects of traveling influence the selection of a destination and are therefore an important consideration. Safety and security are fundamental because even minor security incidents can have a major impact on the way destinations are perceived. The WTO and the World Leadership Forum consider it a key strategic issue. Levels of crime and violence pose a major threat to the country's tourism industry. Crime and the offshore perception of South Africa as a crime-ridden environment will have to be tackled far more robustly. Both the perceptions and the realities must be addressed.

South Africa has twice the international average of crimes per capita. Radically inspired interest groups and common criminals often choose to damage the tourist industry as a soft target. Safety and security actions should be addressed by government, otherwise the tourism industry and its potential for jobs are at risk.

A tourism safety task group comprising representatives from the government departments and other stakeholder groups is tackling a wide range of tourism security issues, including the use of more dedicated tourist police and the establishment of a database of tourism security intelligence. For safety purposes, hotels are now required to provide a save haven as part of the total experience. The key challenge is whether South Africa can overcome external perceptions of safety and security as well as service delivery constraints and capture a growing share of the world's tourism market in the future.

From Information Technology to Knowledge Exchange

Information will be crucial to compete effectively in the global marketplace. On a strategic level, information on global trends, competitors, and market opportunities are essential for informed decisions and to facilitate market-driven strategies. Information infrastructure has emerged as an important source of competitive advantage and competitive risk. Technology is the golden thread that runs throughout to spread learning and knowledge and catalyze opportunities.

Technology has enabled on-line reservations to increase dramatically; on-line generated business has grown at unprecedented rates. Much of the growth of ticket sales on the Internet comes from its ability to reflect modern lifestyles. The Internet acts as a *catalyst* to promote basic brand recognition symbols to full-fledged dialogues. Tailor-made to host such dialogues, the Internet provides scope for marketers to integrate their interactions with customers and enables companies to discover and exploit target-audience individual interests.

From a tourist market perspective, destination information can shape market segmentation strategies. The expectation goes beyond this to also provide information on trends and information on international and local tourism market developments, as well as e-commerce opportunities and commercial marketing opportunities on the World Wide Web. E-commerce, the value of which is expected to reach $1 trillion in the next three to five years, is ideally suited to small- and medium-sized firms. Start-up costs in establishing a Web site are relatively inexpensive, certainly when compared to opening a shop or office in a city space.

Steps have been taken toward creating an integrated tourism information management framework (TIMF) for South Africa. Creating a shared vision and a common focus are at the heart of the TIMF. A further goal of the TIMF is to contribute to the empowerment of local communities through information to enable them to become active and knowledgeable stakeholders and entrepreneurs in the industry. The whole TIMF process is based on strong public-private sector collaboration to ensure accountability.

In a bid to align with global destinations, Satour is currently upgrading its tourism information infrastructure. The planned Web site will improve on the current site by providing a showcase of South Africa, and it is envisaged to be at the forefront of Web site destination marketing in the global marketplace. This will be crucial to ensure strong growth relative to other global destinations.

From Policy to Delivery

Despite the tourism policy framework for South Africa (White Paper, 1996) and the tourism in GEAR (growth, employment, and redistribution) implementation strategy, the industry has not yet been able to deliver on the indicated targets. This concurs with a comprehensive analysis of the impact of tourism on the South African economy and on the region done by the WTTC (1998 and 1999). Integrating the policy and delivery dimensions issues in a regional context aligns with best practice trends. While the tourism industry has been in an expansion phase since the transition to democracy, it is now at the crossroads. The future prosperity of the tourism industry hinges on bridging the gaps and applying innovative solutions. The gaps between what worked in the traditional market and the new cyber market require timely actions.

While there are many opportunities in the growing world tourism market to tap into, and our product base compliments global trends and market needs, there are serious implementation weaknesses. Fragmentation and weak institutional capacity at all tiers are some of the real challenges. An implementation mode that will improve the quality of life at the community level by expanding business and employment opportunities and that capitalizes on scientific and technological progress is the best option to pursue. Creating the future requires partnerships, networks, and alliances.

This partnership approach provides a menu of opportunities by matching the needs and requirements with potential partners that are often competitors as well (Kruger-Cloete, 1995). South Africa's banking and finance industry is not yet geared to meet the demands of small- and medium-sized tourism enterprises. Core impediments to financial services include lack of economies of scale and lack of good information.

The opportunities and possible applications in support of infrastructure and transport systems include, among others, internodal and rail transport systems to enhance travel in the southern African region. For tourism development to branch out into peripheral areas, there will have to be a commitment to target technologies that harness water purification, effluent treatment, and renewable energy technologies.

Community Empowerment

Tourism is presently far from fulfilling its role as a catalyst for rural development. A case study of ten different community models in southern Africa by De Beer and Elliffe (1997) was mainly concerned with how the existing models could meet empowerment objectives while ensuring financial, institutional, and environmental sustainability. There are no easy answers, but generally, the empowerment models have to be tailored to the specific requirements of the location and the resource base and needs of the community.

Experience shows that community involvement in tourism-related projects is extremely demanding and challenging. Participatory projects take time and need dedicated management. Some demonstration projects have been confounded by constraints originating far from the project itself. To secure financing requires concrete steps on project design and management and a clear demonstration that a project is sustainable, replicable, and cost effective (Kruger-Cloete, 1995).

Donor resources can provide the initial impetus through institutional, community, and private sector development; improved infrastructure; and comprehensive policy formulation. The Business Trust is developing a program to support initiatives at the local level. In addition, the European Union has been approached to provide assistance to facilitate the involvement of communities and emerging entrants into the tourism sphere. The Wild Coast was selected as a pilot project for this purpose.

Community-based tourism projects require accessible and effective communication in order to reach their target markets—also through Internet access. Information that entices the potential tourist to Africa is readily available in the tourism origin countries in the form of multimedia videos, TV documentaries, CD-ROMs, and other printed media. A number of films have captured the mood and enticed visitors to the African setting.

A joint venture between a division for roads and transport technology (Transportek) and Satour offers a new tourism CD-ROM series. This is an integrated approach toward packaging and marketing South Africa as a tourist destination. This holistic approach offers advantages to the end user, such as interactive functionality, that allows tourists to plan a trip for specific interests and needs and also allows them to book through the Internet from the comfort of their own home. The package will contain three CDs.

Harnessing Technology

Globalization is forcing tourism stakeholders to come to terms with new standards, a capacity for adaptation to local needs, multiple cultures, and collaboration across national and regional boundaries. For this, speed of reaction is of the essence. Speed is also an element in how efficiently a company learns new technologies and integrates them with those already in use. Increasingly, the focus has to shift toward innovation in business models.

In an era of rapid and continuous change in the economical, political, social, and technological environment, a new competitive landscape has emerged. Software applications are transforming entire business models and stimulating the discovery of new products and markets. While the canvas available to today's strategies is large and new, tourism stakeholders need to understand global forces, react quickly, and become innovative.

Exploring the broad contours of the future we recognize the trends—the desire for mobility and travel, access to information, and the relentless spread of the Web. The problem is not information about the future but interpreting it to gain insights about how these trends will unfold to transform the tourism industry and to identify what new opportunities may emerge.

Concluding Remarks

The global economy is being transformed by political and social forces as well as regional trading blocs, global alliances of airlines, and deregulation. Global forces of competitiveness, information technology, and social-cultural dynamics are significantly impacting and shaping tourism destinations. Global shifts in the economy are driven by new waves of technology, the Internet, and electronic commerce. Places, culture, and identities seem to converge in the world of international travel. Understanding the powerful driving forces that are creating the future are necessary to realign and reframe the policy agenda.

Countries, institutions, and individuals are faced with significant shifts in the global environment, characterized by changing patterns of trade and competition, technological innovation, exponential growth of knowledge, and worldwide social concerns for "quality of life." In the global economy, business solutions require innovations tailored to these technologies. All these trends have ramifications for the tourism industry.

At the same time, travelers are becoming more knowledgeable, informed, and demanding. Competition has shifted from improving productivity to value-added quality, to flexibility and agility in the marketplace, and meeting customer demands anywhere, anytime, with customized solutions. Decisions and reaction times are becoming shorter, meaning that success will relate to the ability to position products and services and to respond rapidly to customer needs.

The accelerating global trends and technological convergence is disrupting traditional industry structures. Tourism industry players will have to come to terms with the nature of transformation that technological convergence and digitalization will have on the dynamics of the industry. This calls for a new mind-set. The impact of the World Wide Web and the Internet is just beginning to be felt.

Stronger ecological sensitivities and the emergence of nongovernmental organizations are also new dimensions in the competitive landscape. These discontinuities are changing the nature of the industry structure—the relationships between consumers, competitors, collaborators, and investors. Increasingly, the distinction between local and global tourism business will be narrowed. Tourism businesses will have to be locally responsive and, at the same time, will be subject to the influences and standards of global players. The explosive growth of multimedia and its impact on tourism, as well as the capacity of the Internet to become the main conduit of travel business for the future, supplemented by electronic commerce, is compelling.

But while global economic and technology shifts provide new challenges for sustainable tourism development, they also offer new opportunities and have made open participatory processes essential for long-term success. The country is finding balance in sustainable tourism development. Competition and collaboration are needed for efficiency, innovation, and customer satisfaction. Strengthening institutions and building capacities to deliver tailormade services harnessed by new and emerging technologies are the catalysts to drive the tourism economy into the new millennium. To promote the country and the region as a preferred tourist destination celebrating diversity, as a destination that will draw and satisfy global and local tourists alike, the creation of a truly memorable African experience is essential.

References

Camagni, R., R. Capello, and P. Nijkamp. 1998. ANALYSIS Toward sustainable city policy: An economy-environment technology nexus. *Ecological Economics,* 24:103–118.

Chang, T. C. 1999. Local uniqueness in the global village: Heritage tourism in Singapore. *Professional Geographer,* 51:91–101.

Collins, J. 1999. Turning goals into results: The power of catalytic mechanisms, *Harvard Business Review.* Internet Access: www.hbsp. harvard. edu./ products/hbr/julaug99/99401.html (September 5, 2001).

Dawe, S., P. Bryden, and J. M. Bryden. 1998. Competitive advantage in the rural periphery: Redefining the global-local nexus. Paper presented at the 2nd International Conference on Urban Development—*A Challenge for Frontier Regions,* Beer Sheva, Israel. April 4–7, 1998.

De Beer, G., and S. Elliffe. 1997. Tourism development and the empower-
    ment of local communities. Working Paper 11. *Development Policy
    Research Unit*, University of Cape Town.
Dini, L., and J. D. Wolfensohn. 1999. Let's start taking the benefits of cultural
    identity seriously. *International Herald Tribune*, Paris, October 6.
Fayos-Solá, E. 1996. Tourism policy: A midsummer night's dream? *Tourism
    Management*, 17:405–412.
Janssen, H., M. Kiers, and P. Nijkamp. 1995. Private and public development
    strategies for sustainable tourism development of island economies.
    In H. Coccossis and P. Nijkamp eds., *Sustainable Tourism Develop-
    ment*. Ashgate: Aldershot, England, pp. 65–83.
Kanter Moss, R. 1997. *Rosabeth Moss Kanter on the Frontiers of Management*
    (Harvard Business Review book). Cambridge, MA: Harvard Univ.
    Press.
Klitgaard, R. 1995. World Bank Discussion Paper 303. Institutional adjust-
    ment and adjusting to institutions. Washington: World Bank.
KPMG, 1999. Review of infrastructure in support of international and
    domestic tourism development—Final report: Tourism infrastruc-
    ture investment framework. Pretoria: Commissioned by the Gov-
    ernment of South Africa Department of Environmental Affairs and
    Tourism.
Kruger-Cloete, E. 1995. Viewpoint: Funding the development of tourism in
    South Africa. *Development Southern Africa*, 12:751–767.
Pine II, J. B., and J. H. Gilmore. 1998. Welcome to the experience economy.
    Harvard Business Review, 76:97–105.
Sealey, P. 1999. How e-commerce will trump brand management. *Harvard
    Business Review*, Internet access: www.hbsp.harvard.edu./products/
    hbr/julaug99/99409.html (September 5, 2001).
Soros, George. 1998. The Crisis of Global Capitalism. New York: Public Affairs.
South Africa, 1996. White Paper: Development and promotion of tourism
    in South Africa, 1996. Pretoria: Government of South Africa, Depart-
    ment of Environmental Affairs and Tourism.
South Africa. 1997. Tourism in GEAR: Tourism Development Strategy 1998–
    2000. Preoria: Government of South Africa, Department of Environ-
    mental Affairs and Tourism.
World Bank 1997. *World Development Report 1997: The State in a Changing
    World*. Washington, DC: Oxford University Press, World Bank.
World Tourism Organisation (WTO). 1999. *Tourism 2020 Vision: A New
    Forecast*. www.selectbooks.com.sg/titles/30305.html (September 5,
    2001).

World Travel and Tourism Council (WTTC). 1998. *South Africa's Travel and Tourism—Economic Driver for the 21st Century.*

World Travel and Tourism Council (WTTC). 1999. *Southern African Development Community's Travel and Tourism—Economic Driver for the 21st Century.*

World Tourism Organisation Newsletter. 1995. Government and business: Partners in tourism (November-December).

World Tourism Organisation, WTO News. 1996. Huge turnout for Bali Forum (November–December).

World Tourism Organisation Press Release. 1995. Charter for Sustainable Tourism. Adopted in Lanzarote, May 8.

World Tourism Organisation Press Release. 1997. Asian Nations Pledge to Protect the Environment, February 17.

Part 2

Economic Aspects of Tourism in Frontier Areas

Chapter 4

The Economic Impact of Tourism in the Central and Outlying Regions of Israel: A Multiregional Input-Output Model

Daniel Freeman and Esther Sultan

The number of incoming tourists to Israel increased at an annual rate of 15 percent over the period 1990 and 1995. Their expenditures in 1995 were 30 percent of the value of export of services and about 11 percent of the total exports. The number and the expenditures of domestic tourists has also increased simultaneously with the continuing rise in personal incomes. The impacts of domestic tourists in outlying regions such as the North and South (Galil and Negev) is greater than that of the incoming tourists.

The development of tourism as a means to widen the export base and generate more employment is of primary importance. Policymakers in the government need to know the magnitude of the impact of international and domestic tourist expenditures on the Israeli economy in order to make decisions about budget allocations for the development of tourist facilities.

In response to this need, the Ministry of Tourism conducted several studies concerning the magnitudes of direct purchases of incoming and domestic tourists from the economic branches, and their regional distribution.

The objective of the present paper is to assess and estimate the magnitude of the contribution to GDP of the intra- and interregional impacts caused by tourist purchases and expenditures. This analysis will allow the government to establish policy objectives for the development of tourist facilities in the different regions of Israel, and especially in the North and South. The policy analyst might be interested in responding to such questions as: How much additional income is to be generated? How many jobs will be created? What will be the magnitude of the addition to GDP? What is the impact of direct demand in one region on the output in other regions? Does the greater impact of Israelis in the outlying regions reduce the disparity between them and the central regions in their favor? And what is the extent of the feedback mechanism whereby increased production in the originating region is met by successive rounds of reimports in order to satisfy this demand. An estimate of tourism's economic impat is complex because it entails an analysis of the direct purchases from several branches in several regions simultaneously.

Literature Review

Archer (1976) developed regional multipliers as a tool for analyzing the economic impact of tourism at the single region level. These regional multipliers were based on the Keynsian model and thus were highly aggregated. Liu and Var (1982) reformulated Archer's model by disaggregation of the accommodation sector. Briguglio (1993) claimed that the Keynsian model and an input-output (IO) model yield the same results at an aggregate level. However, an input-output model was chosen here due to three advantages: first, IO models have the ability to evaluate the impact on each branch separately; second, they can disaggregate the impact by contribution of each region; and third, they are able to measure the returning repercussions from contributing regions in response to the demand from the originating region and the successive rounds of repercussions between them.

Fletcher (1989) and other researchers (Blaine, 1992; Wanhill, 1994; Lundberg et al., 1995) proposed the use of single table IO analysis as a tool, the results of which respond to the foregoing questions due to its ability to evaluate the simultaneous impacts of sectoral interdependencies. They applied single table IO models at both national and regional levels.

As described by Blaine (1992), the single table modelers at the regional level assumed that only some of the leakages from the region reenter the region. However, it may very well be that the "imports" from other regions into the region and its "export" leaks to other regions, resulting from the need to fulfill demand, are not accounted for in the multiplier impact. Also, more importantly, the indirect and induced impacts created in other regions are ignored as part of the multiplier. This leads to a downward bias in the estimation of regional multipliers.

Nordstrom (1996) found that quantitative and monetary data from tourists' surveys about their expenses differed from the reports of the suppliers of goods and services. These discrepancies are largely due to differences between the reports of the suppliers' prices and the consumers' prices and the consumers' tendency to classify expenses into different classes, as well as items they have forgotten. The same problem was encountered in the present study, so adjustments were made in order to align the final uses obtained from the aforementioned two types of sources.

The multiregional input-output model (MRIO) that was used in this research adds to the IO framework the capability of evaluating the impacts due to tourist expenditures on interregional interdependencies simultaneously with sectoral ones. A MRIO model has been used in Israel previously in evaluating national level and regional development projects (Freeman et al., 1990), but evaluate the impacts of tourism it was more recently used to (Freeman and Honigbaum, 1995). The estimates of the magnitude of the economic impacts of the expenditures are then expressed both in monetary terms and in number of employees (see also Fleischer and Freeman, 1997). The results are then expressed as multiregional input-output multipliers. Therefore, this model takes into account the possible returns of the leakages and the impacts in other regions, since it includes a multiregion trade flow matrix, thus evaluating the full impact.

The MRIO Model

The classical definitions of national-level or single-region IO multipliers were presented by authors such as Miernyk (1965), and the multiregional definitions by Polenske (1972) and Dipasquale and Polenske (1977). These authors defined three levels of impacts: direct, indirect, and induced.

While the principal objective of the national IO model is to identify and analyze the interbranch structure of the economy, the objective of the MRIO model is to give content to spatial elements in order to study the structures and linkages of individual branches within a region and the inter-relationships with other branches in the region and in other regions.

As such, MRIO models are most useful for analyzing and assessing different investment strategies and their direct and indirect impacts on the economy of the target region and, simultaneously, on other regions. A further advantage is the flexibility of the model to suit the objective at hand. Thus, branches which are important to the study of tourism can be highly disaggregated while the remaining sectors can be aggregated to keep the size of the model manageable.

The model is composed of two multiregional direct column coefficient matrices: an IO matrix and a trade flow (TF) matrix.

The "services" column of the IO matrix is disaggregated into ten branches that are prominent in tourist expenditures: international air transport, air transport authority, three classes of hotels, two classes of restaurants, car rentals, sight-seeing tour buses, and domestic flights. The other branches of the economy are highly aggregated, so as to reduce the size of the table to a 24x24 matrix for each of the six regions of the country.

The Technological Matrix

The structure of the matrix is based on the assumption that the intermediate uses of branch j from branches i are constant ratios of the output of branch j. It should be noted that the model has a certain weakness, since it does not contain a mechanism that responds to substitution between intermediate resources due to price changes. Yet its use is justified because the rate of change over time of the direct coefficients is very slow. Thus, the error in measurement of the impacts of interbranch dependencies, caused by using a model from former years in a current one, is relatively slight.

The regional IO technological matrices ($A^n = A^n_{ij}$) are arranged along the diagonal of the matrix in a $NM * NM$ multiregional matrix (N regions and M branches), while the off-diagonal parts of the table are zeroes.

The matrix expression of interbranch relations, and between them and the final uses (i.e., Private and Government Consumption, Investments and Exports) and the gross output in an IO table is given in equation 1:

$$X = AX + Y \tag{1}$$

where: X = gross output
              A = direct coefficients
              Y = final uses.

It is quite obvious that equation 1 does not show a regional breakdown.

The Integration of InterRegional Trade Flows

The technological matrix of intermediate uses that describes interbranch relationships in the production process is combined with a trade flow matrix where $C = C_m{}^{gh}$ is the flow of a good in branch m from region g to region h, that has the above dimensions $NM * NM$ and includes $N * N$ trade submatrices, and in each, the trade flows are expressed along its diagonal.

Equation 2 combines the two matrices through multiplication:

$$X = CAX + CY \qquad (2)$$

where: C is the trade flow matrix.
  This can be rewritten as follows:

$$(I - CA)X = CY \qquad (2a)$$

Both sides of the above have to be multiplied by the Leontief Inverse in order to reach a solution:

$$(I - CA)^{-1} (I - CA)X = (I - CA)^{-1}CY \qquad (2b)$$

Equation 2b reduces to show the dependency of gross output on the final uses, as shown in equation 3:

$$X = (I - CA)^{-1}CY \qquad (3)$$

The output multiplier B is derived from equation 3 as shown in equation 4:

$$B = (I - CA)^{-1}C \qquad (4)$$

Data Sources

The sources of data of the expenditures of tourists that were used in this research are discussed in detail by Freeman and Sultan (1997). Thus, a brief discourse seems to be sufficient here.

Data Sources of International Tourists

Statistics on incoming international tourists to Israel are collected from both the tourists and the local businesses that serve them.

All incoming tourists are requested to fill personal questionnaires at the frontier control points. The data are analyzed and published by the Central Bureau of Statistics (Israel CBS Tourism in Israel Series).

Three surveys of tourist expenditures are available (Israel, Ministry of Tourism, 1993):

1. Forty thousand tourists were handed questionnaires to fill out upon their departure. They contained questions concerning the purpose of visit, type of visit, demographic profile, and the amount and components of their expenditure. The response rate was about 40 percent.

2. A diary questionnaire was handed to ten thousand tourists on their arrival in Israel by air (70 percent of tourists arrive in Israel by air). They were asked to make daily entries and return the diary on departure. The response rate was only 6 percent.

3. A sample of thirty package tours was analyzed. The expenditures were separated into the appropriate economic categories.

Two major sources of data by the businesses that serve the tourists are the following:

1. Monthly reports by all hotels on the numbers of available rooms and beds, numbers of guests, and person nights of international and domestic tourists. About 50 percent of the hotels (180) report every three months on revenue, persons employed, and wages (Israel CBS, 1996).

2. Since 1981, the Israel Central Bureau of Statistics (CBS) has been conducting surveys of the income, expenditure, and product for the Ministry of Tourism, Israel CBS, 1991–1992. These surveys present data on the economic accounts of the hotels by level, size, number of rooms, and annual occupancy (Israel CBS, 1993, 1995).

Domestic Tourism

The data on domestic tourism were taken from the following sources:

1. Stays of Israelis by person nights in hotels, youth hostels, and other accommodation from the foregoing sources of tourist hotels (Israel CBS, 1995a).

2. A household survey by telephone of a sample of one thousand households was conducted by the Ministry of Tourism in 1991 and 1994 (Israel Ministry of Tourism 1991; 1994).

3. From November 1991 to April 1992, a time budgeting survey was conducted by Israel CBS (1995b) of leisure activities of persons aged

fourteen and over. Two types of diaries were used: (1) recollection of expenses and purchases from the previous day through an interview by the enumerator, (2) a diary filled out by the interviewee on a specific day after the interview. Two types of questionnaire were used to provide information on the frequency of participation in specific activities: (1) a family questionnaire, (2) a personal questionnaire.

A Supplementary Survey of other Tourist Services

A supplementary survey on income, expenditure, and product of restaurants, domestic flights, excursion buses, and car rentals was conducted in 1993 (Freeman and Honigbaum, 1995). One objective was to examine the share of incoming tourists in their output. The second objective was to find out the expenditure pattern of the different businesses. The third objective was to find out the multiregional distribution of the output and the costs. The surveyed populations were relatively small: one domestic flight airline, six car rental companies, seventeen companies operating as tour operators, and fifteen restaurants. The data were cross-checked with other sources, such as CBS and the income tax authorities.

The Technical Coefficients

A MRIO model of Israel for 1990 (Freeman and Honigbaum, 1995) was adjusted to the needs of this research. The 1990 model was constructed from the former study from the national table for 1988 (Israel CBS, 1994) in four steps:

Step 1: Aggregation of the national table of 191x191 branches into a 16x16 table that was then adjusted to the 1990 price level.

Step 2: The transactions of eight tourist branches from some of the foregoing surveys (namely hotels, restaurants, car rentals, sight-seeing buses, domestic flights) were adjusted to the 1990 price level and then implanted in the table while simultaneously being deducted from the appropriate aggregated branches.

Step 3: The resultant 24x24 size table was adjusted by an RAS* (Univ. of Cambridge, 1971) method and then converted into direct column coefficients.

Step 4: The coefficients were adjusted up by wholesale indices to the 1994 price level by multiplying table rows by wholesale price indices of

---

* RAS is a mathematical method for adjusting input-output tables. The letters represent matematical symbols (see Toh 1998).

the branches by adjusting the sum of the intermediate uses in each column to their original sum (before the multiplication of the rows by the indices). These national level coefficients were applied in all the six regions of the country because the same advanced technologies were used in all the regions.

The Sources of Trade Flows

The trade flows of the agricultural and industrial branches were derived from a truck transportation survey (Israel CBS, 1993). The trade flows of the services were derived by the difference between supply of each branch of services in each of the regions and the demand for that service in each of the regions.

The Tourism Multipliers

The model that is used here has been constructed especially for the present study on the basis of the above sources. The values are expressed in New Israeli Sheqels (NIS) in 1994 prices. The values of goods and services purchased by tourists are introduced into the final use column and then multiplied by the MRIO inverse-matrix.

The model yields various multipliers of output, income, employment, etc., which are presented as two types:

Type I (open model) multipliers which express the ratio of direct + indirect impacts to direct impacts (Lundberg et al., 1995; Myernyk, 1965).

Type II (closed model) multipliers which express the ratio of direct + indirect + induced impacts to direct impacts.

This paper presents the results of a study of the impacts of incoming and domestic tourist expenditures on the Israeli Economy (Freeman, Zeif, and Freeman, 1996). The distributed impacts of twenty-four branches among the six districts and the differences in each of the impacts of incoming and domestic tourists are presented.

Levels of Analysis

First, at the level of the national economy we shall present the tourist expenditures (final use) and their impacts on the economic branches and their recursive impacts on the branches of the direct demand. Second, at the intraregional and interregional level, we shall present the final uses from branches in each region and its impact on the branches within the region, interbranch and interregional impacts and their returning repercussions on the final use branches in the originating region. Third, at the level of the tourist segments, the differences between the impacts of the direct demand of the two tourist segments will be presented. Fourth, at the sectoral level, we will present the results for hotels, restaurants, car rentals, excursion buses, and domestic flights. Then, we will show to what extent the tourist expenditures in these branches generate production in the whole economy.

Multipliers of Two Segments of Tourism

In addition multipliers are collected for two segments.

First, a multiplier representing a weighted average of two segments of domestic tourists: lodging tourists and day trippers.

Second, a multiplier representing a weighted average of five segments of international tourists: holidays, sightseeing, pilgrimage, visiting, and others (Israel, Ministry of Tourism, 1993).

Major Empirical Findings

National Level Multipliers of Tourism

National level impacts are presented in table 4.1a in two separate subtotals. First, the sum of the final uses of the two segments from the economic branches in 1994, which was 10.9 billion NIS, is presented. The derived output was 19.1 billion NIS and the compound output was 37.6 billion NIS.

Second, the rent from apartments rented to international tourists is estimated to be an output of 693 million NIS. The weighted average of 1 NIS of the final uses from the economic branches of international and domestic tourists generates a type I multiplier of 1.76 NIS at the national level, inclusive of the direct expenditure; i.e., each 1 NIS of direct expenditure generates an addition of 0.76 NIS of indirect expenditure. The rent paid by international tourists for apartments adds the output which is also the value added, but the multiplier declines slightly to 1.71 because the rent does not generate indirect impacts.

The type II multiplier from the economic branches was 3.46, which indicates that 1 NIS of direct demand generated an extra 2.46 NIS. The multiplier declines slightly to 3.31 with the addition of the rent.

Table 4.1b presents the share of labor costs in the final uses, in the derived output, and in the compound output. Two versions of multipliers are presented.

First, multipliers entitled Miernyk type (output multipliers). These are

1. The outcome of the division of the derived labor cost from the derived output by the labor cost in the final uses. The weighted average of the two segments was 1.92, which means that each 1 NIS of direct labor cost generated an extra 0.92 NIS of indirect labor costs.

2. The outcome of the division of labor cost in the compound output by the labor cost in the final uses. The weighted average of the two segments was 2.94, which means that each 1 NIS of direct labor cost generated an extra 1.94 NIS of indirect labor costs.

Second, multipliers entitled Polenske type (MRIO multipliers). These are the ones that other authors (see Fletcher, 1989) call income multipliers; i.e., the total of a distributed MRIO multiplier due to final uses in any region is equivalent to the so-called income multiplier, and they are the following:

1. The outcome of the division of labor cost in the derived output by the final uses—each 1 NIS of final uses generated 0.52 NIS of returns to labor.

2. The outcome of the division of labor cost in the compound output by the final uses. The weighted average of the two segments was 0.80—each 1 NIS of final uses generated 0.80 NIS returns to labor.

Table 4.1c presents the magnitude of the other value added (OVA), which includes the returns to capital and the indirect taxes in the derived and compound outputs.

The magnitude of the Miernyk Multiplier is 1.66, which means that each 1 NIS of OVA in the final uses generated an extra 0.66 NIS in the derived output. The average of the multiplier in the closed model is 3.45, which indicates that an extra 2.45 NIS of OVA was generated in the compound output by 1 NIS of OVA in the final uses.

The magnitude of the Polenske multiplier is 0.28—thus, each 1 NIS of the final uses generated 0.28 NIS in the derived output. The average of the multiplier in the closed model is 0.59, which indicates that 0.59 NIS was generated in the compound output by 1 NIS of final uses.

Table 4.1d presents the value added (VA) as a sum of the components of the labor costs and OVA.

The Miernyk multiplier of the economic branches of the open model was 1.95 and that of the closed model was 3.49, but the addition of rent from apartments reduced them to 1.81 and 3.14, respectively.

The Polenske multiplier of the open model of international tourists was 0.78 and that of the closed model was 1.40, but the weighted average with the rent from apartments and domestic tourists is 0.83 and 1.43, respectively.

Table 4.1. National Level Multipliers

Economic Segments	Tourist Segments	Final Uses	Final Uses & Output Derived Output	Compound Derived Output	Miernyk Type Multipliers Derived Output	Compound Derived Output	Polenske Type Multipliers Derived Output	Compound Derived Output
			Millions NIS 1994 Prices					
			Part A					
Final Uses & Output	Domestic	3,861	6,827	13,078	1.77	3.39		
	International	7,012	12,309	24,521	1.76	3.50		
	Sub total branches	10,873	19,136	37,599	1.76	3.46		
	Rent from apartments	693	693	693	1.00	1.00		
	Total	11,566	19,829	38,292	1.71	3.31		
			Part B					
Labor Costs	Domestic	1,025	1,922	2,945	1.88	2.87	0.50	0.76
	International	1,940	3,768	5,762	1.94	2.97	0.54	0.82
	Total	2,965	5,690	8,707	1.92	2.94	0.52	0.80
			Part C					
Other Value Added	Domestic	422	896	2,099	2.12	4.97	0.23	0.54
	International	873	1,704	4,062	1.95	4.65	0.24	0.58
	Rent from apartments	693	693	693	1.00	1.00	0.06	0.06
	Total	1,988	3,293	6,854	1.66	3.45	0.28	0.59
			Part D					
Value Added	Domestic	1,447	2,818	5,044	1.95	3.49	0.73	1.31
	International	2,813	5,472	9,824	1.95	3.49	0.78	1.40
	Rent from apartments	693	693	693	1.00	1.00	0.06	0.06
	Total	4,953	8,983	15,561	1.81	3.14	0.83	1.43
			Part E					
Employed Persons			Number of Employed Persons					
	Domestic	20,593	33,638	49,610	1.63	2.41		
	International	35,613	60,208	91,357	1.69	2.57		
	Total	56,206	93,846	140,967	1.67	2.51		

The three levels of VA in percentage terms of the Israeli GDP of 223 billion NIS were in the following economic segments:

1. Share in the final uses = 2.2 percent;
2. Share in the derived output = 4.0 percent;
3. Share in the compound output = 7.0 percent.

These results indicate that the contribution of tourism to the economy is greater than the direct impact only.

Table 4.1e demonstrates that 56,206 were employed in the direct supply of final uses in 1994, while the estimated number is 93,846 in the derived output (including those in final uses) and is 140,967 in the compound output. These numbers represent 3 percent, 5 percent, and 7.5 percent of the 1.87 million civilian labor force in Israel, respectively. The magnitudes of the multipliers were respectively 1.67 and 2.51. These results indicate that the employment impact of the tourist industry is much greater than the direct impact itself, but it is smaller than the output multiplier which includes the impact of the imported resources, and also smaller than the income multiplier, due to the fact that the average wage in the tourist branches was higher than the average in the country.

Regional Level Multipliers

The impact of the two tourist segments—international and domestic—on the six districts of Israel is a function of the resources and their interregional trade flows. For example, most of the food for tourists in Eilat is transported from the central regions. The final uses of tourists in the hotels in the North generate demand for goods and services from other regions, such as kitchen utensils, textile goods, etc. The final uses in both the peripheral regions include airline services that are supplied in the central region. Thus, the final uses of tourists in one region that does not produce a sufficient quantity (or none at all) of the requested goods generate an import of those goods from other regions.

The magnitude of the multipliers due to final uses of tourists who visit each region are between 1.76–1.77 as estimated by the national level magnitude presented in table 4.1a. This magnitude is the sum of the impacts in the six columns that show the interregional distribution of this multiplier due to final uses of tourists in one region. The multipliers of visitors in each of the other regions are similar in total magnitude and vary in distribution. One can see that the share of domestic tourists in the North is 0.83 (see table 4.2a) and that of international tourists is 0.71. Both are less than the magnitude of the final uses, but the rest of the multiplier is distributed between the other regions. Because of the equality of the magnitude of the multipliers of each region and the similarity of their multiregional distribution, the following tables will not present the multipliers of each region in order not to burden the reader.

Tables 4.2 and 4.3 present respectively the share of each region in type I and type II multipliers, due to final uses of tourists that visit that region. The right-hand column in both tables presents the magnitude of the multiplier at both the national level and that of each of the six regions. Table 4.2 presents the type I multipliers and contains four parts, parts a through d; table 4.3 presents the type II multipliers and also contains four parts, parts a through d. The upper three lines in each of the four parts present the multiplier shares, while the three lower lines present these shares as percentages of the magnitude of the multiplier. In the following discussion, the significant findings are expressed as shares of the multiplier, beside which the same share in percentages is stated in parentheses.

Table 4.2a shows a share of each region in the total of the type I multiplier of domestic tourists of 1.77 and of international tourists of 1.76; such as the second column in the table presents the magnitudes of the shares of the North, and so on. The magnitudes of the multipliers due to final uses in each region are separately equal because the intermediate direct coefficients are equal. Though the shares of the other regions in the multipliers of final uses in each region are not shown here, their sum is the difference between the total and each region's share. The main findings with respect to the output multiplier are as follows.

1. The share of the multiplier of derived output due to final uses of domestic tourists in any of the six regions ranges between 0.83 (47 percent) in the North and 1.11 (63 percent) in Haifa.

2. The shares of Haifa and of Tel Aviv in their multipliers due to domestic tourism are greater than those of the remoter regions of the South and North.

3. The largest share of 1.11 (63 percent) due to domestic tourists in any region was in Haifa, as the supplier of all the fuel for both traveling and production in all the branches and since it supplies its own fuel; a slightly lower share of 1.03 (58 percent) occurs for Tel Aviv, since it supplies its own services and is also the major service supplier to all the other regions, with hardly any need to purchase them from other regions.

4. The largest share of 1.11 (63 percent) of the derived output multiplier due to international tourists is in the Central region, where the inter-

Table 4.2. Tourism Open MRIO Model: Internal Share of Each Region in Its Multipliers. Derived Output Due to Final Uses of International and Domestic Tourists, 1994

Tourism Segments Multipliers	Regional Final Uses	Six Districts of Israel						Each Region Multiplier
		North	Haifa	Center	Tel Aviv	Jerusalem	South	
Part A: Derived Output Share of Each Region in Its Multiplier								
Domestic Tourism	1.00	0.83	1.11	0.83	1.03	0.90	0.95	1.77
International Tourism	1.00	0.71	0.92	1.11	1.06	0.85	0.69	1.76
Total Tourism	1.00	0.77	1.01	0.98	1.05	0.86	0.84	1.76
				Percents				
Domestic Tourism		47	63	47	58	51	54	100
International Tourism		40	53	63	61	49	39	100
Total Tourism		44	58	56	60	49	48	100
Part B: Derived Income Share in Polenske Multiplier of Each Region								
Domestic Tourism	1.00	0.27	0.30	0.27	0.34	0.31	0.30	0.50
International Tourism	1.00	0.23	0.29	0.37	0.34	0.30	0.23	0.54
Total Tourism	1.00	0.25	0.29	0.32	0.34	0.30	0.27	0.52
				Percents				
Domestic Tourism		54	61	54	69	63	61	100
International Tourism		43	53	69	64	56	42	100
Total Tourism		47	56	62	66	57	52	100
Part C: Derived VA Polenske Multiplier Share of Each Region								
Domestic Tourism Multiplier	1.00	0.38	0.44	0.39	0.48	0.44	0.42	0.73
International Tourism Multiplier	1.00	0.33	0.41	0.51	0.51	0.40	0.31	0.78
Total Tourism	1.00	0.35	0.43	0.45	0.50	0.41	0.37	0.76
				Percents				
Domestic Tourism		52	61	53	66	60	58	100
International Tourism		42	53	65	65	52	40	100
Total Tourism		46	56	59	66	54	49	100

con't.

Table 4.2 continued

		Six Districts of Israel						
Tourism Segments Multipliers	Regional Final Uses	North	Haifa	Center	Tel Aviv	Jerusalem	South	Each Region Multiplier
Part D: Share in Employment Multiplier of Each Region								
Domestic Tourism Multiplier	1.00	1.02	1.19	1.02	1.20	1.13	0.97	1.63
International Tourism Multiplier	1.00	0.94	1.14	1.15	1.23	1.02	0.93	1.69
Total Tourism	1.00	0.98	1.16	1.09	1.22	1.03	0.96	1.67
				Percents				
Domestic Tourism		63	73	62	73	69	60	100
International Tourism		55	68	68	73	60	55	100
Total Tourism		59	70	65	73	62	57	100

national airport is located; and the share is a little smaller—1.06 (61 percent)—in Tel Aviv. These magnitudes indicate that those two regions produce more for themselves in response to their own direct final uses than do other regions.

Table 4.2b presents the Polenske income multiplier, the total of which, 0.52, is equivalent to the income multiplier of all the foregoing quoted single-region multipliers. (The national level total of the Polenske multiplier is equal, by definition, to the income multiplier in the quoted single-table studies before deduction of leakages by some researchers.) The multiplier of 0.54, due to international tourism, is greater than the 0.50 due to domestic tourism, especially because of the high import content of the fuel that the domestic day trippers use.

However, in domestic tourism, as in the case of the output, the magnitude of the shares in the multiplier varies slightly between the regions— 0.30 (61 percent) in Haifa and 0.34 (69 percent) in Tel Aviv. But a noted difference from the shares in the output multiplier is that the income in the peripheral regions is larger in percentage terms: 54 percent in the North, 61 percent in the South, and 63 percent in Jerusalem. This is explained by a greater share of labor cost in these regions, because the number of employed persons is larger, as shown in table 4.2d below.

The shares due to international tourism that stand out were in the Center, 0.37 (69 percent) and in Tel Aviv, 0.34 (64 percent), but there is a smaller percentage increase of family income in the North, in the South, and in Jerusalem. The conclusion is that, in these regions, domestic tourism generates more employment and income per 1 NIS of output.

Table 4.2c presents each region's share in the derived value added multiplier of the open model. The sum of labor income plus the OVA is the VA, which is the contribution to the GDP. The VA at the national level is 0.76, deriving from each 1 NIS of final uses in the open model. The more prominent regions in relation to each region's final uses of domestic tourists were Haifa, 0.44 (61 percent); Jerusalem, 0.44 (60 percent); and Tel Aviv, 0.48 (66 percent), while those of international tourism were Tel Aviv, 0.51 (65 percent), and the Center, 0.51 (65 percent). The conclusion here is parallel to that above regarding the greater impact of family income.

Table 4.2d presents the multiplier of the number of the employed persons in the open model. The national level totals of the multipliers are smaller than those of the output multipliers, but the regional shares of the North, the South, and of Jerusalem were even larger than those of family income in table 4.2b. An explanation of this is that the weighted average labor cost per employed person in the peripheral regions is smaller.

Table 4.3a presents the shares in the type II multiplier of the compound output (closed model) due to final demand in each of the regions. Its monetary magnitude is greater proportionately in all the regions than in the derived output (open model). However, in the case of domestic tourists, the shares and percentage shares of 1.74 (51 percent) in Haifa and of 1.82 (54 percent) in Tel Aviv were more than half of the multiplier of the derived output but smaller than in the open model. But since the percentage shares of the peripheral regions were also smaller, the ratio between the shares of the central to the peripheral regions has not changed. The smaller shares of the remoter regions reflects also the differences in impacts between them and those of the center.

In the case of the effect of international tourists, the shares and percentage shares of 1.84 (53 percent) in the Center and of 1.89 (54 percent) in Tel Aviv were more than half of the multiplier of the derived output, but smaller than in the open model. However, the percentage shares of the peripheral regions were also smaller, thus the ratio between the shares of the central vis-à-vis the peripheral regions was unchanged.

A conclusion here is that the percentage shares of each region's compound output, due to final uses of tourists in it, decline, while those of other regions increase. However, it should be noted that the absolute value of the output increases in each of the regions, but more so in the other five regions in comparison to each region.

Table 4.3b presents the results of the income multiplier of the closed model. The multiplier of 0.80 varies slightly between 0.76 for domestic tourists to 0.82 for international tourists. However, the percentage shares of the

Table 4.3. Tourism Closed MRIO Model. Internal Share of Each Region in Its Multipliers. Derived Output Due to Final Uses of International and Domestic Tourists

Tourism Segments Multipliers	Regional Final Uses	North	Haifa	Center	Tel Aviv	Jerusalem	South	Each Region Multiplier
				Six Districts of Israel				
Part A: Derived Share of Each Region in Its Multiplier								
Domestic Tourism	1.00	1.34	1.74	1.38	1.82	1.48	1.50	3.39
International Tourism	1.00	1.18	1.55	1.84	1.89	1.42	1.13	3.50
Total Tourism	1.00	1.25	1.64	1.63	1.87	1.42	1.34	3.46
				Percents				
Domestic Tourism		39	51	41	54	44	44	100
International Tourism		34	44	53	54	40	32	100
Total Tourism		36	48	47	54	41	39	100
Part B: Derived Income Share in Polenske Multiplier of Each Region								
Domestic Tourism	1.00	0.33	0.39	0.34	0.46	0.39	0.37	0.76
International Tourism	1.00	0.29	0.37	0.46	0.47	0.37	0.28	0.82
Total Tourism	1.00	0.31	0.38	0.41	0.47	0.37	0.33	0.80
				Percents				
Domestic Tourism		43	51	45	60	51	48	100
International Tourism		35	45	56	57	45	34	100
Total Tourism		38	47	51	58	47	41	100
Part C: Derived VA Polenske Multiplier Share of Each Region								
Domestic Tourism	1.00	0.54	0.65	0.58	0.76	0.63	0.60	1.31
International Tourism	1.00	0.48	0.62	0.75	0.80	0.60	0.46	1.40
Total Tourism	1.00	0.51	0.64	0.67	0.79	0.60	0.54	1.37
				Percents				
Domestic Tourism		42	50	44	58	49	46	100
International Tourism		35	44	54	57	43	33	100
Total Tourism		38	47	49	58	44	39	100
Part D: Share in Employment Multiplier of Each Region								
Domestic Tourism	1.00	1.22	1.46	1.24	1.55	1.36	1.15	2.41
International Tourism	1.00	1.14	1.41	1.45	1.58	1.24	1.12	2.57
Total Tourism	1.00	1.18	1.44	1.35	1.57	1.26	1.14	2.51
				Percents				
Domestic Tourism		51	61	52	64	57	48	100
International Tourism		44	55	57	61	48	44	100
Total Tourism		47	57	54	63	50	46	100

central regions Tel Aviv, the Center, and Jerusalem, due to domestic tourism, are larger than those in the compound output.

Table 4.3c presents each region's share in the derived multiplier of 1.37 of the compound VA in the closed model at the national level. This means that the compound output generated a greater VA than the final uses as a contribution to the GDP of Israel. The results of the distribution are proportionately parallel to those in table 4.3b.

Table 4.3d presents the national level of employment multipliers of the closed model. They are relatively smaller than the output multipliers, due to the fact that the household component of wages in the private consumption column is very small indeed and does not generate much extra employment. The percentage shares of employment in all the regions are smaller than in the open model, but the estimate is that the numbers of employed persons has increased by about one half.

Summary

This article reports the major findings of a research project of the impacts of international and domestic tourism expenditure in 1994 on the economy of Israel at both the national level and the regional levels. A MRIO model was used to estimate the impacts simultaneously at three levels:

1. the final uses: the direct expenditures of the tourists;
2. the indirect derived output: the indirect recursive interaction (inclusive of the direct final uses) between branches that supply the goods and services that are used as resources and the branches that respond to the direct final uses;
3. the compound outputs (inclusive of the derived output): the added induced impacts due to the productive repercussions deriving from the household consumption of the persons employed in direct and the indirect production.

The contribution to employment was estimated (direct + indirect + induced) and the compound number of employed persons was 7.5 percent of the total number of the 1.87 million of the labor force in the country.

The derived output (open model) that was estimated for each of the six regions, due to final uses on the basis of domestic tourists ranged between 47 percent in the North to 63 percent in Haifa. This means that about one half up to almost two thirds of the derived output due to final uses is produced in each region.

The derived output (open model) that was estimated for each of the six regions due to final uses on the basis of international tourists ranged between 39 percent in the North to 63 percent in Center. This means that the peripheral regions of North and South produce relatively less than that due to the final uses of tourists in them.

The compound output (closed model) due to direct expenditure of tourists in each region was larger in absolute terms than the derived output in all regions. It is evident in the case of domestic tourists that Haifa and Tel Aviv produced relatively more of the derived and the compound output than any other region, due to the volume of their direct expenditure in these areas. In the case of the international tourists, the Center and Tel Aviv produced relatively more than any other region in response to their own direct final uses. However, although the shares of all regions in the compound output, due to final uses in any region, are smaller in percentage terms, the magnitude in absolute terms of the compound output is more or less double.

The household incomes and the derived VA (open model) due to domestic tourism in the peripheral North and South regions were proportionately larger than the output estimated, because the increase in the numbers of the employed persons was relatively larger than that of the output. However, there was a relatively smaller international tourist increase in those regions. The percentage shares of all the regions in the compound output were smaller, but the ratio between them remained the same.

Conclusions

The above results lead to the following conclusions: First, the sum of the VA due to final uses was 2.2 percent of GDP of 223 billion NIS; that due to the indirect output was 4 percent and that due to the induced impacts was 7 percent, while the number of the employed persons were respectively 3 percent, 5 percent, and 7.5 percent of the labor force of 1.87 million. These secondary—and especially the tertiary impacts indicate that the indirect contribution to GDP is much greater than the direct one.

Second, the differences in the three levels of impacts within and between the regions where the final uses originate illustrates the need for such studies. The final uses of incoming foreign tourists generate most of their derived output in the central regions of Israel, but the proportionately greater impacts of domestic tourism in the outlying regions of the North and the South balance out this lopsided impact. This is a significant finding for tourism-based economic development.

Third, the analysis of the multiregional impacts through the use of an MRIO model enables researchers to estimate simultaneously the magnitude of the impacts within each region, the reverberating impacts in the other regions, and the returning impacts to the originating region due to the other regions' demands on it.

Fourth, including indirect plus induced impacts in the multiplier estimates illustrates that the share in the compound multipliers of each region is larger than the final uses of tourists who visit it. But the other regions also produce output due to final uses in that and any other region. Thus, any increase in output in one region encourages an investment in other regions in order to supply the needs of the initiating region. This conclusion explains why there is a need for an investment in the Central regions as a result of an investment in the peripheral regions, and also why the rate of development of the peripheral regions is slower than predicted and faster in the central regions. The explanation is that regional economic development plans for investments in the peripheral regions do not account for the need for the extra investment in the Central regions. This also causes a faster rate of growth in the Center, due to both the investment for its output and that due to demands from the other regions. The outcome is that faster growth is generated in the center and the investments in the peripheral regions are unlikely to be sufficient to significantly improve the local conditions.

This raises the question of the policy implications resulting from those findings. We can suggest that the above results point to the following guidelines for regional economic development:

First, an attempt should be made to transfer to the peripheral regions activities that have strong IO linkages between them and the central regions.

Second, a successful policy would need to promote activities with strong IO linkages in the region itself.

Third, there is a need to ensure that as much VA as possible is added locally before demand leaks out.

Finally, there would seem to be a need to exploit underutilized and un-utilized local resources. These normative recommendations raise the issue of suitable investment policy for effecting these measures.

This brings up a final question: how can the state activate such a policy? Further research is needed in order to devise the needed procedures, because policy decisions by government only pave the way and point out the regional objectives, but private investors must take the larger share of any investment. Thus, it is necessary to initiate a research that will define the type of projects that should be taken up by government participation and those to be initiated by private investors.

Acknowledgments

The authors thank Daniel Felsenstein from the Department of Geography of the Hebrew University in Jerusalem for his valuable assistance in streamlining this paper.

References

Archer, B. H. 1976. The anatomy of a multiplier. *Regional Studies*, 10:71–77.

Bachrach, M. 1970. *Bi-proportional Matrices and Input-output Change.* Cambridge: Cambridge University Press.

Blaine, T. W. 1992. Input-output analysis: Application to the assessment of the economic impact of tourism. In M. A. Khan, M. D. Olsen, and T. Var eds., *VNR's Encyclopedia of Hospitality and Tourism.* New York: Van Norstad Reinhold.

Briguglio, L. 1993. Tourism multipliers in the Maltese economy. In I. Johnson, P. and B. Thomas eds., *Perspectives on Tourism Policy.* London: Mussel Publishing.

DiPasquale, D., and K. R. Polenske. 1980. Output, income, and employment input-output multipliers. In S. Pleeter ed., *Economic Impact Analysis: Methodology and Applications.* Boston: Martinus Nijhoff, pp. 85–113.

Fleischer, A., and D. Freeman. 1997. Multiregional input-output analysis— A tool for measuring economic impact of tourism. *Annals of Tourism Research*, 24:990–1001.

Fletcher, J. E. 1989. Input-output analysis and tourism impact studies. *Annals of Tourism Research*, 16:514–529.

Freeman, D., and E. Sultan. 1997. The economic impact of tourism in Israel: A multiregional input-output analysis. *Tourism Economics*, 3:341–361.

Freeman, D., and M. Honigbaum. 1995. The impact of incoming tourism on the economy of Israel—A multiregional and multibranch study of segments of tourism. Jerusalem: Ministry of Tourism of Israel.

Freeman, D., H. Talpaz, A. Fleischer, and O. Laufman. 1991. A multiregional input-output model for Israel and extensions: Methodology and experience. In D. E. Boyce, P. Nijkamp, D. Shefer eds., *Regional Science Retrospect and Prospect.* Berlin: Springer Verlag, pp. 425–445.

Freeman, D., O. Zeif, and J. Freeman. 1996. The impacts of incoming and domestic tourist expenditures on the Israeli economy. Jerusalem: Ministry of Tourism of Israel.

Israel CBS (Central Bureau of Statistics). 1993. *Survey of Trucks 1990*. Special publication no. 924, Jerusalem.

Israel CBS. 1994. *Input-Output Tables 1988*. Special publication no. 972, Jerusalem.

Israel CBS. 1995b. *Time Use in Israel: A Time Budget Survey 1991/2*. Special series no. 996.

Israel CBS. 1995a. *Tourism in Israel 1994*. Special publication series no. 1010, Jerusalem.

Israel CBS. 1996. *Tourism and Hotel Services Statistics Quarterly*. A tri-monthly publication, Jerusalem.

Israel CBS. 1993 and 1995. *Tourist Hotels—Income, Expenditure, and Product 1987–1988*. Publications no. 938.

Israel CBS. 1993 and 1995. *Tourist Hotels—Income, Expenditure, and Product 1991–1992*. Publications no. 1013.

Israel Ministry of Tourism. 1991. Jerusalem: Domestic Tourism: Current, desired and expected (survey conducted by the Dahaf Institute).

Israel Ministry of Tourism. 1993. Jerusalem: Survey of Expenditures of Foreign Tourists (survey conducted and reported by the Taskir Company).

Israel Ministry of Tourism. 1994. Jerusalem: A survey of domestic tourism (survey conducted by Mertens Hoffman Consultants).

Liu, J., and T. Var. 1982. Differential multipliers for the accommodation sector. *Tourism Management*, 3:177–187.

Lundberg, D. E., M. Krishnamoorthy, and M. H. Stavenga. 1995. *Tourism Economics*. New York: John Wiley & Sons.

Miernyk, W. H. 1965. *The Elements of Input-Output Analysis*. New York: Random House.

Nordstrom, J. 1996. Tourism satellite accounts for Sweden 1992–93. *Tourism Economics*, 2:13–42.

Polenske, K. R. 1972. The implementation of a multiregional input-output model for the United States. In A. Brody and A. P. Carter eds., *Input-Output Techniques*. Amsterdam: North-Holland.

Toh, M. 1998. Projecting the Leontief Inverse Directly by the RAS Method: http://inforoomweb.und.edu/WorkPaper/IOPAP/method.pdf (September 10, 2001).

University of Cambridge, 1971. *The Financial Interdependence of the Economy, 1957–1966*. Published for the Department of Applied Economics by Chapman and Hall.

Wanhill, S. 1994. The measurement of tourist income multipliers. *Tourism Management*, 15:281–283.

Chapter 5

Legalization of Casino Gambling in a Frontier Region: The Israeli Experience

Tomer Goodovitch

Casinos are an international phenomenon that have gained recognition worldwide as a legitimate industry. However, several countries, including Israel, are struggling with the decision as to whether to legalize casino gambling. In this situation, they tend to experiment with casino legalization in frontier regions and to expose the phenomenon to public scrutiny in densely populated urban areas. In this paper, I identify a worldwide pattern of casino development that has been echoed in the attempts to legalize casino gambling in Israel. Casinos have developed from periphery to core. This pattern has increased the availability of casino gaming to wider populations and has facilitated its economic growth on both regional and international levels. Nevertheless, the spatial diffusion of casino gambling involves an inherent conflict with social and environmental protectionism, religious sentiments, and, especially, the public fear of crime and problematic gambling. As a result, the Israeli government had taken an extreme approach in order to prevent the perceived evil, although there is no clear evidence that such activity actually increases crime rates or that casinos in themselves increase criminal activity and antisocial behavior.

Casino gambling has grown at spectacular rates worldwide in the last few years. Gambling is for many an entertaining and amusing pastime, but some people gamble for more than just pleasure: they gamble for profit. Other gamblers become addicted to gambling and this becomes a problem both for them and their families. Gambling also crosses social and economic boundaries: people in Africa gamble as much as people in America, although the amount of money spent differs according to their income and the availability of gambling facilities. In general, however, there is little or no gender or race discrimination in a casino (Polders, 1995).

In order to understand casino geography, one must also understand why people gamble. Most people find gambling fun, competitive, and potentially profitable. Although this may not always be true, surveys have confirmed that 51 percent of the sampled population gambled for amusement and excitement and 38 percent gambled for competition or profit. The remaining 11 percent are considered to be habitual gamblers (Hugick, 1989). Thus, we can find three general types of visitors to a casino:

- the economic gambler
- the social gambler
- the habitual gambler

The first of these gambles to beat the system and make a profit. However, the *house* advantage in a casino alters the odds so that, in the long run, returns to the gambler from winning bets are generally less than losses from unsuccessful bets; nevertheless, some professional gamblers can make a living out of the casino (Eadington, 1987; Walker, 1992). Although winning increases the entertainment value of gambling, winning is neither absolutely necessary nor expected for the social gambler. There are indications that social gamblers often put limits on their bets, as they would do for other discretionary activities (Downes et al., 1974). This is especially true for holiday trips, when people decide on a budget limit and expenses are allocated by category. In this case, casino gambling is only one of several activities. The habitual gamblers are obsessive, compulsive, and addicted, and are termed by professionals as problem gamblers (Walker, 1992). These are people for whom gambling is a way of life. The social effect on individual gamblers is one issue, but casino gambling must also be evaluated on the basis of its environmental impact.

Several questions arise with respect to the environmental and social effects of casino gambling. Do casinos cause an increase of crime? Do casinos encourage crime and criminals? Do casinos effect the quality of life and do their activities put pressure on the local infrastructure? The answers to these questions are not straightforward. Friedman et al. (1989) reported that crime rates increased due to casinos in Atlantic City, but such effects were reported neither in the Netherlands nor in Austria. In Vienna and in Cannes, there is evidence that casinos even helped to decrease crime rates, due to the added security, round the clock activity, and the attraction of respected people to the casino vicinity (Gavish, 1995). Casinos also have an effect on the environment, as would any other economic activity or tourist attraction. The opposition to casinos is not always aimed at the casino in particular, but rather at all economic development that might change the character and demography of an area. The size of the casino industry and the size of the population in the whole region both affect crime rates. Small casinos in large metropolitan areas, such as Vienna, have relatively little influence on crime rates, whereas large casinos in small cities, such as Atlantic City, may have a significant impact on crime rates (Braunlich, 1996). This is partly because crime rates are measured in relation to the number of people living in the area and not the number of people visiting the area, and partly because it is much more difficult to control criminals in large facilities.

Similarly, the effect of the casino on the quality of life is another double-sided issue. One would expect a casino to have less of an effect on the quality of life in large areas with major economic and tourist activities. Yet, if large casinos were to be introduced in small communities with few economic activities, there would no doubt be dramatic changes and a significant decline in the quality of life. The decline is subjective not only because the new environment may still have a relatively high lifestyle, but also because it is a dramatic change to the previous way of living. This may be why about 22 percent of Atlantic City residents left the city after the first casino opened in 1978. Most of them simply moved to more distant neighborhoods, while in the 1990s, the number of residents in the city rose due to decreasing crime rates and infrastructure investment (Goodman, 1995). It is important to note that the case of Atlantic City is quite unique and that similar consequences were not recorded in other places (Gavish, 1995).

The Location of Casino Gaming

From a historical perspective, the locations of casinos were influenced by two main factors: gambling acceptance and holiday preferences. For these reasons, casino resorts tend to be found in geographically peripheral areas with some medicinal or recreational amenities such as a spa. Those members of the upper class who frequented spa resorts wanted some kind of amusement to fill in the time between treatments. Typically, amusements included eating, socializing, and gambling (Lowenthal, 1962). In such resorts, upper class society was able to keep itself apart from the lower and middle classes. This isolation also helped to avoid public scrutiny and contributed to continuation of operations, even when society values had turned against gambling.

The geography of casino gambling shows distinct differences over time and space. Whereas entrepreneurial innovations originated in the very largest cities (Moseley, 1974: 56) and spread from core to periphery, according to Perroax's (1964) "growth pole theory," the spread is from periphery to core in the case of casinos. Central locations typically adopt innovations first (Brown and Cox, 1971:559), since they are more cosmopolitan and have larger business opportunities, but the adoption of legalized casino gambling is based on the need to minimize political and economic risk. The introduction of a new process or product is inherently a risky business for its originator. Policymakers can reduce the economic and social risks by encouraging exclusiveness in peripheral locations. Thus, casino policies are, in effect, deliberately channeling growth to certain experimental peripheral sites under the guise of regional development.

Australia is one example of this process. The first casino was opened in 1973 in Hobart, Tasmania, a tourist resort, followed by the first mainland casino in the peripheral region of the Northern Territory in 1979—both peripheral locations. Only in 1992 was the first casino opened in the main population centers of Canberra, Melbourne, and Sidney (Beagle, 1993; Mossenson, 1991). Similar patterns can also be found in the United States and Europe. Bugsy Siegel started his gambling casino in 1946 in the isolated Las Vegas desert. The first casino in the populated northeast corridor in Atlantic City, New Jersey, opened only in 1978 (Loverseed, 1995). In Europe, this geographic pattern repeats itself. Greece is a recent example of this phenomenon, when it was decided to open up twelve new casinos in 1995 on the mainland, in addition to the old historic and only casino that was operating on the island of Rhodes (Adler, 1995). This geographical trend has brought about a substantial increase in the number of available casinos, but it has not solved the moral dilemma. As one observer commented: "It seems as if gambling is a theme like religion, which is commented upon in public mostly by those who feel passionate enough either to promise it whole heartedly or to down it fervently" (Rubner, 1966:1).

Various styles of gambling establishments have emerged, each with different reasons for the legalization of gaming. In Europe, traditional casino houses tend to be small and luxurious, aimed at the upper classes and making it difficult for lower classes to gain access. The American casino has a different style and atmosphere. With the exception of underage gambling, the American casino has no limitations on class or type of client. It is very large in size and attempts to lure as many patrons as possible (Goodovitch and Zemah, 1995).

The Economics of Casino Gambling

According to our worldwide survey (Goodovitch and Zemah, 1995) over 100 countries have legalized casino gambling. As of 1999, at least twenty more countries were considering the legalization of casino gambling. Figure 5.1 shows that during the '80s and '90s, the casino industry showed a tremendous growth, which led in several places, such as the United States and Canada, to cutthroat competition with a number of takeovers leading to a more mature industry. The results are shown in the declining curve of the number of new casinos opened in the late '90s.

The world regional distribution of casinos and their gross revenues is presented in figure 5.2. In 1999, there were over 1,200 casino-resorts worldwide. Europe is the largest market, with over 650 casino houses and gross revenues of more than 20 billion dollars. North America is the second largest market with fewer than seventy large casinos and few dozen more small operations, with gross revenues of over 12 billion U.S. dollars (Goodovitch and Zemah, 1995).

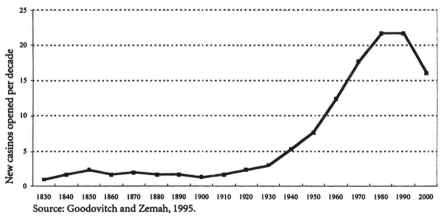

Source: Goodovitch and Zemah, 1995.

Figure 5.1. The Development of the Casino Industry Worldwide

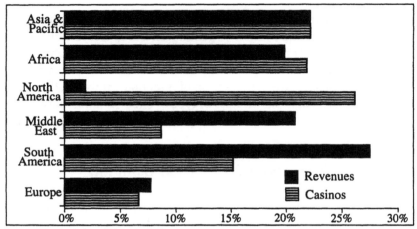

Source: Goodovitch and Zemah, 1995.

Figure 5.2. Regional Distribution of Casino Resorts and Gross Revenues

The economics of casino gambling shows important geographic differences, and its revenues depend on several economic factors. In most countries, over 80 percent of casino customers are locals and not foreigners (Gavish, 1995). Therefore, the population size and average disposable income are the most important factors affecting the total sums wagered. As table 5.1 shows, the highest casino revenues come from areas with a relatively large population and high gross national product (GNP) per capita. Tourists are also an important clientele for gaming. Thus, major tourist countries, such as Germany, France, or Britain, produce relatively large casino revenues. The degree of market maturation and the number of casino operations also affect such income. Competition is increased by a large number of casinos and consequently, average revenues decrease. The number of gaming opportunities can facilitate market growth, especially in the case of a new development. For example, only two casino houses were operating in Louisiana in 1993, but by 1994, seven new casinos had opened. As a result, annual gaming admissions increased twenty times from 500,000 to almost 10 million, and gaming revenues increased twenty-eight times from 16 million dollars to over 440 million dollars (Adler, 1995).

In mature markets, such as New Jersey, increased competition has leveled out the revenue statistics. Gross revenues between 1992 and 1994 almost remained unchanged and increased by less than 2 percent, totaling 3.3 billion dollars. However, in such a competitively saturated market, the size of the industry increases and, as a result, wins per gambling position decrease.

Table 5.1. Europe Casino Economic Data, 1994

Country	Casino Revenues (million $)	Number of Casinos	Population (millions)	Tourist Arrival (millions)	GNP per Capita ($)	Lottery Revenues (million $)
Spain	9,000	22	39	13	4,800	11,000
U.K.	3,500	120	58	20	8,900	11,500
Germany	1,600	40	80	70	12,000	7,500
Netherlands	1,000	14	15	15	10,000	750
France	650	140	57	55	10,700	10,000
Turkey	350	75	60	3	1,100	250
Hungary	50	4	10	3	2,000	185
Greece	20	2	10	12	3,500	1,000
Europe	*20,000*	*700*	*750*	*250*	*8,000*	*150,000*

Source: Goodovitch and Zemah, 1995.

In the case of New Jersey, in the same period of time, wins per gambling position declined by 5 percent from $296 to $282 (Adler, 1995).

A relatively large number of casinos in a country point to a small type of operation. Such small establishments are usually characterized by a modest design and atmosphere and thus cater to local gambling needs. Large establishments cater to both foreign and local tourists, and they are designed to attract as many visitors as possible.

It should be remembered that casino gambling competes with other forms of gambling, such as the lottery, football pools, and horse racing. In places where casinos are discrete and not so popular a game, revenues tend to be greater in more accessible gambling opportunities such as the lottery. For example, table 5.1 shows that the Greek lottery produces over fifty times the revenues of the two small casinos available in Greece. In Europe, lotteries are more accessible and popular than casinos. Lottery stands are available on almost every major street corner, and although casino houses are sometimes relatively accessible, such as the twenty club-style casinos in London, in other places, few, if any, are available at all, such as the one and only casino operating in Lisbon. Therefore, in 1994, Europe lotteries produced seven and a half times ($150m) the revenues ($20m) of the 700 casino houses available throughout Europe.

The History of Casino Gambling in Israel

Governments considering casino legalization, such as is the case in Israel, must balance the social and environmental objections to casino gambling against its economic and development potential (Felsenstein, 1999; Israeli and Mehrez, 2000). A set of rules and regulations is necessary that not only controls casino operations but also ensures that the benefits are not concentrated in one group (i.e., the entrepreneurs), while another group (i.e., the local population) carries the costs (i.e., implementation and infrastructure). Experience shows that governments do not always appreciate the complexities associated with casino gaming. There is a major risk of loss of control over the industry, unless the key policy issues, such as increased tourism, employment, and development are effectively dealt with.

This has led many governments to adopt an unbalanced view of casino gambling. Some countries are so concerned with the negative side of casinos that they follow a policy of "it is so wicked, we will do it ourselves." At the other extreme is the policy of "the public is less efficient"—which leads the way to privatization of casino gambling. Yet neither of these approaches can successfully safeguard the values, which they claim to uphold. That is why a combination of government ownership together with private management and operation is thought to be the most effective regulatory environment.

Casinos are not legal today in Israel, but the country is no stranger to them. Israelis are well known as gamblers, as many of them came from countries, such as Germany, with a long tradition of casino gambling. There is also a long history of contact with other cultures in Israel. One can point to Roman baths and gambling establishments, Turkish dice rollers and card player in cafes, and more recently, the British army Naafis, where one could have a drink and also play pinball machines or bingo.

In the early 1920s, casinos were established in Tel Aviv and Haifa with the idea of stimulating late night activity by offering music, dancing, drinks, and some pinball machines as entertainment. These were very fashionable places but never really became true casino houses. Other localities were envious of this activity and began to consider genuine gambling establishments. An example was the new German settlement in Nahariya, which wanted to establish a casino in 1935; today it is one of the potential sites for casino legalization. Andreas Mayer, one of the first settlers of Nahariya, recalled that the economic depression of the 1930s and the low profits from agriculture products were the main reasons for the search for other sources of income. The lively Bat Galim casino, further south in Haifa, was a good model, but at the time, the settlers could not find a foreign investor. Sixty years later the plan is being revived (Goodovitch, 1996).

The idea of an *Israeli* casino was occasionally brought up as an element in the image of a modern European culture, a goal of many founders of the Israeli State. But one or other of the orthodox religious parties almost always rejected it, even in the period of the first prime minister David Ben-Gurion. This opposition has remained fairly constant, although it has begun to weaken in recent years.

Legalizing Casino Gaming in Israel

When the Israeli government first looked at legalization of gambling, its intention was to shut down illegal operations. Many illegal operations are still functioning, although the police have lately taken a much stronger stand against them. They consist of installing poker machines in video game halls or placing slot machines in service stations and rest areas along the intercity highways. On one occasion, an owner of a service station near Tel Aviv was interviewed on television and asked whether the police knew about his slot machines. His reply was: "Of course they know, and they come in once in a while, but as far as I know, they have never won anything." These machines are minor problems when compared to illegal casino houses, operating even in residential areas and ordinary apartments.

In 1994, the illegal casino operations were flourishing: an estimated 100 casinos were operating in Israel with almost half of them in Tel Aviv alone. At the peak period, almost 500 professionals were employed: dealers, pit bosses, and casino managers. Many of these people came from the United Kingdom to work and train local staff: dealer agencies in London could offer them two and sometimes three times their U.K. salary and the risk looked well worth taking. Most of them had worked in various countries around the world, but usually the younger dealers were not well trained. Such illegal operations attracted many Israeli gamblers to their roulette and blackjack tables but took a very high house advantage—up to 25 percent (Gansh, 1995).

The police raided some of these casino houses, but the owners were organized and well prepared and were often linked to other criminal activities. Policemen were bribed, venues were changed frequently, and even if caught, someone without a criminal record could always be found to take the blame. The penalties and sentences were not very severe in any case.

Some of this activity took advantage of the minimal offshore policing in Israel. The rough Mediterranean Sea does not allow for comfortable conditions, but for a while, there were up to six casino boats in operation in the Gulf of Eilat. They did a very good business. However, there are no international waters in the Red Sea and once the police decided to intervene, only one or two boats remained for occasional cruises out of Eilat harbor (Goodovitch, 1995).

The Israeli Industry Economic Potential

In a recent paper, Goodovitch (1998) analyzed the Israeli gambling industry's economic potential as follows. More than 2.5 million Israeli tourists travel abroad each year. Each of them spends an average of $800 on holiday expenses, and some 20 percent of them spend their holidays in the Mediterranean resorts of Greece, Egypt, Cyprus, and Turkey. In these countries, a flight and a four-day holiday in a deluxe hotel with full board costs only $300 per person. With costs as low as these, it can be very tempting to spend the remaining $500 of one's planned vacation money on amusements, such as those that can be found in a casino. Using these figures, the potential yearly revenues for a competitive casino in Israel would be on the order of $1.25 billion. This is not to say that Israelis gamble *only* $1.25 billion every year. In fact, as noted above, many Israelis gamble within their own country. A large illegal casino in Tel Aviv typically includes up to ten tables and a few slot machines and can take in $20,000 to $50,000 a night, which averages $10 million a year. Using police raid statistics, it is estimated that in the roughly 100 illegal casino operations that exist in Israel, the combined annual total gambled amounts to an additional $1 billion (Goodovitch, 1998).

A Palestinian casino on the autonomy border now lures Israeli gamblers and competes on both the domestic and the international markets. The closure of the Turkish casinos in early 1998 only adds to the attractiveness of a nearby casino. Jericho is only a thirty-minute drive from Jerusalem and ninety minutes from Tel Aviv. It is within close proximity to three million people. The Egyptian casino in Taba serves as a good example of a border casino that lures Israeli gamblers. It is just across the Israel-Egypt border and a ten-minute drive from Eilat. The one million tourists, most of them domestic, that visit Eilat every year generated an average of half a million patrons for the Taba casino in 1997. Of them, 95 percent were Israelis who had crossed the border for a few hours of entertainment and gaming. Each of the half-million patrons spent an average of $100, creating annual revenues for the casino of about $50 million (Goodovitch, 1998).

Conclusions

Casino gambling is a world phenomenon that has grown at spectacular rates in the last few years. Gambling crosses social and economic boundaries, although the amount of money spent by different communities differs according to their income and the availability of gambling facilities. The proliferation of casinos has affected casino revenues and has prevented the development of the type of attractive facility that could only be economic with high profit margins and monopolistic status.

Several countries, including Israel, are struggling with whether to legalize casino gambling. In this endeavor, they tend to experiment with casino legalization in frontier regions and to expose the phenomenon to public scrutiny in densely populated urban areas. I identified a worldwide pattern of casino development, which has been repeated by the attempts to legalize casino gambling in Israel. Casinos have developed from periphery to core. This pattern has opened casino gaming to wider populations and facilitated its economic growth on both regional and international levels. Nevertheless, the spatial diffusion of casino gambling involves an inherent conflict with social and environmental protectionism and, especially, the public fear of crime and problematic gambling. As a result, the Israeli government had taken an extreme approach in order to prevent the perceived evil, although there is no clear evidence that such activity actually increases crime rates or that casinos in themselves increase criminal activity and antisocial behavior.

References

Adler, J. N. 1995. *Global Gaming Almanac.* New York: Smith Barney.

American Heritage. 1992. *Dictionary of the English Language.* Washington: Houghton Mifflin Company

Beagle, J. 1993. Casino play monopoly. *Gaming and Wagering Business,* 14:15–18.

Braunlich, C. G. 1996. Lessons from the Atlantic City experience. *Journal of Travel Research,* 34:46–56.

Brown, L. A., and K. R. Cox. 1971. Empirical regularities in the diffusion of innovation. *Annals of Association of American Geographers,* 61:551–559.

Downes, D. M., B. P. Davies, M. E. David, and P. Stone. 1974. *Gambling Work and Leisure: Study Across Three Areas.* London: Routledge and Kegan Paul.

Eadington, W. R. 1987. Economic perceptions of gambling behavior. *Journal of Gambling Behavior,* 3:264–273.

Felsenstein, D. 1999. *The Great Local Gamble: The Casino As an Instrument of Local Development in Israel.* Jerusalem: The Floersheimer Institute for Policy Studies.

Friedman, J., S. Hakim, and J. Weinblatt. 1989. Casino gambling as a growth pole strategy and its effect on crime. *Journal of Regional Science,* 29: 615–623.

Gavish, M. 1995. The public committee on the evaluation of casino gambling in Israel. Jerusalem: Ministry of Finance.

Goodman, R. 1995. *The Luck Business, the Devastating Consequences and Broken Promises of America's Gambling Explosion.* New York: Simon and Shuster.

Goodovitch T. 1996. The case for casinos in Israel. *Intergaming*, 2:17–25.
——. 1998. Legal Israeli casinos. *Intergaming*, 4:21–26.
Goodovitch, T., and M. Zemah. 1995. The impact of legalizing casino gambling in Eilat. Jerusalem: Ministry of Tourism.
Hugick, L. 1989. Gambling on the rise. *Gallup Report*, 285:32–39.
Israeli, A., and A. Mehrez. 2000. From illegal gambling to legal gaming: Casinos in Israel. *Tourism Management*, 21:281–291.
Loverseed, H. 1995. Market segments: Gambling tourism in North America. *Travel and Tourism Analyst, No. 3*. Washington: Economist Intelligence Unit.
Lowenthal, D. 1962. Tourists and thermalists. *Geographical Review*, 52:124–127.
Moseley, M. J. 1974. *Growth Centres in Spatial Planning*. Oxford: Pergamon Press.
Mossenson, D. 1991. The Australian casino model. In W. R. Eadington and J. Cornelius eds., *Gambling and Public Policy*. Reno: University of Nevada Institute for the Study of Gambling and Commercial Gaming.
Perroax, F. 1964. *L'Economie du XX Siecle*. Paris: Presse Universitaire de France.
Polders, B. 1995. *Gambling in Europe: Unity in Diversity*. Hague: European Association of the Study of Gaming.
Rubner, A. 1966. *The Economics of Gambling*. London: Routledge.
Walker, M. B. 1992. *The Psychology of Gambling*. Oxford: Pergamon Press.

Chapter 6

Gambling on the Border:
Casinos, Tourism Development,
and the Prisoners' Dilemma

Daniel Felsenstein
Daniel Freeman

The emergence of casino gambling on the economic development landscape has forced elected officials and practitioners to confront a host of public policy issues that were hitherto ignored. The first relates to gambling as a sustainable economic development strategy. For which kinds of community is it suited, if at all? The second relates to gambling as a tourism and leisure activity. Can it be categorized as such and under which circumstances? These are not simply questions of classification and definition. They depend heavily on the circumstances of the community in question, the sources of demand for gambling, and the supply of casino facilities. Almost overnight, the fortunes of casinos can change and with them, the economic futures of those communities that gambled heavily on the casino; from being export-based economic development activities serving external demand in a regulated or monopolistic environment, they can turn into local service-based activities in a ruthlessly competitive market.

Casino operators will, of course, try to ensure the former scenario. One way of ensuring such a development trajectory is by establishing casinos at border locations. This chapter uses the case of gambling at border locations in order to illustrate this point. The border is a favorite site for the development of casinos, particularly if a large market exists on the other side. For the casino operator, this means a large source of demand stemming from more than one national or state jurisdiction. For the local community, a border casino represents the ultimate in export-based activity—appropriating local taxes from casino operators and the direct, indirect, and induced impacts of local casino-based expenditures. For national or state governments, the border casino means the import of tax income and the reexportation of all the negative externalities that accompany the gamblers as they return to their homes on the other side of the border: gambling-induced addiction, bankruptcy, reduced productivity, and social pathologies.

However, the border location is also a gamble. Its attraction is generally contingent on special (regulated) circumstances. In their absence, the border can turn into a relentlessly competitive battleground for reasons similar to those that made it popular. Casinos on opposite sides of the border compete over proximity to markets, attempt to capture external sources of demand, and to "roll over" negative externalities to neighboring jurisdictions. In such circumstances, the stage is set for the classic "prisoners' dilemma"[1]: competitors on both side of the border would be better off if there was voluntary cooperation between casinos. But in practice, the outcome is likely to be far from the collective optimum solution, as no casino operator is likely to trust another and no community wants to opt out voluntarily and leave the market in the hands of the neighboring jurisdiction.

This chapter examines the issue of casino development at border locations, highlighting the above mentioned prisoners' dilemma that this situation encourages. After examining how this dilemma impacts on the regional dynamics of casino and tourism development, we present a (hypothetical) empirical analysis of the outcome of such competition between two tourist locations on the Israeli-Egyptian border: Eilat (Israel) and Taba (Egypt). The latter has a land-based casino that feeds almost totally off the Israeli market on the other side of the border. Recently, Eilat has started seriously to consider the option of promoting casinos. This will, of course, detrimentally affect the captive market that Taba now enjoys. Based on some simplifying assumptions, we present some numerical estimations of the impacts likely to arise from the different combinations of competition and no-competition over casino development at this border location. First, we consider the case of a casino in Taba but not in Eilat (the existing situation). Then we proceed to consider the reverse case of a casino in Eilat but not in Taba. Finally, we present estimations for the most likely future scenario of casinos in both Taba and Eilat. Using simulation-generated data for Eilat and estimations for Taba, we show that the most probable outcome falls short of also being the welfare-maximizing outcome.

Economic Development and Border Areas

State or national boundaries are often locations of economic opportunity (Krakover, 1997). This is especially the case if the existence of the border is itself the source of monopoly or noncompetitive conditions that favor one side over the other. Unequal tax regimes, business incentives, and restrictions on the movement of goods or people may serve to divert economic activity from one side to the other. More frequently, however, it is the combination of state or national regulation and a large captive market on one side of the border that is enough to create economic opportunity for agents operating in an unregulated environment on the other side.

However, while the existence of unequal economic conditions is a necessary condition for favoring one side of the border over the other, it alone is insufficient. In order to generate economic development on one side of the border, it is not enough simply to have a large source of (export) demand on the other side. The revenues generated by this cross-border demand must be spent within the area in order to have a local economic development effect. If they leak out to other areas, very little will have been achieved. Furthermore, even if these revenues are spent locally, for example as payroll, it is important that those doing the spending are local residents. If they are nonlocal employees, then this is likely to be another source of leakage from the local economy. Finally, even if revenues find their way to local employees who reside locally, their effect can still be diminished if these local residents are new in-migrants, rather than long-term residents. In the context of casino development at the border, these conditions are portrayed graphically in figure 6.1. The border casino that feeds off external demand is only likely to have a local economic development impact if casino revenues are spent locally, find their way into the pockets of local residents, and generate income for locals who were resident prior to the introduction of the casino (Grinols and Omorov, 1996).

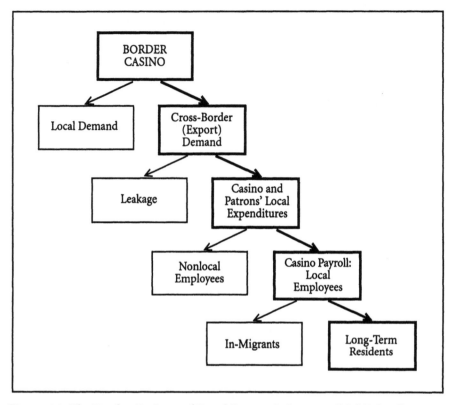

Figure 6.1. The Border Casino and Local Economic Impacts (highlighted)

In practice, state and national borders often serve as favorite locations for casino activity. Invariably, this is the result of the existence of a large, untapped market on one side of the border in a relatively gambling-regulated environment and an unregulated environment on the other side. This combination of conditions repeats itself time and time again. For example, the casino at Windsor, Canada is directed at the casino-free Detroit market (Deloitte-Touche, 1995). The riverboats of northeast Indiana feed off the Chicago market, where no casino exists (Przybylski and Littlepage, 1997), while those of southern Indiana are aimed at the metropolitan market of Louisville, which has resisted casinos in order to protect its horse-racing industry (Przybylski, Felsenstein, Freeman, and Littlepage, 1998). Illinois riverboats are aimed at the urban market of St. Louis (Grinols and Omorov, 1996), the Macau casinos service the Hong Kong market (Hobson, 1995), and the Nevada casinos (outside of Las Vegas) target the large population concentrations of northern California (Eadington, 1995). Similarly in Israel, the Jericho casino within the autonomous territory of the Palestinian Authority is dependent on the urban populations of some of Israel's largest cities, such as Tel Aviv, Jerusalem, and Beer Sheva, where casinos are illegal.

In all of these situations, the success of the border casino is assured as long as regulated conditions continue to operate over the border. However, once these regulations are eased, the monopoly situation turns to a highly competitive one. If casinos begin to develop on both sides of the border, it is obvious that one casino's gain is at the expense of the other. This is the classic zero-sum condition in local economic development that results in pure redistribution rather than economic expansion (Blair and Kumar, 1997). In the case of casino development, however, there is a further twist. Not only is the economic development cake simply redistributed, but each side of the border now has to deal with the negative externalities generated by casino gambling on the other side. In this situation, not only are the slices of the cake cut to different sizes, the cake itself might actually shrink.

Faced with such a situation, the obvious solution might seem to be a mutually agreed moratorium on casino development on both sides of the border in an effort to preserve market shares at current levels. In practice, however, such a cooperative solution is unlikely to be attained. This is because in the cross-border gambling situation, authorities (cities or regional or national governments) are locked into a form of prisoners' dilemma. The essence of this dilemma is that while locations on both sides of the border would prefer some form of collaboration and cooperation, in practice the competition between them is likely to intensify. This is due to the lack of trust and information between them and the prospect of "cheating" or "defection" even in the presence of some collective solution.

The prisoners' dilemma metaphor has been used as a framework for understanding the "bidding wars" between states and countries and the prevalence of public subsidies for economic activity. Once cities and states are caught up in this competitive spiral, it becomes increasingly difficult to opt out unilaterally (Ellis and Rogers, 1997). Despite the fact that the welfare-maximizing strategy for all players is to disengage from the bidding wars and to promote some kind of noncompetitive collaboration, the incentives of the situation, in practice, force the players into higher and higher bids. The interstate diffusion of gambling in the United States has similarly been examined in this framework. Thompson and Gazel (1997) have shown how the hypothetical case of casinos in both Chicago and northern Indiana leads to a situation in which locations on both sides of the state border lose out. It would seem that the only situation in which casinos generate positive economic impacts is the (unrealistic and temporary) monopoly situation in which one side has a casino and the other side does not.

The Setting

We now proceed to present an empirical estimation of the impacts of cross-border competition around casino development. An analysis is presented of the likely regional economic impacts arising from two casinos in frontier tourist locations (Taba, Egypt and Eilat, Israel) on opposite sides of an international border (figure 6.2). Taba is an Egyptian tourist resort in the northern Sinai desert adjacent to the Israeli border. At present, there is one hotel operating, with six more under construction within a ten kilometer radius, totaling over 4,000 additional rooms. Foreign visitors are composed of Israelis and European winter charter vacationers (mostly from Switzerland and Germany). In this respect, the Taba resort competes in the market with Eilat, although its main market is still Israeli vacationers and especially family weekend vacationers.

The differences in magnitude and function between Taba and Eilat should be noted. Taba is primarily a hotel resort location. It has none of the features of an urbanized area with all that this implies: flows of population and visitors, transportation and tourism infrastructure—all of which exist in Eilat. While it has its own airport with twice weekly flights to Cairo, it is to a large extent dependent on Eilat for markets and access. Were it not for the international border, it would be considered a suburb of Eilat.

The Taba Hilton Casino operates from a building adjacent to the Taba Hilton hotel and is owned by London Clubs International, a publicly traded company with casinos in London, Las Vegas, Belgium, South Africa, the Bahamas, Lebanon, and Egypt. The present casino was established in 1994 and has thirty tables and eighty slot machines. This represents roughly 300 gaming positions, although the gaming areas can accommodate 2,000 people at full capacity. It employs 230 people, the vast majority of whom are Egyptians from Cairo and Alexandria.

Patrons at the Taba Hilton Casino are almost exclusively Israeli tourists. The Taba border crossing serves as the main gateway for entry from Israel to the Sinai desert. Border control registered 301,000 and 372,000 Israeli exit crossings to Egypt in 1997 and 1998, respectively. Of these, roughly 77 percent were visitors crossing the border whose destination was Taba. The identification of these visitors is possibly due to the fact that they are exempt from paying border tax. The Egyptian authorities, recognizing the revenue potential of these visitors, have reduced border-crossing formalities for those

Figure 6.2. Taba and Eilat Casino Research Area

entrants who are going no further than Taba. We estimate that 90 percent of these visited Taba for the purpose of gambling. It should also be noted that Taba is only ten to fifteen minutes away from Eilat by car and that the casino also provides a bus service to and from the border.

Eilat is immediately adjacent to Taba. It is Israel's premier tourist resort with over 1.27 million visitors in 1996, of whom 33 percent were foreign tourists and 66 percent were Israelis. The former stay an average of four nights in Eilat and the latter an average of two nights. The city has a well-developed tourist infrastructure with a wealth of water and sun-related attractions, 7,500 hotel rooms, and a further 2,000 at present under construction. It has a rapidly growing population and many of the characteristics of a tourist resort in terms of a high crime rate, a rather transient population, and a large rental housing stock (see Felsenstein and Freeman, 1998).

While land-based casinos are illegal in Israel, between five and eight casino boats operate out of Eilat port and engage in gambling activity outside the territorial waters of Israel. The patrons of these boats are exclusively vacationers in Eilat and Israeli gamblers who come to Eilat for this purpose. This, along with the fact that the vast majority of the patrons at the Taba casino are Eilat vacationers, means that the city of Eilat provides the infrastructure for local gambling activity without seeing any visible returns. In some respects, gambling activity in the Taba casino and on the boats has all the features of a classic export-base activity whereby the casinos appropriate all revenues and the city of Eilat bears all the externality costs. After some years of ambivalence toward the issue of promoting a casino in Eilat, city hall, the local chamber of commerce, and the Eilat hotel association have all firmly supported the idea. A further impetus would seem to be the recent establishment of a Palestinian Authority-controlled casino in Jericho, whose presence has cut in to the revenues of both the Taba casino and the Eilat casino boats.

The development of the tourism and gambling sectors in this part of the Red Sea over the last decade illustrates a fascinating chronology of competition and trade diversion. Initially, the Eilat monopoly position in the region was challenged by the development of the Taba tourism resort, which eroded some of the Israeli hegemony over the European winter tourist market and deflected some of the Israeli tourism market through the opening of a casino. The Eilat gambling ships were a partial response to this challenge, at least in terms of the Israeli gambling market. Recently, both gambling locations have been challenged by the Jericho casino. The response has been a concerted effort by the city of Eilat to lobby for a permit to establish Israel's first land-based casino. The cycle has thus turned full circle.

Method and Data

The Accounting Approach

In order to illustrate the prisoners' dilemma facing casino development in border areas, we set up a simple four-scenario case, outlining the various combinations of competition and cooperation between Taba and Eilat over the establishment of casino gambling. Using a transparent accounting system, we attempt to estimate, for each case, the direct economic impact of the casino (composed of positive and negative economic outcomes). We then expand this outcome by a suitable regional multiplier that yields the total economic impact. Finally, we adjust this economic impact to account for the social cost of gambling. This result gives us the overall impact in monetary terms. Note that no attempt is made to assess the nonpecuniary issues that accompany casino development, such as the quality of the working environment and job satisfaction (Blair, Schwer, and Waddoups, 1998). These are important issues that deserve serious consideration but are beyond the scope of the present study.

The four cases considered here are as follows:

1. *Both locations agree to a moratorium on gambling.* In this instance, no casinos develop in either location. No estimation is needed here as overall impacts are zero in both Taba and Eilat. This is the welfare-maximizing, but highly improbable, solution to the prisoners' dilemma for both locations.

2. *Taba has a casino while Eilat does not.* This represents the existing situation and provides one short-term and unstable solution to the dilemma. We estimate the economic impacts as outlined above for this situation.

3. *Eilat has a casino while Taba has none.* This is the mirror image of the previous situation and represents the desired outcome on the part of Eilat. As above, this solution is unlikely to occur.

4. *Both Taba and Eilat have casinos.* This represents the most likely outcome and the longer-term solution. In the absence of mutual trust between the two locations, it is likely that each will promote gambling, despite the fact that in this situation, both may stand to lose.

The four potential solutions to the prisoners' dilemma are represented graphically in table 6.1. As can be seen, the impacts of gambling are obviously zero when neither location has a casino. When a casino is located in Taba and not in Eilat, we expect the net gain to Taba (positive minus nega-

Table 6.1. Four Potential Solutions to the Prisoners' Dilemma: Gambling in Taba and Eilat

		EILAT	
		No Casino	Casino
TABA	No Casino	0	T -
		0	E +
	Casino	T +	T -
		E -	E -

T = Taba; E = Eilat
0 = no impact
+ = positive impact; - = negative impact

tive economic impacts) to outweigh the economic impacts in Eilat which are nearly all negative spillovers from Taba. When the situation is reversed (Eilat has the casino and Taba does not), we expect a reversal of outcomes. The net economic impacts in Eilat (positive minus negative outcomes) will exceed the economic impacts in Taba. These latter effects are likely to be all negative due to demand diversion and opportunities forfeited in Taba when Eilat opens a casino. Finally, in the instance that both locations open casinos, we expect negative economic outcomes in both. Because of the limited volume of visitor flows to Taba and its dependence on Israeli patrons, we expect these negative outcomes to be higher than in Eilat.

The first stage of the analysis is to estimate the *volume of visitors* to the Taba casino and to the hypothetical Eilat casino. In the latter case, our estimations are based on the existence of a stand-alone casino with 75 tables, 300 games (i.e., 750 gambling positions), and employing 350 people. Visitors to the Taba casino are estimated using data on Israelis crossing the border. Visitors to the Eilat casino are based on actual data on foreign tourists and Israeli tourists, the propensities to gamble for these two groups and for local Eilat residents, and estimates of the extra demand generated by the presence of a casino in Eilat.

The second stage relates to estimating the *within-casino expenditure* by patrons and the *casino cost structure*. Within-casino expenditure is composed of the casino "drop" (revenues from gambling), plus ancillary revenues from the sale of food and beverages and the collection of entrance fees. Casino costs relate to wages and salaries paid, national gambling tax, corporate tax, property tax, sales or value-added tax, and the costs of inputs (goods and services).

The *direct economic impacts (positive and negative)* are distilled from the casino revenue and cost structure in the third stage. The positive impacts include all those casino-related expenditures that remain locally. Amongst them we can include wages and salaries, the proportion of gaming tax that gets transferred to the city, the proportion of the entrance fee that is transferred to the city, local property tax paid by the casino, and visitors' additional expenditure induced by the presence of the casino. The negative impacts are deadweight spending (i.e., nongambling spending by locals or visitors that would have occurred in the absence of the casino) and demand that is displaced by the casino (displacement of other local gambling revenues such as lottery, displacement of local residents demand, and displacement of visitors' demand). Subtracting negative from positive impacts yields total direct economic impacts arising from the casino.

This direct impact is then *expanded by a suitable regional income multiplier* in the fourth stage in order to account for the indirect and induced impacts triggered off by the presence of the casino. This gives an estimate of the *total economic impact*. This figure is further adjusted (downwards) in order to represent the monetary cost of the local social effects generated by the casino (cost of treating local gambling addicts, local productivity loss, and negative spillovers generated locally). Once this sum is subtracted from the total economic impact, we arrive at the *overall impact*, which is a statement of the various outcomes arising from the prisoners' dilemma situation of adjacent and competing casinos.

Data Sources and Assumptions

Our accounting approach is based on a series of simplifying assumptions and estimation parameters. As far as possible, these have been based on real data gathered from tourism, hotel, municipal, and gambling representatives in Taba and Eilat; simulation-generated data from previous work (Felsenstein and Freeman, 1998); and informed estimations when none of the former are available. These assumptions are broadly outlined in the notes to table 6.2. The guiding principle is to generate parameter values on the basis of local data and only failing that to use literature-generated parameters. Thus, for example, numbers of visitors to Eilat and their expenditure patterns comes from the Central Bureau of Statistics data (CBS, 1999) and from surveys commissioned by the Bureau (Taskir, 1993). Israeli visitors to Taba are calculated from data made available by the Taba border terminal. Expenditure within the casino is based on an industry-confirmed figure of $125 per visitor that is distributed across casino drop ($100), entrance fee ($10) and food and beverages ($15). Tax rates for the Taba casino are those presently prevailing. In the case of Eilat, hypothetical tax rates are taken from the recommendations of the government commission into gambling (Gavish Commission, 1995). Property tax rates are based on Eilat city existing rates for hotels and assume both gambling floorspace and other unbuilt space (e.g., parking). For Eilat, we based our estimations on gambling floorspace of 3,500 m² and open space of a further 2,500 m².

The employment structure for the purpose of estimating wages and salaries was based on 230 employees for Taba and 350 for Eilat. In both cases, top level management comprises the top 5 percent earning $48,000 per annum, a middle-level strata of 15 percent of all employees earning $30,000 (in Eilat only), and the remaining 80 percent (or 95 percent for the Taba casino) earning $18,000 yearly, net of tips. All wages and salaries are assumed to be spent locally. For Eilat, inputs purchased locally are estimated as 5 percent of net revenues after netting out wages and taxes. In the case of Taba, all local purchases are done in Eilat. These are estimated as 1 percent of net revenues and are counted as a leakage (negative impact) for Taba. These small shares of local inputs reflect the limited nature of the local economy. Visitors' additional expenditure over and above what they would have spent in the absence of the casino is calculated in the Taba case as 40 percent of the occupancy of the Taba Hilton on an annual basis at a rate of $166 per day (Felsenstein and Freeman, 1998). In the Eilat case, this expenditure is estimated as the within-casino expenditure of the visitors diverted to Eilat as a result of the casino (i.e., their food and beverage spending alone).

The negative local economic impacts are deadweight expenditure and local demand displacement. For both Eilat and Taba, we assume that all hotel expenditure would have happened in the absence of a casino in either place. Eilat's visitors would continue to come to the city: they would just gamble elsewhere, either at Taba or on the gambling boats. Similarly, Taba's patrons would continue to stay (in the main) in Eilat. Displacement is calculated on the basis of the presence of truly additional visitors. Those that are assumed to gamble elsewhere in the absence of the casino do not displace existing demand. Rather, it is the expenditure of those that cannot be expected to go elsewhere that will displace existing demand. In the case of the casino in Taba, displacement rate is calculated as 10 percent while in the Eilat casino case, it is estimated as 24 percent. Local positive and negative economic impacts are both expanded by a regional output multiplier of 1.3 (Felsenstein and Freeman, 1998).

On the social costs account, we quantify three separate costs. The first is the cost of treating local gambling addicts. We assume (conservatively) that 3 percent of the local gambling population has compulsive tendencies and that one year's treatment (not including hospitalization) costs $5,000. These estimates are based on figures provided by professionals working in the area of gambling addiction in Israel. We assume a local negative spillover effect comprising local crime, disturbances, and the costs that accompany this. This is calculated on the same basis of local compulsive gamblers, assuming that only half of them are involved in criminal activity and that of these, only half will commit crimes locally. The cost per crime is estimated as $2,000, which is less than half the accepted figure (BGA, 1992). Finally we estimate a local productivity loss parameter based on the local population of compulsive gamblers, assuming this time that half the regional GDP per employee is lost within this subset of the population (i.e., $17,500 per addict). This figure is again a very conservative estimate, at 65 percent of the accepted productivity loss figure at the beginning of the 1990s. As above, this is expanded by a multiplier and combined with the two other social costs to yield the overall local social cost of gambling.

Gambling in Taba and Eilat: Estimates of the Impacts

The above accounting system yields results for three of the four outcomes described above. These are presented in table 6.2. The first case deals with the present situation: a casino in Taba and none in Eilat. In this instance, visits to the casino add up to over 200,000, comprising local Eilat residents and Israelis crossing the border for the purpose of gambling. These visitors generate revenues of over $26 million and casino costs add up to over $18 million. Direct positive impacts generated locally greatly outweigh the negative economic impacts as we only assume 10 percent demand displacement. In addition, all social costs are passed on to Eilat, the point of origin for all Taba gamblers. As a result, total economic impacts in the Taba area sum to over $7 million.

In this situation, Eilat loses even more than Taba gains. Lost economic opportunities in diverted demand add up to over $5 million and to $6.6 million when indirect impacts are considered. Hotel revenues are not considered forfeited as nearly all casino visitors stay in the Eilat hotels. Social costs arising from Israeli visitors addicted to gambling and the attendant crime and productivity loss generate an estimated local cost of over $12 million. Obviously, this is not a situation that Eilat wants to encourage.

Case 2 describes the hypothetical situation of a casino in Eilat but none in Taba (table 6.2). Under this scenario, over 1.6 million visits are expected at the casino, comprising visits by local residents, Israeli tourists, foreign tourists, and demand diverted to the casino from other gambling locations (gambling boats, Jericho casino, illegal casinos, etc.). The volume of tourist traffic in Eilat combined with the larger casino that we are positing make for a much greater revenue flow than in the previous case. The casino visitors are expected to generate within-casino expenditures (casino drop, admission fees, and food and beverages) of $198 million. Casino costs, on the other hand, (wages and taxes) add up to $63.7 million.

The amount of casino-generated revenues that stays in the local economy is the sum of all the positive and direct impacts such as local revenues from the casino, property tax paid by the casino, casino spending on local inputs, and additional visitor expenditure promoted by the casino. This adds up to over 17 percent of all casino-generated revenues ($35.1 million). From this figure, the negative direct impacts need to be subtracted in order not to count spending that would have occurred anyway and casino-induced

Table 6.2. Economic Impacts in Three Hypothetical Situations

	CASE 1: Casino in Taba: None in Eilat	CASE 2: Casino in Eilat: None in Taba	CASE 3: Casino in Taba: Casino in Eilat	
	TABA IMPACTS	EILAT IMPACTS	TABA IMPACTS	
1. Visits to Casino (Th)[1]	209	1,639		70.0
2. Casino Revenues + Costs ($m)				
2.1 Within-Casino Expenditure[2]	26.2	198.0		8.7
2.2 Casino Cost Structure[3]	18.3	63.7		8.2
3. Direct Economic Impacts ($m)				
3.1 Positive Impacts[4]	8.4	35.1		5.5
3.2 Negative Impacts[5]	0.9	9.9		0.5
Balance	7.5	25.2		5.0
4. Total (Direct + Indirect) Impacts[6]	9.7	32.8		6.5
5. Social Costs[7]	0	(30.6)		0
	EILAT IMPACTS	TABA IMPACTS	EILAT IMPACTS	
1. Direct Economic Impacts ($m)			1. Visits to Casino (Th)[1]	1,569
Diverted Demand[8]	(5.1)	(21.8)	2. Casino Revenues + Costs ($m)	
Hotel Revenues Forfeited[9]	(0)	(5.8)	2.1 Within-Casino Expenditure[2]	196.2
2. Total (Direct + Indirect) Impacts[6]	(6.6)	(36.0)	2.2 Casino Cost Structure[3]	63.3
5. Social Costs[7]	(12.1)	(0)	3. Direct Economic Impacts ($m)	
			3.1 Positive Impacts[4]	33.9
			3.2 Negative Impact[5]	13.1
			Balance	20.8
			4. Total (Direct + Indirect) Impacts[6]	27.0
			5. Social Costs[7]	(30.6)

Notes to Table 6.2

1. Volume of visits to the Taba casino is calculated on the basis of 80 percent of the Israelis using the Taba border crossing whose destination is Taba. For the Eilat casino, visitor volume is composed of foreign tourists, Israeli tourists, local Eilat residents, and demand diverted to Eilat from Taba and from the gambling boats. In the case where both locations have casinos, we assume 20 percent

of the Taba visitors will continue to frequent the location. Hotel visitors (10 percent of border crossings) are assumed to visit twice per visit.

2. Within-casino expenditures are estimated on the basis of a gambling "drop" of $100 per visit, $10 entrance fee, and $15 on food and beverages, per visit.

3. The casino cost structure is composed of employees' wages and salaries, gambling tax, admissions tax, value-added tax (on food and beverage sales), and property tax based on the size of the casino (floorspace and unbuilt areas).

4. Direct positive impacts are the sum of the following factors: wages and salaries (all employees are assumed to be local); 33 percent of revenues from the gaming tax; 33 percent of revenues from the admissions tax; all the property tax; inputs purchased locally, which in the case of Eilat are assumed to be 5 percent of net revenues after deducting wages and taxes and in the case of Taba are assumed to be 1 percent of net revenues, all of which is spent in Eilat; visitors' additional expenditure (i.e., non-deadweight spending), which is assumed to be only the expenditure on food and beverage arising from the new demand diverted to the casino. All other expenditure is assumed to have occurred even in the absence of the casino (visitor expenditures in Taba and Eilat). In the case of casinos in both locations, the volume of Taba visitors' extra spending is subtracted from the Eilat total.

5. Negative economic impacts represent the local demand displaced by the casino. In the Taba casino case, we assume that 90 percent of visitors would gamble elsewhere in the absence of the casino (i.e., 10 percent displacement). In the case of the casino in Eilat, we estimate a displacement rate of 24 percent, assuming that half of the additional demand diverted from the gambling boats would gamble elsewhere; 20 percent of the demand diverted from Taba; and 33 percent of the demand from local Eilat residents. All the rest is assumed to be displacement. In the case of a casino in both Eilat and Taba, the nonadditional spending figure in Eilat is adjusted upwards to reflect the volume of visitors going to Taba.

6. Total impacts are calculated as direct impacts expanded by a regional income multiplier of 1.3 (see Felsenstein and Freeman, 1998).

7. Local social costs represent the monetary cost of treating compulsive gamblers, their productivity loss locally, and the local spillover cost (crime, etc.) generated by all casino visitors. Social costs are assumed to relate to 3 percent of all local visitors (not visits) to the casino at a cost of $5,000 per gambler (for one year, without hospitalization costs). Local spillover costs generated by all gamblers (crime, etc.) are estimated as the number of addicted visitors (3 percent) multiplied by $2,000 per addict. We assume that only half of those addicted will commit crimes and of these, only half will be committed in Eilat. The local productivity loss is estimated as half of gross regional product per employee ($17,500) for each of the local addicted gamblers. This latter figure is expanded by a regional multiplier.

8. Diverted demand represents income lost to Taba or Eilat through not having a casino when the other location has one. In the case of no casino in Taba it is calculated as number of cross-border visits for the purpose of gambling multiplied by $125 per visit (drop, entrance fee and food and beverages). In the case of no casino in Eilat, it is assumed that with 90 percent of Taba visitors gambling elsewhere in the absence of the casino (see note 5 above), 50 percent of this proportion would go to the Eilat boats, 15 percent to other locations (Jericho, illegal casinos), and the remaining 25 percent represents the demand diverted from Eilat. In addition, food and beverage expenditure for all Taba visitors are taken as demand diverted from Eilat.

9. Hotel revenues forfeited are calculated for Taba on the basis of 10 percent of the Israelis crossing the border for the purpose of gambling, spending two nights in Taba at a cost of $166 per night (hotel and ancillary expenditures). This would be lost if there was no casino in Taba. In the case of no casino in Eilat, we assume no hotel revenues are forfeited (no reduction in Taba casino patrons staying in Eilat).

spending that displaces other spending in the local economy. Subtracting these effects still leaves positive direct balance of $25.2 million. Once this is expanded to account for indirect and induced local spending that it triggers, we are left with a total impact of nearly $33 million.

Local social costs, however, have to be taken into consideration. Conservative estimations of the propensity to gamble (and become addicted) amongst visitors to Eilat, the cost of treatment for this addiction, the productivity loss that this addiction implies, and the spillover costs of the casino result in total social costs adding up to over $30 million. Thus over 90 percent of the positive local effect is eroded by the local social costs arising from hosting the casino in Eilat. It should be noted that this narrow margin of local profitability is achieved under the most favorable scenario from Eilat's perspective. The absence of a casino in Taba results in lost direct economic opportunities (gambling demand diverted to Eilat and hotel revenues forfeited) of $27.6 million. This figure expands to $36 million once the indirect impacts are counted.

The most likely outcome is Case 3: casinos on both sides of the border. Under this scenario, we assume the same size casinos as in Cases 1 and 2. With the presence of a large casino in Eilat, visits to the Taba casino are reduced drastically. As a result, casino revenues fall and barely cover costs (table 6.2). In terms of local economic impacts (composed of salaries and additional expenditures), the Taba casino generates a positive balance $5.0 million which expands to $6.5 million when indirect effects are accounted for.

The impacts in Eilat derive from slightly reduced demand (1.569 million visitors) due to the presence of the casino in Taba. As in Case 2, casino revenues far outweigh costs. The slight diversion of demand to the Taba casino means that local positive economic impacts are marginally reduced (less local expenditure) and the negative impacts are slightly increased (more deadweight or nonadditional expenditure). This means that the overall positive balance is reduced to $27 million (including multiplier effects). This sum, however, is not sufficient to cover the local social costs of gambling ($30.6 million), which remain constant. Even when demand is slightly diverted from Eilat, the city still has to deal with the social cost of gambling that is taking place over the border. This slight deflection is enough to cancel out the positive local impacts of the casino and leave Eilat with a negative balance of $3.6 million.

Conclusions

While our empirical results support the outcomes hypothesized in table 6.1 (above) in the case where one location has a casino and the other does not, the peculiarities of the Taba-Eilat situation are such that even when Eilat has no casino, it still has to shoulder heavy social costs. This explains why contrary to the simple prisoners' dilemma hypothesis, Taba reports positive impacts in the instance when both locations promote casino gambling (Case 3). All social costs simply flow back over the border to Eilat along with the returning gamblers.

The results have significant implications for the use of gambling as a tourist development strategy in three respects. First, in the absence of cross-border cooperation, the kind of competitive situation described above is likely to lead to both locations losing, as hypothesized by the prisoners' dilemma. The situation described above with competition between two remote locations is, however, a highly simplistic representation. In reality, prisoners' dilemma-type situations can emerge in more complex settings, such as metropolitan areas where multiple locations are involved. For example, metropolitan Chicago is within the orbit of both the Iowa and Indiana borders and thus a tristate competitive situation, involving Illinois, Iowa, and Indiana emerges. Locating a border casino in any one of these states immediately has ramifications in the others. A similar situation could potentially develop if a casino where to open in Aqaba (Jordan). This port city adjoins Eilat to the east, and any gambling activity there would promote a more complex dilemma with nine possible outcomes involving Egypt, Israel, and Jordan.

The second implication relates to the limited size of the market for gambling in a small country such as Israel. While the monopoly-type situation of a casino in one location and not in the other yields large revenues and local impacts, once a competitive situation merges, using casinos as a tool for tourist development quickly become a zero-sum game. Our findings illustrate just how susceptible positive local casino impacts really are. A slight diversion in demand across the border is enough to negate any positive local effects. In a more competitive situation, the likelihood of each new entrant to the casino market benefiting only at the expense of all the others only increases.

Finally, our findings point to the heavy monetary weight of social impacts. These effects are often glossed over (either deliberately or unintentionally) in many impact analyses. The results above have shown that even when employing particularly conservative assumptions, these impacts can turn a local positive effect into a negative one. In the heat of the economic development debate, it is often assumed that the very large revenues that casinos generate automatically create positive local impacts that are large enough to cover the negative externalities generated. Our particular case study has illustrated that this margin might be smaller than anticipated. Furthermore, faced with moderate social costs, it may evaporate altogether. Even a modest deflection of demand may be all that is needed to effect this turnaround. In a competitive border situation, the likelihood of this demand-diversion is increased. In this uncertain environment, locating casinos on the border may indeed be a gamble.

Notes

1. The prisoners' dilemma story, as used in game theory (Gibbons, 1992), tells of two suspects accused of a crime by the police. Each one is held separately and is faced with the dilemma of whether to cooperate with the police (in return for a reduced sentence) while not knowing the behavior of his partner. In the absence of sufficient evidence for an indictment, each prisoner is confronted with the following dilemma. He can incriminate his accomplice and hope that the accomplice does not incriminate him. This is the best possible outcome for the prisoner. Failing that, he can remain silent and hope that the other prisoner will do the same. This is the welfare-maximizing strategy for both prisoners. However, there is no guarantee that the accomplice will act in the same way. The third choice is to implicate his fellow prisoner and be incriminated himself. This strategy is a great deal worse for both prisoners as they will both be subjected to some form of punishment. Nevertheless, it is likely to be the dominant strategy, in that it minimizes the risk of "cheating" or "defection" on the part of his accomplice. Finally, the prisoner can remain silent and be indicted by his fellow prisoner. Few prisoners are likely to opt for this strategy.

References

BGA. 1992. Casino gambling in Chicago. Staff White Paper, Better Government Association, Chicago, IL.

Blair, J. P., and R. Kumar. 1997. Is economic development a zero sum game? In R. D. Bingham and R. Mier eds., *Dilemmas of Urban Economic Development*. Thousand Oaks, CA: Sage.

Blair, B. F., R. K. Schwer, and C. J. Waddoups. 1998. Gambling as an economic development strategy: The neglected issue of job satisfaction and nonpecuniary income. *Review of Regional Studies*, 28:47–62.

C.B.S. 1999. Quarterly statistical report on tourism and lodging, 27. Jerusalem: Central Bureau of Statistics.

Deloitte-Touche, L. L. P. 1995. *Economic Impacts of Gambling on the State of Michigan.* Chicago: Deloitte-Touche Tohmatsu International.

Eadington, W. R. 1995. The emergence of casino gaming as a major factor in tourism markets: Policy issues and considerations. In R. Butler and D. Pearce eds., *Change in Tourism; People, Places and Processes.* New York: Routledge.

Ellis, S., and C. Rogers. 1997. Local economic development as a game: We're caught in a trap, I can't walk out . . . Research Paper 9706, Regional Research Institute, West Virginia University, Morgantown, WV.

Felsenstein, D., and D. Freeman. 1998. Simulating the impacts of gambling in a tourist location: Some evidence from Israel. *Journal of Travel Research,* 37:145–155.

Gavish Commission. 1995. Report of the public inquiry into legalizing casino gambling in Israel. Tel Aviv (Hebrew).

Gibbons, G. 1992. *Game Theory for Applied Economists.* Princeton, NJ: Princeton University Press.

Grinols, E. L., and J. D. Omorov. 1996. Development or dreamfield delusions? Assessing casino gambling's costs and benefits. *Journal of Law and Commerce,* 16:49–87.

Hobson, J. S. P. 1995. Macau: Gambling on its future? *Tourism Management,* 16:237–246.

Krakover, S. 1997. A boundary permeability model applied to Israel, Egypt and Gaza strip tri-border area. *Geopolitics and International Boundaries,* 2:28–42.

Przybylski, M., and L. Littlepage. 1997. Estimating the market for limited site casino gambling in northern Indiana and northeastern Illinois. *Journal of Urban Affairs,* 19:319–334.

Przybylski, M., D. Felsenstein, D. Freeman, and L. Littlepage. 1998. Does gambling complement the tourism industry? Some empirical evidence of import substitution and demand displacement. *Tourism Economics,* 4:213–232.

Taskir, 1993. Survey of expenditures of foreign tourists. Taskir Surveys and Consulting, prepared for the Ministry of Tourism, Jerusalem (Hebrew).

Thompson, W. N., and R. Gazel. 1997. The *Last Resort* revisited: The spread of gambling as a "prisoners dilemma." In W. R. Eadington and J. A. Cornelius eds., *Gambling Public Policies and Social Sciences.* Reno: Institute for the Study of Gambling and Commercial Gaming, University of Nevada, Reno.

Part 3

Tourism Frontiers in Rural Areas

Chapter 7

The Training Needs of Small Rural Tourism Operators in Frontier Regions

Abraham Pizam and Randall S. Upchurch

Rural Tourism

Defining rural tourism has been problematic due to the lack of a comprehensive body of knowledge and a theoretical framework. This is largely attributed to (a) little agreement among experts on a working definition of "rural tourism," (b) the paucity of databases on rural tourism enterprises, (c) inconsistency in measuring small rurally based tourism enterprises, and (d) reduced visibility that smaller operations command relative to their traditional counterparts (Oppermann, 1996). For example, on this latter point, bed and breakfast operations are often a best-kept secret in many rural communities versus their branded counterparts in the lodging industry, not only in terms of size, but also in their impact upon the community (Boger and Buchanan, 1991; Brown, 1990). Of course, the fact that national accounting firms monitor the economic impacts of traditional lodging operations and totally ignore the contributions of small rural properties contributes to the obscurity of these enterprises. Therefore, it is no surprise that the small, and often independent, rural operator is omitted in public documents.

The body of literature linked to small rural tourism development is relatively diverse in composition. For the purposes of this paper, small rural tourism in frontier regions, also known as farm tourism, can best be described as a range of activities, services, and amenities provided by farm operators to attract tourists to their homesteads with the direct intent of generating additional income for their business operation (Gannon, 1994). So with this working definition in mind, small rural tourism becomes a robust segment of the tourism industry that includes of bed and breakfast (B&B) facilities, recreational services associated with frontier regions, festivals and events, and selling of hand-crafted materials (figure 7.1).

Fee fishing	Orchard tours
Hunting	Motorcycle trails
Primitive camping	Farm vacations
Farm animal zoos	Farm museums
Horseback riding	Golf
Boating and canoe rentals	Bridle trails
Ski slopes	U-pick fruits, vegetables, trees
Nature walks	Snow mobiling
Calf roping	Western-wear shopping
Bird watching	Livestock auctions
Antique auctions	Ostrich farming
Spelunking	Sheep herding
Lamb shearing	Picnicking

Source: Dice, Eugene (1999). Michigan State Extension. Tourism Educational Materials #33839810 & #33839801.

Figure 7.1. Potential Recreational Services Available in Rural Tourism Facilities

After perusing this list of recreational activities, it should be no surprise that recreational services such as these will appeal strongly to various city and urban dwellers who are seeking experiences that satisfy their psychological, social, and cultural needs. Therefore, small rural operators can capitalize on these unique "tourist" desires as a means of reducing fluctuating commodity prices while increasing their diversity of profitable farm activities. So with this logic in place, it is no revelation to find that farm operators are playing the host to paying recreational and leisure consumers (Fact Sheet, 1997).

In reviewing small tourism research, it was found that the most common form of rural tourism is an operation that combines leisure activities with limited boarding, food and beverage offering, and limited retailing services. For the rural tourist, this type of accommodation is better known as a bed and breakfast operation. This form of rural tourism has gained great acceptance over the last twenty years in both the United States and Canada (Lanier, 1982). Furthermore, Fleischer and Pizam (1997) suggest that small rural tourism is on the advance in frontier regions of numerous other countries. In particular, Fleischer and Pizam noted that the number of small rural tourism operations is on the increase in Israel and in the United Kingdom due to heightened demand for frontier types of experience.

In general, there are two common types of small rural endeavors. First, there are small rural tourism operators who market their facilities as a means of generating income that is supplemental to the revenues generated from raising crops or livestock. Second, there are operators who make the rural tourist experience their main economic source of income. For either of these small rural tourism operations to be economically feasible, the operator must have access to a relatively large consumer base and, at the outset, a sound production and marketing scheme (Dice, 1999; Oppermann, 1996).

However, other researchers have shown that small rural tourism operators have been beset by problems. For the small rural entrepreneur desiring to enter the industry, the fact that 67 percent of new small business entrants have failed within the first four years is quite alarming. (Dunkelberg, 1995). Therefore it is of utmost importance that the reasons for success and failure in this business be identified and studied. A rudimentary review of current rural tourism literature reveals that the common reasons for failure of small businesses are: (a) poor financial understanding, (b) lack of proper capitalization, (c) poor identification of a specific target market, (d) ineffective advertising and sales promotion activities, (e) lack of understanding of the service dynamics, and (f) inability to compete in a trading area (Pizam and Pokela, 1980; Kwansa and Parsa, 1990; Upchurch, 1997; Moore, 1998).

In reviewing the literature on small rural tourism operations, one is inclined to conclude that this type of operation is increasing in popularity from both demand and supply perspectives. In 1991, the *Journal of Tourism Recreation Research* [Volume 16(1)] and in 1994, the *Journal of Sustainable Tourism* [Volume 2(1&2)] dedicated respective issues to rural tourism research. The overall message that emanated from this international collection of research is that rural tourism attracts a small but growing number of motivated visitors. The tourists who stay in these places are generally interested in local culture and social interaction with rural natives. Conversely, the residents of these rural communities are quite content to share their knowledge, crafts, and "way of life." Furthermore, the residents of these communities benefited from improvement in roads and public facilities, increased local revenues, generation of new jobs, development of new attractions, heritage protection, and land conservation (Emerick and Emerick, 1994). Juxtaposed with these benefits, there are reported downsides to small rural tourism development. These range from negative influences upon sociocultural characteristics, strains on the environment, strains on physical and natural resources, outward migration of young adults to urban and city areas, reduced privacy, and restructuring of economic and social stratification in the host environment (Davis and Gilbert, 1992). Overall, this body of rural tourism impact literature asserts that it is the duty of the small rural tourism developer to plan the development in such a way as to neither damage the physical and social environment nor negatively influence the community. Hence, the literature suggests that tourism entrepreneurs must be socially responsible when embarking upon small rural tourism developments. But most important is the notion that small rural tourism operators can respond in a civically and socially responsible manner only if they possess the proper skills to address these issues. Therefore, it is vital that small rural tourism operators acquire the knowledge and skills necessary for financial success that is achieved in a socially responsible manner.

Competencies and Skills Required for Successful Operation

Researchers and operators alike have tried time and again to identify the competencies, skills, and knowledge that are necessary prerequisites for successful operation of small rural tourism businesses. Furthermore, these individuals have proposed methods of implementing such skills in ways that can lead to the vitalization or revitalization of the community's economy, the creation of jobs, the practice of social and cultural development and sensitivity, the preservation of the natural environment, and the perpetuation of community arts, history, and handicrafts.

Our research has identified six competencies that entrepreneurs must possess before embarking upon starting a rural tourism business. These are:

* determining the motive for entering the rural tourism business
* understanding financial and capital requirements
* being able to prepare a business and marketing plan
* developing a service orientation
* understanding regulatory requirements
* identifying sources for external assistance.

Motive for Entry into the Rural Tourism Business

Many rural tourism operators and farming communities have unrealistic expectations as to the benefits that may accrue from engaging in small rural tourism businesses. Small farmers are motivated to go into tourism operations to make a profit. However, in many parts of the world, small rural tourism operations are not financially successful and therefore new entrants cannot expect to be necessarily financially profitable in the short term. For example, Dawson and Brown (1988) reported that midwestern B&B businesses had low occupancy levels and poor gross revenue. They noted that in order to increase gross revenue, these operators had to spend money on promotion, continue to "stay" in the business (i.e., have a high level of commitment), add more rooms and offer private bath facilities. Gruidl et al. (1990), Boger and Buchanan, (1991) and Dawson and Brown (1981) also conducted B&B research in the Midwest region of the United States and found that these operations were not very profitable. When examining occupancy, income, and expenditures levels, they found that B&B operations in the Midwest were not as profitable as their West and East Coast counterparts. Typically, B&Bs in the Midwest had fewer rooms, charged less, and were more seasonal than their coastal counterparts.

Overall, these studies indicated that the average B&B operator needed to have more than eight rooms to generate a profit, something that most small farmers do not possess. Others researchers (the Professional Association of International Innkeepers, 1992; Poorani and Smith, 1995) studied B&B operations on the East and West coasts of the United States and found that these operations could be profitable, but operators had first to focus on establishing a market within their geographical area; second, to realize that running a B&B is a long-term engagement that requires long hours; and third, had to have a strong command of the accounting and investment process.

As previously indicated, high profitability was not the norm in such ventures. Yet many farmers enter this business and they do it for other reasons, such as earning supplemental income and social interaction. For the majority of tourism farmers, as suggested by Denroi (1983, 1991), rural tourism predominately serves as a means of supplemental income. This finding was supported by Pizam and Pokela (1980), who found that engaging in rural tourism produced supplemental income and at the same time did not distract farmers from their normal farming activities. As to social interaction, studies conducted by Gruidl et al. (1990), and Pizam, Richardson, and Seymour (1980) suggest that one of the primary reasons for entering into the rural tourism business is the opportunity for "social interaction with the guests." This is especially true for those farmers who considered their tourism operation to be only a minor source of income.

From the rural community perspective, the motivation to engage in rural tourism development is mostly economic. Rural communities encourage these types of enterprises because they expect that through them, jobs will be created, roadways and transportation will be improved, and outward migration of community residents will diminish. Yet experience in the United States and other countries shows that these expectations are somewhat unrealistic and such major economic impacts do not normally occur.

In summary, research shows that the profit motive is not and should not be the main incentive for most rural tourism operators. Apparently, the primary reasons for entering into this business are supplemental income, social interaction, and improving one's quality of life.

Financial and Capital Requirements

Accounting Practices

It is of paramount importance for the operator to master a few accounting fundamentals to avoid failure during the early stages of market entry. Indeed, one of the most predominant reasons for failure was found to be the operators' inability to manage their finances. At the most fundamental level, operators must monitor their income and expenses to ensure that there is an adequate return on their investment. In order to arrive at a gauge of what is an acceptable price to charge and what are acceptable operational costs, the new operator need only look at comparable rural tourism operations (Upchurch, 1995). For example, operators who want to determine what is an acceptable return on their investment can review the annual report produced by the Professional Association of Innkeepers International. Also, most states have associations that were formed to provide "starter packs" for individuals considering entering the rural tourism market. In general, the use of national or state association statistics is critical in estimating cash flow projections by providing guidelines for monthly revenues and expenses. From these projections, operators should be able to construct a monthly revenue and income budget for the first year of operation. Of course, the prices charged would have to be in balance with the supply of consumers and the demand for services offered. Moreover, the operator must consider revenue (sales) gains or shortfalls relative to the budget. This review process enables the operator to make necessary corrective adjustments in pricing, advertising, or promotional activities in relation to consumption rates (e.g., demand). Still, at the minimum, the prices charged must cover all operational costs.

Furthermore, looking at national or state revenue or expense projections is but one element in determining the price-value relationship. There are other costs that many new operators do not often consider as a "cost of doing business." Such costs as furniture, fixtures, equipment, construction, guest supplies, cleaning supplies, necessary food and beverage storage equipment, and legal and accounting consultation may be needed in the early stages of business development. Hence, these start-up costs occur before the business is in operation and in many cases are overlooked by the farmer as an initial capital request.

Second, as part of operating under normal business conditions, rural operators must consider their sales levels. This is necessary, because as sales increase, there is a concomitant increase in variable expenses associated with increased sales. As sales volume increases, utility fees, staffing/personnel, advertising and promotional activities, and taxes increase as well.

Third, in all rural tourism operations there will be certain fixed expenses associated with conducting business unassociated with sales levels. For example, insurance, business or association fees, and payment on debt schedule (assuming a loan was taken out) have to be paid out, regardless of level of sales. Again, just as with variable expenses, fixed expenses are a cost of doing business and, therefore, must be accounted for in the pricing structure.

Finally, the monthly revenues minus variable and fixed expenses result in net profit. This process sounds fairly complex, but with the appropriate costs accounted for, the new entrant is not very likely to become surprised or shocked at the end of the year.

Overall, the most common way of tracking the profits of a business is by construction of a monthly income statement and a balance statement. Once these have been prepared, state and national statistics from tourism associations should be consulted in order to compare one's performance with national or regional averages.

Given the low profit nature associated with bed and breakfast operations, there is rarely sufficient discretionary income to put into the operation. Unfortunately for the bulk of the small rural farmers, this is indeed the case. Therefore, at the outset, sufficient capital to sustain the operation within the first few years is a necessary prerequisite portion of the operation's business plan. First and foremost, this initial capital investment is a significant, though not large, consideration before the entrepreneur can start operations. Such working capital is required to acquire a building, land, or structures or to renovate the present facilities, making them suitable for commercial usage

Table 7.1. Initial Cost: Original Construction

	Minimum Investment	Maximum Investment	Average Investment
Original Construction	$31,400	$977,000	$276,663
Converted Property	$6,440	$490,500	$ 108,025

Adapted from: Upchurch, R. (1995) *1994–1995, Profile and Performance of Wisconsin's Bed and Breakfast Industry*, University of Wisconsin, Menomonie, WI, page 58.

Table 7.2. Investment Profile: Original versus Converted Properties

	Average Costs: Original Construction Properties	Average Costs: Converted Properties
Construction	$97,461	$54,130
Furniture	$31,638	$39,746
Equipment	$4,998	$6,728
Linen & Guest supplies	$2,981	$2,161
Advertising and promotion	$2,882	$2,118
Auto and travel expenses	$3,674	$422
Miscellaneous	$2,239	$1,680

Adapted from: Upchurch, R. (1995) *1994–1995, Profile and Performance of Wisconsin's Bed and Breakfast Industry*, University of Wisconsin, Menomonie, WI, p. 58.

and hence more attractive to the consumer. For instance, a study of rural and urban B&B operations in the state of Wisconsin yielded data on initial capital investments for either an original or a converted property. In reviewing these tables, it is obvious that there is a fairly substantial initial capital outlay that must be accounted for in advance (tables 7.1 and 7.2).

These costs appear to be somewhat alarming for the first time investor; however, it need not be assumed that all operations require this amount of initial outlay. Still, it is important for operators to specifically list all potential investment costs for their project. In essence, one should begin with a comprehensive list that might look something like the following:

- Renovation of building facade
- Entry way improvements
- Parking enlargement (per city or county code; typically one space per guest room)
- Privacy fence
- Assorted cleaning supplies
- Water heater upgrade

- Additional plumbing
- Furniture, fixtures
- Inspection costs to meet city and county codes (fire, safety, utilities)
- Promotional literature
- Advertising
- Accounting software or services for the business portion
- Additional food and beverage costs
- Linen supplies
- Yard equipment
- Serving area and other kitchen equipment improvements
- Addition of a bathroom or toilet (a minimum of two each is the typical standard code)
- Addition of smoke detectors and fire extinguishers (per city or county code)
- Addition of property signage (within city or county height, size, and placement regulations)
- Transportation (will you be needing a new vehicle due to business activities?)

Again a review of such an exhaustive list can be quite threatening to the first time entrant. Yet how extensive this list is will depend on the age of the facility; compliance with city or county health, fire, safety, and other governing bodies' codes; the pricing structure of retailing establishments in the area (e.g., standard retailer versus a wholesaler); and cost of living in the area.

Financing the Project

As soon as the costs have been estimated, operators need to find sources for financing the operation with enough capital to purchase and then remain solvent over the first few years of operation. Typically, government-guaranteed commercial loans are available, that offer a reduced rate of interest that is sufficient to keep the operation solvent. In addition, there may also be subsidized loans available from the federal, state, or county governments prepared to provide expertise and dollars to support the development of rural tourism projects. Such loans can be accessed through the local agricultural extension service. As extracted from a national rural tourism study, Poorani and Smith (1995) identified four basic means of loan acquisition from external lending authorities. They suggested that a typical loan should offer the operator approximately a 33.9 percent return on equity and extend for about three years (table 7.3).

Table 7.3. Loan Sources

	1–3 rooms	4–8 rooms	9 or more rooms
Commercial bank	59%	71%	73%
Savings & loan	31%	19%	11%
Credit company	3%	0%	3%
Small Business Administration	0%	6%	11%
Other	7%	4%	2%

Adapted from: Poorani and Smith. Financial Characteristics of Bed and Breakfast Operations. *Cornell Hotel and Restaurant Administration Quarterly*, 36:57–63, 1995.

To obtain the necessary finances, the prospective operator must provide the appropriate requested information. First and foremost, the loaning authority will request the reason for the loan. The standard categories are to establish or purchase a new or existing business, to finance the acquisition of real property, to remodel or expand an existing business, to purchase or lease equipment, to provide working capital, or to restructure an existing loan.

Next, it is a standard practice to request personal and business-related information. This requested information will cover an application form and letter of request from the lender, previous three years' financial statements (if applicable), previous three years' tax returns (if applicable), current personal financial statements, cash flow and income statement projections, inventory listing (as is necessary), an aging of accounts receivable (as is necessary), an aging of accounts payable (as is necessary), an appraisal of the property (if applicable), a history of the business, a detailed marketing plan and sales projections, and a review of management and ownership (Bank of South Dakota, 1999).

Next, the rural operator should be prepared to provide approximately 15 percent tangible equity toward the business. However, upwards of 25 percent might be needed if the business is less than two years old. In addition, the loaning authority might also request collateral for the business venture. This collateral is necessary to protect the interest of the loaning agency by guaranteeing that repayment of the loan is assured.

The repayment schedule for a small business development loan will vary with the terms of the loaning agency and by the complexity of the business proposed. In general, the operator can expect loan maturities of twelve to fifteen years for a real estate loan, five to seven years for equipment loans, and three to five years for working capital stipulations.

In closing, seeking out a loan is a very arduous process that requires a thorough assessment of operational skills, full disclosure of assets and liabilities, analysis of supply and demand, and the development of a balance sheet, monthly budgets, and allocation of initial capital to seed the project. So in determining which type of loan is most suitable for one's operation, it is advisable to seek out guidance from a seasoned loan advisor.

Business and Marketing Plans

To develop a successful business, entrepreneurs must develop a sound business plan and implement it carefully and meticulously (Schermerhorn, 1993). Operators who address each step of their business plan are able to position their new business venture in a manner that will ensure its success in the marketplace. As listed in figure 7.2, these business-planning points are critical to positioning the rural tourism enterprise in the marketplace. Basically, these business-planning elements start with the development of a reason for the business (description of products and services), what assets (financial, physical, and human resources) the individual is bringing to the project, what services will be provided, how the business will fit within the community, who is the projected consumer, what is the level of competition, and a detailed analysis of short- and long-term financial projections.

Marketing Plan

If seriously addressed, the preceding elements will enable operators to understand the level of complexity that is required to make a business enterprise successful. Still, once this process is completed, there are a number of marketing activities that rural tourism operators must undertake as part of their ongoing responsibility to ensure that their operations continue to be successful. To market their products successfully, small rural tourism operators need to prepare a comprehensive marketing plan that determines the different activities to be undertaken under the four marketing mix variables. These variables are:

- price—at what level of price should the product be offered;
- product—how should the product be packaged and positioned;
- promotion—what specific program should be undertaken to promote the product to the consumer;
- place—what specific channels of distributions will be used to offer the product to the consumer.

Regarding promotion, rural tourism operators have at their disposal a set of tools (communication mix variables) that include advertising, sales

Steps for Success

Executive Summary

  description of product or service

  description of target market

  description of channel of distribution

  summary of revenue and profit in dollar value for the projected periods
  summary of human resource involvement and deployment

Background of business

  analysis of the advantages and the disadvantages of your product or service

  analysis of competitor advantages and disadvantage of product or services

  description of where your current markets are located

  description of how your product is used

Description of strategic, tactical, and operational planning for target segment

  description of target segments

  detailed description of your marketing strategy

  discussion of human resources involved for the strategic, tactical, and operational plans

  discussion of the channels of distribution analysis of current geographical target markets

Promotional literature

  state the techniques that you intend to use in promoting the product or service

  state the types of media utilized

  project costs of the promotional tactics

  establish budget for promotional tactics

  develop sales forecasts by periods of business

Detailed analysis of management's role

  discuss management involvement in the marketing plan administration

  discuss requisite skills needed by management and employees

Adapted from: Schermerhorn, John, *Management for Productivity.* John Wiley & Sons, New York. 1993, p. 658.

Figure 7.2. Marketing and Business Plan

Table 7.4. Advertising Media by Small-Scale B&B Operators
(Two Separate B&B Studies)

	Effectiveness rating		Effectiveness rating
Local brochure	60.3%	Local brochure	67.5%
Referral/friends	53.4%	Referrals/friends	59.0%
State B&B guide	48.3%	State B&B guide	34.5%
Newspaper	13.0%	Newspaper	39.5%
National travel guide	14.7%	National travel guide	17.5%
Chamber of Commerce	25.3%	Chamber of Commerce	23.0%
Travel agency	4.65%	Travel agency	7.0%

Note: The B&Bs surveyed had less than 20 guest rooms each, offered breakfast only, and were located in cities, urban, and rural locations.
Adapted from: Upchurch, Randall. Conduct of midwestern bed and breakfast operations in the U.S.A. *International Journal of Contemporary Hospitality Management*, 9:40–43, 1997.

promotions, publicity, and public relations. Advertising activities serve as a means of formulating a favorable impression in the prospective tourist's mind. Hence, a combination of tangible and intangible cues is very important in the formation of an image about the leisure or recreational services offered. In general, the effectiveness of various advertising media will vary with the specifics of the situation. In the case of rural B&B operations, experience shows that word of mouth is extremely powerful and that a combination of targeted printed advertisements is helpful as well (see table 7.4) However, another study indicated that cooperative arrangements between various tourism enterprises enabled rural operators to use printed publications and a shared reservation system that could not have existed without a collaborative effort. In two cases and in two separate rural settings, researchers found that cooperative advertising and promotional activities were very effective for small rural tourism operators. First, Koth (1995) found that spending from 4 percent to 6 percent of an operator's gross sales on cooperative advertising in newspapers, magazines and brochures for local chamber of commerce and visitor bureaus was productive in stimulating first-time awareness. Second, the Farm Holiday Bureau (FHB), a government-funded agency in the United Kingdom, found that farmers were typically lacking in a pre-determined strategy for advertising or promotion activities. The net result of collaborative advertising and promotional activities increased regional and national exposure, leading to positive economic impacts for the participating communities (Clarke, 1996).

Clarke (1996) acknowledged the level of importance that the marketing communications mix plays in the economic success of the small rural tourism operation. In particular, she found that advertising and personal selling were effective elements for attracting and conveying images to tourists, but public relations and sales promotions were of lesser importance. However, what is interesting to note is the use of cooperative agreements in actualizing the communications mix. For example, promotional literature was prepared on an annual basis by a cooperative group of rural tourism operators in order to gain price and distribution efficiencies. The above mentioned cooperative produced brochures that were printed in French and German as part of its European campaign. To offer another example, regarding the advertising portion of the communications mix, a consortium or cooperative arrangement brought about economic and distribution efficiencies. In particular, the FHB in the United Kingdom served as the vehicle for disseminating joint advertisements for a European market. Of course, projects on such a relatively grand scale offer the small and independent operator outreach capabilities that cannot be afforded otherwise. In the United States, the Rural Development Service of the U.S. Department of Agriculture specifically advocated the creation of vacation farm cooperatives and produced a brochure in which the fundamentals of operating such cooperatives were listed (Pizam, Richardson and Seymour, 1980).

In summary, attention to detail in the initial business plan is in the operator's best interest. More specifically, the preparation of a marketing plan and participation in marketing cooperative ventures, such as those utilized in the United Kingdom and the United States, have improved the rural tourism operators' ability to promote their products in the marketplace. Hence, the primary message is that a cohesive business plan, which includes a structured marketing plan, leads to economic gain for the operator and the host community.

Service Orientation

A major means of competing in the marketplace is to continually concentrate on providing the types of services that will meet consumer expectations. This is by no means an easy task, given that consumer expectations of the type and quality of services offered have continually risen. From the consumer's perspective, there is a certain "price-value" relationship for the type and quality of services offered. The challenge for management then is to stay in tune with the expectations of the consumer (Lovelock, 1996).

The provision of quality service is founded on the following premises:

1. Consumer expectations of products and services are constantly changing. This implies that rural tourism operators have constantly to evaluate the extent to which their services meet the expectations of their tourists.
2. Management actively promotes a "climate" that rewards and fosters a level of service that meets established service standards.
3. Service staff is fully empowered to administer and make service decisions.

These three premises serve as the foundation for quality service for a variety of operations in the tourism industry.

Basic Components of a Service Program

Service programs should cover the entire service experience, which can be divided into three distinct phases—before, during, and after service actions. Each service phase is unique in the types of actions that occur in response to satisfying tourists' expectations.

Before service actions: Establishing a climate of goodwill with the guest (tourist) is extremely important in setting a service message that should occur early in guest-staff interactions. Greeting guests with a pleasant smile, asking them how their day is going, and asking how one can be of help can accomplish this. Casual conversation concerning the guests' attire, the weather, or a meeting that they will be attending is also valuable in setting a personal tone with the customer. Experience shows that personalizing the guest interaction by using the guest's name in conversations makes the guest feel comfortable. Listening to the needs of the guests at all times is also an effective means of increasing guest satisfaction. The process does not stop with listening, but continues with attempts at predicting guest needs as ascertained during the conversation. Given the fact that guests are likely to be staying in the farmer's home, it is very likely that a reasonable degree of social interaction will occur. And since current trends show that the sharing of social, cultural, and historical "items" are the main reasons for seeking out a rural tourism experience, it is of great importance to attend to the guest's social and service needs (Davies and Gilbert, 1992).

During the service experience: The "during" phase is also a time to gain feedback from the guests who experience the services. If any performance does not meet established service standards, then a thorough analysis should be made so corrective actions can prevent substandard performance in the future. Then and only then can guest satisfaction be improved in the future. In the long term, it is much more damaging to a rural tourism operation's image to ignore a problem than to admit to an error and address the problem directly. Naturally, this will involve making amends with the guests and reassuring them that the lapse of service was an unfortunate oversight and has definitely been corrected. A general rule is to thank the guest for bringing the problem to the your attention, for without this input, the "inefficiency" of service could not have been improved so quickly! The result of this process is to reinforce the guest's choice of doing business with this operation.

After the service is offered: This is a phase of the service process that is often neglected with unfortunate results. The general impression is that the "beginning" and "during" process are usually sufficient to gain a competitive edge over other operators. However, this is not necessarily true and requires further attention. Even if an interaction with a guest went without any service errors, one cannot assume that the service was impeccable or could not have been improved. It could be that the guest simply did not bring the problem to the operator's attention and never intends to come back.

Attending to guest needs is still a vital part of the "after" phase. This means that programs must be developed that can acquire information from the guests after the service experience has ended. For a rural tourism operation, this could be a casual inquiry as to how the guests liked their experience, or it could entail a more formal but brief survey of the guests' perceptions of the overall experience (see Figure 7.3).

Regulatory Requirements

Before blindly investing in a rural tourism operation, entrepreneurs should study the multitude of city, county, or state regulations that affect their planned operation. In the United Sates, it is advisable to contact the zoning office or planning commission in one's own community to obtain a starter pack for the type of proposed operation. This starter pack will include valuable information relating to residential versus commercial type of zoning; health, fire, safety; and building codes and other things. In addition, it would be beneficial to contact one's neighbors and other community residents to determine their views on the proposed operation (Leones et al., 1994).

Municipality Zoning Regulations

The main reason for contacting the local municipal office is to determine if there are any special ordinances regulating the type of operation proposed

To our Valued Guest: We hope that our B&B meets or exceeds your expectations. Please take a moment to complete this postage-paid comment card. Your comments are very helpful.

Thank you for your patronage.

Please circle your choice for each item

Your Room

Décor	Excel	Good	Fair	Poor
Cleanliness	Excel	Good	Fair	Poor
Comfort	Excel	Good	Fair	Poor
Amenities	Excel	Good	Fair	Poor
Price and value	Excel	Good	Fair	Poor

Breakfast

Quality of food	Excel	Good	Fair	Poor
Menu variety	Excel	Good	Fair	Poor
Atmosphere	Excel	Good	Fair	Poor
Service	Excel	Good	Fair	Poor
Price and value	Excel	Good	Fair	Poor

Overall

How would you rate our B&B overall?	Excel	Good	Fair	Poor
Would you return for another visit?	Yes	No		

Name:
Address
City
State
Zip code

Figure 7.3. Abbreviated Guest Survey

and to review these thoroughly before making any investments. Even if no zoning regulations exist, one still needs to check whether the proposed enterprise falls under a "general" building ordinance (Farm and Country Holiday Association, 1997). Some localities might have special easement requirements (easement is a right of use over the property of another), parking requirements, traffic restrictions, lighting, hours of operation, noise, up-keep and appearance, type of license that is required to operate (e.g., food license, accommodation license), type of business that is allowed or prohibited in the area, and so on. Either way, farmers should determine what the procedures are for seeking approval before taking any actions to establish their rural tourism operation.

Site License and Building Permits

Each country or state has varying requirements relating to the number of guest rooms permitted for a rural tourism business, visitor cabin, B&B operation, or country inn (Lanier, 1982; Lanier and Berman, 1993). This is an important distinction due to the magnitude of related services that go along with larger units (e.g., country inns) that typically have expanded amenities. For all properties, an inspection by the state department of health, fire marshal, and a building inspector for safe electrical, plumbing, and sewage conditions is a mandatory process. Furthermore, if the operation is to serve food and beverages, a separate inspection process by the local health department is also required. Depending how the operation is classified, a restaurant license may be required as well.

Food and Beverage Handling Regulations

All rural tourism operations require at least a limited amount of cooking and serving of foods. Although this does not require an extensive knowledge of menu planning and food preparation, operators must be familiar with hygiene and food safety handling, storage, preparation, and serving conditions. Furthermore, such operators should possess some rudimentary knowledge of nutrition and meal preparation principles. Figure 7.4 contains a listing of fundamental food handling and preparation practices.

As seen in figure 7.4, there are detailed procedures relative to serving food and beverages in a food-related business. In summary, it is necessary for those handling food to have demonstrated competencies in food preparation, hygiene, storage, and disposal. In general, it is the operator's responsibility to comply with public health regulations related to the correct storage of food, hygienic meal preparation, food handling during meal preparation, and the avoidance of unhealthy contamination of food from chemicals, poisons, pests, or pets (Georgia Division of Public Health, 1999).

Fire and Safety Regulations

As mentioned previously, there are a myriad of fire and safety regulations with which the rural tourism operator must comply. It is advisable to check with the fire marshal to determine the various requirements related to the

General	Food may only be prepared for guests staying in rooms at the bed and breakfast.
Food Supplies	Food shall be in sound condition and safe for human consumption. The use of hermetically sealed containers for food not prepared in a food processing establishments is prohibited.
Food Protection	All food shall be prepared, stored, displayed, dispensed, placed, transported, sold, and served so as to be protected from dirt, vermin, unnecessary handling, and other contamination.
Food Display and Service	When food is displayed for customer self-service, it will not be necessary to have protective sneeze shields. Hazardous foods are kept at or below 41° F. Food is displayed no more than two hours. Tongs or suitable utensils are provided so that there is no hand contact with the food.
Health and Practices	No person while infected with a disease in a communicable form that can be transmitted by foods or a carrier shall work in any capacity in which there is a likelihood of contaminating food. Also, persons engaged in food preparation and service shall wear clean clothing, and wash their hands and exposed portions of their arms thoroughly with detergent. Persons engaged in food preparation shall wear a hair net, cap, or other suitable covering to restrain loose hairs.
Equipment and Utensils	Food equipment, surfaces, and tableware shall be cleaned and sanitized prior to food preparation. Manual cleaning and sanitizing shall use a three-compartment sink. In all cases, five steps of washing shall be followed: pre-rinsing/scraping, application of cleaner, rinsing to remove cleaning chemicals, sanitizing, and air drying.

Source: Tourist Accommodations Rules and Regulations. XVII. 290–5–18.17 Food Service. Amended. Georgia Division of Public Health, 1999.

Figure 7.4. Food Handling Regulations

number and type of fire extinguishers, smoke detectors, means of egress, proper storage of cleaning and flammable materials, CPR training requirements, proper floor coverings, and use of flame-retardant materials. This process not only occurs during the preopening phase of the business, but fire and safety inspections also occur on an annual basis. In summary, the objective of fire and safety regulations is to ensure that there is adequate protection, early warning, and provision for rapid escape for guests, residents, firefighters, and adjacent neighbors (Farm and Country Holiday Association, 1997).

External Assistance Sources

Given the previous discussion of the complex nature of entering into a small rural tourism enterprise, it is no wonder that most farmers or rural residents shy away from the prospect of such an apparently complex undertaking. Clearly, the combination of financial, marketing, human resources, rules and regulatory knowledge, service management, and management skills are a rare combination for the small rural entrepreneur to possess. And indeed, based on several rural tourism failure studies, each of these categories can and does lead to foreclosure (Fleischer and Pizam, 1997). Therefore, it is worth considering educational outlets that can provide information and training relative to skill area deficiencies.

There are numerous avenues available through which to acquire partial or overall skill training. As with any type of training, it is important to match one's budget, convenience, quality of the program, quality of materials, and time constraints. In the area of small rural tourism development, there are small business development centers and agricultural extension centers that are versed in tourism development issues. In addition, various universities have programs or centers that focus on the development of tourism businesses at local, regional, or national levels.

Another avenue of skill training is often provided by state associations or governing tourism bodies (Gruidl et al., 1990). In both cases, these bodies should take to heart the image that tourism has upon the state or the community in general. These sources should not be overlooked, given the findings that poor financial returns are correlated with a lack of operational knowledge, marketing activities, lack of financial resources, and an incompatibility between agricultural values and guest service values. All these educational resources are capable of training the operator in design, implementation, and monitoring functions. An excellent example of governmental support for rural tourist business development is the project undertaken by the Welsh

Tourism Board. From its foundation, this project had the intent to develop rural tourism businesses, develop strategy for this industry, and raise the level of professionalism by providing access to educational sites and materials at participating universities or via a distance learning pack. Clearly, this is an excellent example of government and university support in raising the entrepreneur's knowledge base (Gilbert and Davies, 1992).

Another progressive example is that offered by the New Zealand Association of Farms and Hosts. This association represents a group of rural tourism operators that have banded together to address the educational needs of the growing numbers of rural tourism operators in frontier regions. In particular, this association provides guidelines on a variety of educational topics, current research on marketing, financial and service standards, development of a code of ethics, and related operational issues. Of specific interest are training courses in food safety, food preparation, and hygiene. Also, the New Zealand Ministry of Agriculture and Forestry has actively developed and promoted certification programs that address target market development, product pricing, advertising practices, and promotional activity deployment. Clearly, this external form of assistance addresses many of the skill deficiencies that lead to business failures (Ministry of Agriculture and Forestry, 1994).

Finally, a study conducted by Pizam, Richardson, and Seymour (1981) determined that cooperative arrangements had wide ranging and positive impacts in the areas of greater promotion and publicity activities, greater support from public and private agencies, decreased operating expenses, and improved access to management skill training. And perhaps the most useful element of this document was the construction of a checklist for the first-time entrant regarding the basic skills and competencies required for a successful rural tourism operation, as mentioned in this chapter.

Summary and Conclusions

In concert with Fleischer and Pizam (1997), this chapter alludes to the growth and importance of skill set training for the small rural tourism operator in peripheral or frontier regions. Specifically, entrepreneurs considering entering the business of rural tourism in frontier regions should give strong consideration to acquiring or refining their business development skills (i.e., motivational, financial, marketing, management, regulatory, service delivery, business alliances, and educational assistance) as outlined above.

By now it is possible to conclude that rural tourism is composed of similar business development issues, as portrayed by the other and more established tourism sectors. This, of course, speaks to the advancement of the rural tourism sector through the tourism life cycle. Hence, as the industry continues to progress in size and stature, these and other operational issues will become increasingly complex (Butler, 1980; Richardson, 1991). Therefore, it behooves small rural tourism operators to acquire and maintain the business operation skills necessary to conduct their frontier tourism enterprises with success.

References

Bank of North Dakota. 1999. Small Business Loan Program. *http://www.banknd.com* (October 2, 1999).

Boger, C., and R. Buchanan. 1991. *A Study of Bed and Breakfast Facilities in Indiana.* Indianapolis: Indiana University, the Indiana Extension Service.

Brown, N. 1990. Nine state survey of bed and breakfast establishments. In The Dunbar/Jones Partnership ed., *Proceedings of the 11th Conference of the Censtates Chapter of the Travel and Tourism Research Association.* Des Moines, IA: Iowa Division of Tourism.

Butler, R. 1980. The concept of a tourist area cycle of evolution: Implications for management of resources. *Canadian Geographer,* 24:5–12.

Clarke, J. 1996. Farm accommodation and the communication mix. *Tourism Management,* 17:611–620.

Davies, E. T., and D. C. Gilbert. 1992. A case study of the development of farm tourism in Wales. *Tourism Management,* 13:56–63.

Dawson, C., and T. Brown. 1988. B&Bs: A matter of choice. *Cornell Hotel and Restaurant Administration Quarterly,* 29:18–21.

Denroi, I. 1983. Farm tourism in Europe. *Tourism Management,* 4:155–166.

Denroi, I. 1991. About rural and farm tourism. *Tourism Recreation Research,* 16:3–6.

Dice, E. 1999. Can a farmer make money with an outdoor recreation sideline? Ann Arbor: Michigan State University Extension. Document #3839810.

Dunkelberg, W. 1995. Presidential address: Small business and the U.S. *Business Economics,* 30:13–18.

Emerick, R. E., and C. A. Emerick. 1994. Profiling American bed and breakfast accommodations. *Journal of Travel Research,* 32:20–25.

Fact Sheet. 1997 *Farm and Station Tourism.* Washington, D.C.: Department of Agriculture. *http://agric.wa.gov.au/programs/new/tourism.htm* (October 2, 1999).

Farm and Country Holiday Association. 1997. *Home Hosting for Rural Tourist Accommodation.* Commonwealth Office of National Tourism, New South Wales: P&A Walsh Consulting Pty Limited.

Fleischer, A., and A. Pizam. 1997. Rural tourism in Israel. *Tourism Management,* 18:367–372.

Gannon, A. 1994. Rural tourism as a factor in rural community economic development for economies in transition. *Journal of Sustainable Tourism,* 2:51–80.

Georgia Division of Public Health. 1999. Tourist Accommodations Rules and Regulations. SVII. 290–5–18.17. *http://www.ph.dhr.state.ga.us/manuals/tourist/xvii.htm* (October 2, 1999).

Gilbert, D. C., and E. T. Davies. 1992. A case study of the development of farm tourism in Wales. *Tourism Management,* 13:56–63.

Gruidl, N., R. Cooper, and D. Silva. 1990. *Structure, Conduct, and Performance of the Bed and Breakfast Industry in Wisconsin.* Madison, WI: Recreation Resource Center, University of Wisconsin-Extension.

Koth, B. 1995. Bed and breakfast: Hosting travelers for extra income. In *The Direct Farm Marketing and Tourism Handbook.* Minneapolis: University of Minnesota, Tourism Department.

Kwansa, F., and H. Parsa. 1990. Business failure analysis: An events approach. *Hospitality Research Journal,* 14:23–34.

Lanier, P. 1982. *The Complete Guide to Bed and Breakfasts, Inns & Guesthouses.* New York: Ten Speed Press.

Lanier, P., and J. Berman. 1993. Bed and breakfast inns come of age. *Cornell Hotel and Restaurant Administration Quarterly,* 34:15–23.

Leones, J., M. Worden, R. Call, and D. Dunn. 1994. *Agricultural Tourism in Cochise County, Arizona, Characteristics and Economic Impacts.* Ann Arbor: Michigan State University Extension.

Lovelock, C. 1996. *Services Marketing.* Upper State River, NJ: Prentice Hall.

Ministry of Agriculture and Forestry. 1994. *Thinking of Starting in Rural Tourism? A Resource Book.* Wellington, New Zealand: Ministry of Agriculture and Forestry.

Moore, F. 1998. Forecast: The eighth report of the Tourism Forecasting Council. Office of National Tourism, Commonwealth Department of Industry, Science and Tourism, Australia.

Oppermann, M. 1996. Rural tourism in southern Germany. *Annals of Tourism Research,* 23:86–102.

Pizam, A., and J. Pokela. 1980. The Vacation Farm: A New Form of Tourism Destination. In D. E. Hawkins, E. L. Shafer, and J. M. Rovelstad eds., *Tourism Marketing and Management Issues.* Washington D.C.: George Washington University.

Pizam, A., L. Richardson, and W. Seymour. 1981. Vacation farm cooperatives. Washington, D.C.: United States Department of Agriculture, Rural Development Service Report.

Poorani, A., and D. Smith. 1995. Hotel finance: Financial characteristics of bed and breakfast inns. *Cornell Hotel and Restaurant Administration Quarterly,* 36:57–63.

Professional Association of Innkeepers International. 1994. *1992 Bed and Breakfast/Country Inns Industry Study of Operations.* Santa Barbara, CA: Professional Association of Innkeepers International.

Richardson, S. L. 1991. *Colorado Community Tourism Action Guide.* Boulder: University of Colorado.

Schermerhorn, J. 1993. *Management for Productivity.* New York: John Wiley & Sons.

Upchurch, R. 1995. *B&B's Are the Rage: The Financial Review of Midwestern B&B's for 1994.* Menomonie, WI: University of Wisconsin–Stout.

Upchurch, R. 1997. Conduct of Midwestern bed and breakfast operations in the U.S.A. *International Journal of Contemporary Hospitality Management,* 9:40–43.

Chapter 8

Small Tourism Ventures in Peripheral Areas:
The Impact of Environmental Factors
on Performance

Sigal Haber and Miri Lerner

Most of the tourism businesses in the world in general and in peripheral areas in particular are small (Brownlie, 1994). The advantages of small tourism ventures operating in rural and peripheral areas and their contribution to the people and communities involved are broadly recognized. They provide job alternatives, raise the level of popular participation in the economy, generate secondary income, enhance community stability, and tend to do less harm to the physical environment than other industries (Oppermann, 1996; Hall, 1996; Echtner, 1995). Moreover, small tourism ventures are not necessarily capital intensive and are thus less dependent on massive foreign investment, which limits the financial risk involved. This minimization of risks encourages entrepreneurship and self-employment. They also have the advantage of enabling utilization of underexploited factors of production. For example, small ventures in peripheral and agricultural regions, such as domestic accommodation and home restaurants, make use of existing infrastructure (Oppermann, 1996). The fact that most natural resources are located in the peripheral areas (Swarbrooke, 1995), as well as the unique ways of life of these areas, are still further advantages.

The physical and social environment of the small venture location plays an important role in its subsequent development. Despite the acknowledged importance of venture location, there is still a need to understand its characteristics and their impact on performance, especially among small ventures (Smith, 1995:150).

Statistics on long-term net job creation show that, on average, small firms create more new net jobs than large firms, and they typically produce more than half of the total. The data clearly show that small firms are the primary job creators in the United States (Kirchhoff, 1994). As the world's largest and fastest growing industry in recent years, tourism is a source of new job creation and has the potential to lead to an increase in the number of employees worldwide. According to the World Travel and Tourism Council (WTTC, 1994) 10 percent of the total employees in the world are employed in the tourism industry. For every $1 million of revenue generated by the industry, 20,000 new jobs are created (Lundberg, Krishnamoorthy, and Stavega, 1995; WTO—World Tourism Organization 1994). Since the 1980s, high rates of unemployment have led many governments to see the tourism industry as an important source of job creation.

Increasing government involvement in tourism as a result of its economic importance has important outcomes for tourism itself. Data from the WTTC (1994) show that government expenditures on tourism worldwide are reaching 7 percent of total expenditures. The worldwide income from tourism in 1995 was $372 billion, a growth of 7 percent compared to 1994 (WTO, 1996). Tourism is growing almost twice as fast as world gross national product (GNP) and taxes generated from tourism are 12 percent of total direct and indirect taxes. The total gross output for travel and tourism was over $3.2 trillion in 1994 and the added value from tourism is now calculated at 10 percent of the world's GNP.

In spite of all the macro assessments on the impact of governmental actions in general and on peripheral areas in particular, very few studies have examined the impact of such actions from the point of view of the small venture. Furthermore, in spite of the growing importance of small tourism ventures, the subject of the factors explaining their success has hardly been studied at all.

The study also focuses on the impact of the tourism environment upon the small venture's performance. Examining the tourism location is important due to the fact that establishing a venture in a specific location is a critical decision that may influence the business concept and the type of the tourism experience as well as the venture's performance. Changing such a decision is difficult and expensive. Some large hotels, resorts, and franchise restaurants have sophisticated location models for selecting sites. However, this is not the case for small peripheral tourism ventures (Smith, 1995). Thus, the location's environmental features are assumed to be important for the business success of small tourism ventures.

Following the above introduction, an important theoretical and practical question concerns the main environmental factors that affect the performance of small tourism ventures in peripheral areas and whether these factors affect performance measures differentially. In this study, the question of the factors affecting performance of small tourism ventures in peripheral areas is viewed from the contingency theory perspective.

After referring to the contingency approach and its application to this study, the issue of performance of small ventures is discussed and each of the environmental factors is then reviewed. The research method follows, including the data collection, and the hypotheses are then examined in the context of the case of small tourism ventures in Israel's southern peripheral Negev region. The study concludes with a summary of the results and the interpretations, offering several implications.

A Contingency Framework for Examining the Relationships between External Environmental Factors and Performance

Contingency theory seeks to understand the relationships between the organizational system and its environment and to define patterns of relationships among the variables. In seeking to explain how organizations operate under varying conditions and in specific circumstances, a number of schemes have been suggested within the framework of the theory for classifying the environmental characteristics that may affect organizations: these include political, natural resources, economic, and cultural schemes. The interrelationship with a certain type of environment is determined by the organization's choices and actions (Kast and Rosenzweig, 1986). While contingency theory relates to the various aspects of the environment that impact the organizations operating within it, our current focus is confined to two such external environmental aspects that are assumed to affect the performance of tourism ventures: (a) the governmental or institutional support and (b) the location's attractiveness

Business Performance and the Employment Measure

The perception of venture performance as a multidimensional concept has emerged only recently (Lumpkin and Dess, 1996; Gartner, 1985). Performance is usually measured by indices that reflect the size of the business, generally in terms of revenues and number of employees (Merz and Sauber, 1995; Robinson and Sexton, 1994; Davidsson, 1991; Loscocco and Leicht, 1993; Srinivasan, Woo, and Cooper, 1994; O'Farrell, 1986). In studies on technological and manufacturing industries, researchers have used various financial measures to examine business success, such as revenue volume, net profit, return on investment (Kirchhoff, 1977), and the ratio revenues/income per worker (Bade, 1986; Johannisson, 1993; Miller, Wilson, and Adams, 1988).

Determining a small venture's performance by the number of its employees may be rather problematic because of the nonlinear relationship that quite often exists between the number of employees and financial measures such as revenues and/or profitability. Some may view the number of employees as an input rather than an output for creating the venture's product or service. Therefore, while it is important to include the number of employees in the examination of performance of small ventures, it is necessary to examine this performance measure alongside other financial measures such as revenues, which also determine the size and profitability of the business.

The Institutional Support Mechanisms for Small Tourism Ventures

The institutional support mechanisms include mainly the governmental agencies as well as financial bodies and other organizations designed to promote new venture creation and its performance. According to Elliott (1997: 13), although it is difficult to measure the impact of the governmental and institutional support in a particular region, their contribution is essential and cannot be provided by private sector. Governments affect business ventures by their monetary policy, by instituting infrastructure and superstructures, and by developing advisory and training programs for the owners of small tourism businesses. Hall and Jenkins (1997) identified eighteen types of policy instruments used by governments for promoting rural tourism, among them expenditure, financial incentives, and regulatory instruments. Moreover, the government may provide a general economic, security, and health framework that actively encourages growth and at the same time removes unnecessary restrictions or burdens (Hall, 1996; Hisrich, 1986;

Stonich, 1998). New jobs have often been created with the help of government grants. In Britain, for example, the increase of 18 percent in the number of the self-employed in tourism in the period 1981–1989 led the British government to consider that its role in assisting these new enterprises lay in founding and strengthening the governmental training agencies (Elliott, 1997). In several Third World countries, government is changing its role from active involvement in tourism development to selective involvement as a guiding agent to the private sector at different levels of the tourism industry (Esichaikul and Baum, 1998).

There is a growing recognition of the potential contribution of governmental incubators for promoting new venture creation (Sexton, 1986; Bird, 1989; Gatewood et al., 1985; 1986; Keeble and Wever, 1986; Smilor, 1986). Incubators may serve as a tool for developing enterprises in peripheral areas as well as in cities (Gatewood, Ogden, and Hoy, 1985; 1986). By providing the new firm with access to low-cost facilities and services, such as skilled consultants, government officials, and bankers and venture capitalists, the incubator offers a hospitable environment for entrepreneurs. Incubators strive to fill a perceived gap in venture capital financing by improving the quality of locally based entrepreneurial talent and building indigenous companies (Smilor, 1986). So far, most of the incubators have been established for manufacturing firms, especially technological ones. However, since the beginning of the '90s, the concept of the incubator model has been widely accepted and adopted in the tourism industry.

In tourism, the term incubator should be used in the wider sense of an "incubator without walls." The tourism incubator enables entrepreneurs who usually base and locate their ventures on unique environmental components, such as scenery, to develop the product and sell it within their natural environment. It is assumed that in contrast to the case of research and development and high tech incubators, the tourism entrepreneurs must operate within their tourist environment and thus receive the advisory and training on location. In contrast to many research parks, such as that of the Weitzman Institute in Israel, tourism incubators are usually oriented toward peripheral areas.

The evidence regarding the impact of incubators and other institutional services on venture performance and growth is contradictory from one study to another, from one country to another, and even within the same country. Felsenstein (1992) claims that studies which focused on the effectiveness of different assistance programs found that most of the new employment seemingly generated due to governmental programs would also have been generated in their absence (See also: Fleisher and Felsenstein, 2000). On the other hand, in a study in Bangladesh, Sader, Ghosh, and Rosa (1997) found that firms assisted by governmental as well as nongovernmental support organizations performed significantly better than did nonassisted firms. However, support services played a relatively minor role in enhancing business success compared to other factors.

Solomon and Weaver (1983) found that small ventures using the advisory assistance given by the Small Business Administration in the United States showed growth in number of employees, revenues, and net profit, and a decrease in their labor costs. Similarly, Gatewood et al. (1985) found that ventures assisted from the incubator showed higher performance than the nonassisted ventures (see also: Birley and Westhead, 1992; Levie, 1994; White and Reynolds, 1994).

The findings with regard to financial support given to small ventures are also contradictory. In a survey of 204 incubators in the United States, Udell (1990) found no significant relationships between financially assisted firms and business performance. His conclusion was that financial benefits do not guarantee business success. On the other hand, O'Farrell (1986) found that in Ireland, those firms which were supported financially by external sources were larger and attained a higher level of revenues. Lerner (1989) found meaningful differences between, on the one hand, sponsored Israeli entrepreneurial firms, which enjoyed more favorable conditions, and, on the other, nonsponsored entrepreneurial firms, especially in the number of employees, avenues for raising capital, recruitment, and ownership.

In line with the contingency view (Kast and Rosenzweig, 1986), the impact of two types of institutional support on tourism venture performance will be examined: (1) the use of external financial support, and (2) the use of the advisory services of a governmental tourism incubator. Furthermore, we shall examine the impact of these two different types of assistance on the employment measure, compared to the financial measures. These relationships will be analyzed within the framework of hypotheses testing.

Hypothesis 1a: There is a positive relationship between external financing support and tourism venture performance.

Hypothesis 1b: There is a negative relationship between receipt of advisory support and venture performance.

The rationale in presenting these two hypotheses separately is rooted in the difference in the selection criteria for supplying assistance. Financial support is usually given to those ventures that are considered to have the more promising success potential. This does not assume a causal, but rather a bilateral relationship. In contrast, advisory support from the governmental tourism incubator tends to be provided precisely to those ventures in peripheral areas that suffer difficulties in boosting their business performance and in increasing employment. This policy contradicts that of many profit incubators, especially in high-tech areas, that choose to provide assistance to start-ups having greater growth potential.

The Environmental Attractiveness of Small Tourism Ventures

Tourism and the physical and social environment appear to be inseparable. Therefore, from a contingency perspective, which states the interrelationships between organizations and their environments, the location of the tourism venture is of crucial importance to its performance. A well-established body of literature has dealt with location of entrepreneurial ventures, both rural and urban. Studies examining the location decisions of new ventures show that the meta-variables important to rural as well as to urban locations are labor (availability of cheap skilled labor), locale (convenience, nice area), land (low property prices, availability of water, etc.), climate, availability of

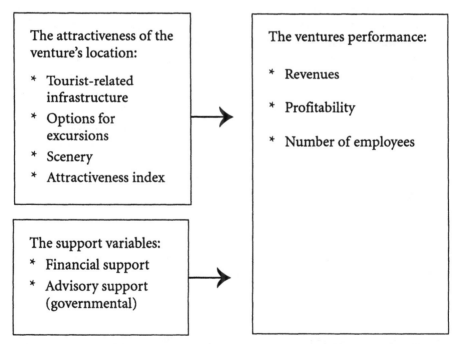

Figure 8.1. A Model of the Environmental Performance Factors of Small Tourism Ventures

state support, and competitiveness (closeness to customers) (Banks, 1991). In spite of the fact that location is both theoretically and practically important in determining the size and success of a tourism firm (Smith, 1995), there is still an unsatisfied need to conceptualize the issue of tourism venture location and its impact on growth and performance.

Obviously, an environment endowed with many tourist attractions is an advantage to the tourist venture (McIntosh et al., 1995; Mill and Morrison, 1992), contributing to growth in financial performance as well as to a potential job increase in the tourism industry. The supply of tourist facilities in the area in the form of natural and man-made attractions and goods and services is likely to encourage visitors, thus increasing demand and creating new jobs. Tourist attractions and popular travel destinations are planned on the basis of unusually pleasing physical, scenic, and geographic components of the environment. Other attractions are sites of historic, cultural, and religious interest; basic infrastructure and higher level infrastructure such as entertainment centers, casinos, theaters, and transportation; and special features of the local culture such as food and tradition, all catering to different groups of tourists (Al-Wahab and Al-Din, 1975; Fridgen, 1984; Hall, 1996; Ley and Madison, 1996). These primary and secondary tourism resources are essential components of the tourism product and experience, and they define the multidimensionality of the tourism environment.

Quantifying features of the tourism environment, such as scenery, and attaching relative weights to each component is problematic (Smith, 1995). Thus, the current research tries to develop an operational instrument in order to examine the association of the environmental factors with tourism venture performance (see the methodology section). This instrument is used to test a location-dependence hypothesis suggesting that various environmental factors such as scenery, climate, proximity of tourist centers, a developed tourist infrastructure, and recreation facilities are important for tourism venture success.

Hypothesis 2: There is a positive relationship between the level of the environmental attractiveness and the tourism venture's performance. The more environmental attractiveness factors there are that characterize the venture location, the higher the venture's performance.

The Israeli Arena

The growth of Israel's tourism industry in the 1990s reached a peak in 1995. Data of the Israeli Ministry of Tourism (1996) show that during 1995, more than 2.5 million tourists visited Israel. The figures in 2000 were 2.7 million tourists, passing the 1995 peak. The Israeli tourism industry is an important source of new jobs. For example, the total growth rate of employees in hotels and other accommodation services in Israel between 1985 and 1995 was more than twice the growth rate for the total work force and almost triple that of the total population and of the manufacturing industries (Israeli Central Bureau of Statistics, 1995).

The Case of the Israeli Desert—The Negev

The Negev is a peripheral area, although it actually constitutes about 60 percent of Israel's land area. It has very great potential for providing tourist facilities from the point of view of natural scenic resources. Nevertheless, its tourism infrastructure is minimal. Even though there has been a significant increase in the number of tourism ventures in the Negev in recent years (a 70 percent growth in accommodation ventures since 1989), figures indicate a relatively early stage of tourism development. Indeed, the Negev may still be said to be a peripheral frontier from the tourism point of view. In many ways, Negev tourism resembles ecotourism in that its uniqueness is based mainly on open areas, unique geological phenomena, scenery, and so on. In contrast to the hotels and resorts in Eilat and the Dead Sea area, the greater part of the ventures in the Negev are small, locally owned, and fairly new. Moreover, statistics on government investments in the Negev, compared to other regions in Israel, indicate that only in 1989 did the Israeli government begin to invest in tourism infrastructure in the Negev. The figures also show that only 6 percent of the total investments in tourism ventures between 1989 and 1995 were made in the Negev, compared to 33 percent in Eilat.

The Negev Regional Incubator

The Negev incubator was the first attempt made by the Ministry of Tourism to establish a new way of supporting small tourism ventures in a peripheral area (Negev Tourism Development Authority, 1995). The incubator, which was established in 1992, came about as a result of cooperation between the government and other public entities. Its aim was to provide guidance and training to existing and new tourism ventures in the Negev during their development and growth stages. The incubator was modeled after incubators in manufacturing and adapted to the special needs of the tourism industry. It finances 75 percent of the entrepreneur's advisory costs, including an examination of the operative plan for establishing the venture, preparation of marketing and operating plans, and a follow-up.

Research Method of This Study

Data Collection

The field population approached consisted of eighty-six small ventures, seventy-six operating in the Negev and ten in Eilat. Of the eighty-six questionnaires distributed, fifty-six were returned, indicating a response rate of 65 percent. Three questionnaires were omitted due to the fact that the ventures were closed. Forty-five were from ventures in the Negev and eight from the Eilat area. A comprehensive and structured research questionnaire was tested in a pilot study, in which five of the respondents were interviewed personally to examine the questionnnaire's clarity and suitability for the tourist industry. The data on the highly representative final research sample were collected during August–November 1995. Sixty-six of the ventures located in the Negev received the questionnaire by mail. A further ten ventures requested face-to-face interviews, which were conducted at the venture location in the Negev. The eight ventures in Eilat were interviewed on site. Since the questionnaire included variables on business performance, the respondents were assured of full confidentiality.

Population Description

The study focused on small businesses in the tourism industry located in the south of Israel, including Eilat. The population did not include sites owned by public institutions such as the National Parks Authority, though ventures sited within these locations and run by private entrepreneurs as well as kibbutz-owned ventures were included. Hotels in Eilat were not included, because they do not fit the research framework's definition of small businesses. All the ventures were eight years old or less, and 60 percent of them were less than five years old. For a detailed population description, see the appendix.

The Research Variables

Dependent Variables: Performance

1. Number of employees in 1995: one open question
2. Profit in 1995: one question scored as 1=loss, 2=break even; or 3=profit
3. Revenues in 1995: one open question

Independent Variables

4. The attractiveness of the tourism venture's location: thirteen questions indicating various environmental factors that express attractiveness. The items were scored by both the respondents and twelve professional raters on a 5-point scale, ranging from 1 = not a strong feature of the venture, to 5 = features very strongly (Hotel Review, 1993). Each of the thirteen attractiveness characteristics received a score composed of the sum of the raters' scores.

Results in the attractiveness of tourism venture location, obtained by a factor analysis carried out on the thirteen features, elicited the following three environment attractiveness factors:

a. Tourism-related infrastructure, which includes auxiliary services such as restaurants, shopping, transportation, places of entertainment, information, and tourist centers that offer these services (a = 0.90).

b. Options for excursions, including organized tours, access to nature and scenic spots, a range of tourism activities in the area, and activities for children (a = 0.82).

c. Scenery, including climate (a = 0.74).

An index of the attractiveness of a tourism venture location, including all the 13 items, was constructed on the basis of the responses of the subjects (a = 0.88).

Institutional Support Characteristics

Sources of Finance

Ventures were classified into two groups: assisted and nonassisted. The assisted group included those ventures that had used institutional and other external sources of finance (e.g., banks, the Ministry of Tourism, the Jewish Agency, local authorities). Analysis of the responses was carried out on a dichotomous basis for each source separately. The nonassisted group consisted of those ventures that did not use external financial resources at all.

Advisory and Training Assistance

The assisted were those ventures that had used one or more of the advisory services of the incubator, such as preparation of a business plan and/or a marketing plan, and support in operating the venture. Respondents were required to give a yes/no answer to each type of assistance. The nonassisted were those ventures that had not used these advisory services at all.

Examination of the Hypotheses

The research hypotheses were first tested by means of t-tests as well as Pearson correlation coefficients between each of the variables appearing in the research model and each of the performance variables separately. Then, multivariate examinations were performed by means of multiple regression analyses for each of the performance variables.

Institutional Support of Tourism Ventures

A t-test analysis (table 8.1) compared the means and standard deviations of the performance of ventures that had obtained external financial support with those that did not. It also compared the performance of ventures assisted by the advisory services of the tourism incubator with that of the nonassisted ventures.

In partial accordance with the hypothesis, the statistical results indeed show that those tourism ventures that are financially supported by external sources, governmental or otherwise, perform significantly better in terms of their revenues than ventures that are not financially supported. However, receiving external financial assistance is not significantly correlated either

Table 8.1. Means and Standard Deviations of Performance Measures of Assisted and Nonassisted Entrepreneurs (t-test)

Number of Employees	Profitability	Revenues	
			Financial Assistance
6.1	2.53	529.1	Nonassisted
(7.5)	(.83)	(661)	Mean (sd)
8.9	2.29	1,155.4	Assisted
(19.1)	(.80)	(1,552)	Mean (sd)
−.76	.97	−1.88 *	t
			Advisory Assistance
9.4	2.54	1140	Nonassisted
(20.9)	(.71)	(1,426)	Mean (sd)
6.1	2.05	512	Assisted
(3.4)	(.88)	(561)	Mean (sd)
.90	2.12 *	2.09 *	t

*P<.05 **P<.01

with profitability or with number of employees, suggesting that revenues do not necessarily assure higher profitability. The average financially assisted firm is larger than the nonassisted firm (nine versus six employees, respectively). However, no significant differences were found between the financially assisted and nonassisted firms in terms of number of employees.

Hypothesis 1b, regarding advisory support, is also confirmed. It is precisely the nonassisted ventures that achieve the better performance scores. These results are significant for the revenues and profitability measures. Although the nonassisted firms are larger in terms of number of employees than the assisted ones, the differences are not significant.

Attractiveness of a Small Tourism Venture's Location

The second hypothesis proposed that the attractiveness of the location of the tourism venture is positively related to the venture's performance: the more attractive the venture location, the better the performance of the venture. A factor analysis elicited three environmental factors: tourist-related infrastructures, options for excursions, and scenery. Table 8.2 shows the Pearson correlation coefficients among these three factors as well as the attractiveness index and the performance measures.

As expected, the three factors of attractiveness, particularly the excursions, are associated with venture performance measures. While the attractiveness index is significantly correlated with two performance measures—profitability and revenues—the tourist-related infrastructure is correlated with revenues ($r=.29$); the options for excursions factor is correlated to revenues ($r=.32$) and to profitability ($r=.30$). The third factor, scenery, is correlated with profitability ($r=.30$), but not with the other performance measures. None of the factors are correlated with number of employees. These findings show the differential correlations between the attractiveness of the environment and the two different measures of the business size: revenues and number of employees.

The stepwise regression analyses (table 8.3) of the revenues and profitability, which include both the contingent external factors—institutional support and attractiveness of the ventures' environment—reveal the significant contribution of the attractiveness index to the explained variance of business performance. Furthermore, they both show a minor impact of the assistance variables on performance relative to that of the attractiveness variables. As the regression analysis on the number of employees measure shows no impact of the attractiveness or of the support measures on it, it is not presented in table 8.3.

Table 8.2. Descriptive Statistics and Correlation Coefficients

Variable	Mean	S.D.	1	2	3	4	5	6	7
1 Revenues in 1995 (in k NIS)	10,002.3	1,407.7	1.00						
2. Profitability in 1995	2.36	.81	.28*	1.00					
3. Number of employees	8.11	16.6	.73***	.10	1.00				
4. Tourist-related infrastructure	2.80	1.15	.29*	.18	.21	1.00			
5. Option for excursions	3.77	1.02	.30*	.32*	.13	.53***	1.00		
6. Scenery	4.11	.82	.18	.29*	.17	.30*	.42**	1.00	
7. Attractiveness index	3.40	.84	.33*	.30*	.22	.90**	.80**	.57***	1.00
8. Advisory assistance	.38	.49	-.22	-.28*	-.10	-.39**	-.11	-.00	-.00
9. External financial assistance	.72	.45	-.13	-.29*	.07	.03	.13	.03	-.06

*P<.05 **P<.01 ***P<.001

Table 8.3. Stepwise Regression of Independent Variables on Performance Measure

AdjR^2	R^2	Fch	Rch^2	beta	Performance variables
.10					Revenues
	.10	5.8*	.10	.26*	Attractiveness index
	.13	1.3	.02	.18	Financial assistance
	.15	1.3	.02	.18	Advisory assistance
.10					Profitability
	.09	5.1*	.09	.25*	Attractiveness index
	.14	2.8	.05	-.21	Advisory assistance
	.15	.8	.02	-.12	Financial assistance

*P<.05 **P<.01

Discussion and Conclusions

In this study, we attempted to assess the impact of two contingent external factors on small tourism ventures success: (1) governmental—institutional assistance, and (2) attractiveness of the venture location. Furthermore, we attempted to distinguish between the impact of these factors on two types of venture performance measures: financial measures—revenues and profitability—on the one hand and the number of employees on the other hand. The theoretical basis for this approach is the contingency perspective, which states the impact of various aspects of the environment on features of organizations in an attempt to understand how organizations operate under varying conditions and in specific circumstances.

The research findings indicate that the attractiveness of the venture's location has a stronger impact on its performance than does institutional support. Thus, the regression analyses show significant contribution of the attractiveness index to the explained variance of business performance, while the support variables do not add any significant contribution. It is worth noting that the environmental variables only explain a small part of the variance of the performance measures. This probably suggests that other variables, organizational as well as managerial, have a greater impact on the performance of small tourism ventures, as was found by Lermer & Haber (2001).

Our findings elicited three environmental attractiveness factors: tourist-related infrastructure, options for excursions, and scenery, including climate. These findings indicate the multidimensional nature of the attractiveness of the environmental milieu of tourism ventures. According to our findings, an environment endowed with highly developed infrastructure, rich scenery, and many options for excursions is likely to yield high financial rewards. This may indicate the importance of the existence of natural and man-made attractions as well as the superstructures and infrastructures for subsequent venture performance. However, although an attractive environment is a vital component of the tourism product (Al-Wahab and Al-Din, 1975; Fridgen, 1984; Hall, 1996; Ley and Madison, 1996; Wall, 1996; Smith, 1995), our findings show that one cannot rely on environmental attractiveness as the sole guarantee of financial business success. This conclusion is based on the relatively low impact of environmental factors on performance, as shown in the regression analyses.

The results indicate the dual nature of the impact of governmental— institutional support upon the tourism venture's performance, confirming the hypotheses regarding the impact of two types of support: (a) the use of external financial sources, and (b) the use of advisory services through governmental incubator programs. As expected, the tourism ventures that are financially supported by external sources perform better than those not financially supported. On the other hand, in the case of advisory support from a tourism incubator, it is precisely the nonassisted ventures that achieve better performance. The findings confirmed our initial assumption regarding the preselection and the differing criteria for receiving these two types of support (see also Sarder, Ghos, and Rosa, 1997).

Obtaining financial support from external sources is evidence of the entrepreneur's success in persuading these external sources that the venture is sound, well planned, and economically viable. By contrast, obtaining assistance from the governmental tourism incubator in the form of business guidance requires no evidence of meeting financial criteria of any kind, insofar as advice is given by the incubator to almost anyone in the area applying for it. Indeed, many ventures take advantage of these services in their early stages. Thus, the explanation for the inferior performance of the assisted ventures may also lie in the fact that these ventures are often younger and smaller than the nonassisted ventures.

These results have implications regarding the nature of the support to be given by the governmental tourism incubator to entrepreneurs operating in the region. In this context, scholars such as Echtner (1995) and Elliot (1997) have indicated that governments have not given appropriate emphasis to the importance of support to small-scale locally owned tourism ventures. The fact that no significant differences were found between the financially assisted and nonassisted firms in terms of number of employees may suggest that the business potential of a tourism venture is not necessarily reflected in the number of its employees, whereas the decision to financially support a venture is dependent on its business potential.

Several potential contributions to the research on performance factors of small tourism ventures are suggested here. The first derives from the attractiveness examination, and the second derives from the performance examination. The operationalization of measures of attractiveness in the tourism location may add to a deeper understanding of the interface of environment and performance in tourism. However, because most of the literature on tourist attractions is descriptive, case-specific, and not explanatory in either the general or specific sense (Stear, 1981:91), further elaboration and refinements are needed in order to improve the usefulness of the instrument suggested here.

The results confirm the multidimensionality of business performance (Cooper and Gimeno-Gascon, 1992; Birely and Westhead, 1990) and reinforce the claim that different measures of performance are associated with different combinations of factors. These findings may strengthen the claim made by many scholars, such as Kirchhoff (1977), that one cannot rely on a single measure in determining business performance or success. Using only one type of business performance measure may lead to a biased conclusion. Each of the two external factors—attractiveness of the tourism venture's location and the financial and advisory support of government incubators and other institutional entities—are correlated differentially to the business performance measures. However, due to the relatively small size of the present research sample and the self-reported data, further research is clearly required.

To sum up, despite the great importance of tourism to the economies of many countries, studies to determine precisely which are the factors that affect performance of ventures in the tourism industry are clearly needed.

Practical Implications

Government assistance for small ventures can be seen as having a dual nature. On the one hand, general data indicate a high failure rate among small businesses and assistance to them becomes a risky investment. On the other hand, the potential of small ventures to create employment and increase wealth at the local and national levels makes them a worthy investment. Thus governments and other institutions should consider the assistance criteria carefully.

In order to increase community-based tourism development, there is a need to provide efficient tailored regional business and management training tools for tourism entrepreneurs. While most tourism activities are provided and controlled by the private sector, the public sector has a crucial role to play in providing and refining the necessary policy guidelines needed by small ventures in this fragile stage.

As for the entrepreneurs, our results clearly indicate the importance of venture location attractiveness to business success. These results imply that the entrepreneurs need to pay close attention to the many facets of the attractiveness of the location during the site selection process.

References

Al-Wahab, A., and S. Al-Din. 1975. *Tourism Management*. London: Tourism International Press.

Bade, F.-J. 1986. The economic importance of small business and medium firms in the Federal Republic of Germany. In D. Keeble and E. Wever eds., *New Firms and Regional Development in Europe*. London: Croom Helm.

Banks, M. C. 1991. Location decisions of rural new ventures. *Frontiers of Entrepreneurship Research*, www.babson.edu/entrep/fer/front_91. html#dem (September 7, 2001).

Bird, B. J. 1989. *Entrepreneurial Behavior*. London: Scott Foresman.

Birley, S., and P. Westhead.1990. Growth and performance contrasts between "types" of small firms. *Strategic Management Journal*, 11:535–557.

Birley, S., and P. Westhead. 1992. A comparison of new firms in "assisted" and "non-assisted" areas in Great Britain. *Entrepreneurship and Regional Development*, 4:299–338.

Brownlie, D. 1994. Market opportunity analysis: A DIY approach for small tourism enterprises. *Tourism Management*, 15: 37–45.

Central Bureau of Statistics. 1995. Jerusalem, Israel.

Cooper, A. C., and J. F. Gimeno-Gascon. 1992. Entrepreneurs, processes of founding and new firm performance. In D. L. Sexton and J. D. Kasarda eds., *The State of the Art of Entrepreneurship*. Boston: PWS-Kent.

Davidsson, P. 1991. Continued entrepreneurship: Ability, need and opportunity as determinants of small firm growth. *Journal of Business Venturing*, 6:405–429.

Echtner, C. M. 1995. Entrepreneurial training in developing countries. *Annals of Tourism Research*, 22:119–133.

Elliott, J. 1997. *Tourism: Politics and Public Sector Management*. London: Routledge.

Esichaikul, R., and T. Baum. 1998. The case for government involvement in human resource development: A study of the Thai hotel industry. *Tourism Management*, 19:359–370.

Felsenstein, D. 1992. Assessing the employment effectiveness of small business financing schemes: Some evidence from Israel. *Small Business Economics*, 4:273–285.

Fleisher, A., and D. Felsenstein. 2000. Support for small scale rural tourism: Does it make a difference? *Annals of Tourism Research,* 27:1007–1024.

Fridgen, J. D. 1984. Environmental psychology and tourism. *Annals of Tourism Research,* 11:19–39.

Gartner, W. B. 1985. A conceptual framework for describing the phenomenon of new venture creation. *Academy of Management Review,* 10:696–706.

Gatewood, E., L. Ogden, and F. Hoy.1985. Incubators centers—Where they are and where they are going. *Frontiers of Entrepreneurship Research,* www.babson.edu/entrep/fer/front_85.html (September 12, 2001).

Gatewood, E., L. Ogden, and F. Hoy. 1986. Incubator center evolution: The next five to ten years. *Frontiers of Entrepreneurship Research,* op. cit..../fer/front86.html (September 12, 2001.

Hall, C. M. 1994. *Tourism and Politics—Policy, Power and Place.* Chichester, England: Wiley.

Hall, C. M., and M. Jenkins. 1997. The policy dimensions of rural tourism and recreation. In R. Butler, C. M. Hall, and J. Jenkins eds., *Tourism and Recreation in Rural Areas.* New York: Wiley.

Hisrich, R. D. (ed.) 1986. *Entrepreneurship, Intrapreneurship and Venture Capital.* Lexington, Mass: Lexington Books.

Israel Ministry of Tourism. 1996. *Tourism to Israel 1996—Statistical Report.* Israel. Jerusalem.

Johannisson, B. 1993. Designing supportive contexts for emerging enterprises. In C. Karlsson, B. Johannisson, and D. Storey eds., *Small Business Dynamics: International, National and Regional Perspectives.* London: Routledge.

Kast, F. E., and J. E. Rosenzweig. 1986. *Organization and Management.* New York: McGraw-Hill.

Keeble, D., and E. Wever, eds. 1986. *New Firms and Regional Development in Europe.* London: Croom-Helm.

Kirchhoff, B. A. 1977. Organization effectiveness measurement and policy research. *Academy of Management Review* 2:347–355.

Kirchhoff, B. A. 1994. Entrepreneurship economics. In W. D. Bygrave ed., *The Portable MBA in Entrepreneurship.* New York: Wiley.

Lerner, M. 1989. Paternalism and entrepreneurship: The emergence of state-made entrepreneurs. *The Journal of Behavioral Economics,* 8:149–166.

Lerner, M. and Haber, S.2001. Performance factors of small tourism ventures: The interface of tourism, entrepreneurship and the environment. *Journal of Business Venturing,* 16:77–100.

Levie, J. 1994. Can governments nurture young growing firms? Qualitative evidence from a three nation study. *Frontiers of Entrepreneurship Research*, www.babson.edu/entrep/fer/papers94/levie.htm (September 7, 2001).

Ley, D. A., and J. Madison. 1996. Romanian tourism—Status, limitations and prospects. In E. Kaynak, D. Lascu, and K. Becker (Eds.), *Restructuring for Global Production, Service Needs and Markets: Business Strategy and Policy Development for a Global Economy*. Proceedings of the 5th International Management Development Association, Congress, Hamilton, Bermuda.

Loscocco, K. A., and K. T. Leicht. 1993. Gender, work-family linkages and economics among small business owners. *Journal of Marriage and the Family,* 5:875–887.

Lumpkin, G. T., and G. G. Dess. 1996. Clarifying the entrepreneurial orientation construct and linking it to performance. *Academy of Management Review,* 21:135–172.

Lundberg, D. E., M. Krishnamoorthy, and M. H. Stavenga. 1995. *Tourism Economics*. New York: Wiley.

McIntosh, R. W., C. R. Goeldner, and R. J. R. Brent. 1995. *Tourism Principles, Practices, Philosophies*. New York: Wiley and Sons.

Merz, R. G., and M. H. Sauber. 1995. Profiles of managerial activities in small firms. *Strategic Management Journal,* 16:551–564.

Mill, R. C., and A. M. Morrison. 1992. *The Tourism System: An Introductory Text*. New Jersey: Prentice Hall.

Miller, A., B. Wilson, and M. Adams. 1988. Financial performance patterns of new corporate ventures: An alternative to traditional measures. *Journal of Business Venturing,* 3:287–299.

O'Farrell, P., 1986. The nature of new firms in Ireland: Empirical evidence and policy implications. In D. Keele and E. Wever eds., *New Firms and Regional Development in Europe*. London: Croom-Helm.

Oppermann, M. 1996. Rural tourism in southern Germany. *Annals of Tourism Research,* 23:86–102.

Robinson, P. B. and E. A. Sexton. 1994. The effect of education and experience on self-employment success. *Journal of Business Venturing,* 9:141–156.

Sarder, J. H., D. Ghosh, and P. Rosa. 1997. The importance of support services to small enterprise in Bangaladesh. *Journal of Small Business Management,* 35:26–56.

Sexton, D. L. 1986. Role of entrepreneurship in economic development. In R. D. Hisrich ed., *Entrepreneurship, Intrapreneurship and Venture Capital*. Lexington, Mass., Lexington Books, pp. 27–29.

Smilor, R. W. 1986. Building indigenous companies: The technology venturing approach. In R. D. Hisrich ed., *Entrepreneurship, Intrapreneurship and Venture Capital.* Lexington, Mass., Lexington Books, pp. 43–69.

Smith, S. L. J. 1995. *Tourism Analysis.* New York: Longman.

Solomon G. T. and M. K. Weaver. 1983. Small business institute economic impact evaluation. *American Journal of Small Business,* 8:41–51.

Srinivasan, R., C. Y. Woo, and A. C. Cooper. 1994. Performance determinants for male and female entrepreneurs. *Frontiers of Entrepreneurship Research,* MA: Babson College. www.babson.edu/entrep/fer/papers94/raji.htm (September 12, 2001).

Stear, L. 1981. Design of a curriculum for destination studies. *Annals of Tourism Research,* 8:85–95.

Stonich, S. C. 1998. Political ecology of tourism. *Annals of Tourism Research,* 25:25–54.

Swarbrooke, J. 1995. *The Development and Management of Visitors Attractions.* Butterworth Heinemann: Oxford.

Udell, G. G. 1990. Are business incubators really creating new jobs by creating new business and new products? *Journal of Product Innovating and Management,* 7:108–122.

Wall, G. 1996. Tourism, environments and business: An essential alliance. In E. Haynak, D. Lascu. and K. Becker eds., *Proceedings Restructuring for Global Production, Service Needs and Markets: Business Strategy and Policy Development for a Global Economy.* Proceedings of the 5th International Management Development Association, Congress, Hamilton, Bermuda.

White, S. B. and P. D. Reynolds. 1994. What can the public sector do to increase new business starts? In *Frontiers of Entrepreneurship Research,* www.babson.edu/entrep/fer/papers94/white.htm (September 12, 2001).

World Tourism Organization (WTO). 1994. Recommendations on Tourism Statistics. World Tourism Organization, Madrid.

———. 1996. World Tourism Market Trends. World Tourism Organization, Madrid.

World Travel and Tourism Council (WTTC). 1994. Strategy 2000: Economic Leadership and Euromonitor. Travel and Tourism Council, London.

Appendix

Population Description

Variable	Frequency (%)
Type of Business	
Active recreation	38.5
Tourist resorts	21.2
Accommodation	21.2
Catering and auxiliary services	19.1
	100.0
Business Age	
Five years or less	60.0
Six to seven years	21.0
Eight years	19.0
	100.0
Assistance from Tourism Incubator	
Assisted	38
Nonassisted	62
	100.0
Number of Times Advisory Assistance Used	
1	45.0
2	20.0
3–4	35.0
	100.0
Type of Advisory Assistance	
Feasibility study	7.5
Business plan	15.0
Marketing plan and promotion	36.0
Assistance in business operation	19.5
	100.0
Support from Financial Sources*	
Assisted from governmental financial sources	43.0
Obtained loans from banks and private investors	28.0
Self-capital	91.0
Profit:	
Gained profit	56.6
Balance	22.6
Loss	20.8
	100.0

con't.

Population Description (con't.)

Variable	Frequency (%)
Number of Employees	
1–2	26.4
3–5	32.0
6–8	19.0
9 or more	22.7
	100.0
Revenues (in k NIS)	
0k–500k	60
501k–3,000k	30
3001k and more	10
	100.0

* Not equal 100%

Chapter 9

Agricultural Land in Frontier Areas: Conflict between Urban Development and Tourism and Recreation Activities

Aliza Fleischer

In recent years, the traditional activities of the rural sector in developed countries have assumed a new significance as a provider of value-added benefits for tourism and recreational activities as well as environmental protection (Hackl and Pruckner, 1997; OECD, 1993). For instance, farmers' agricultural fields offer a beautiful landscape to tourists and recreationalists (Fox and Cox, 1992). Visitors to rural areas tend to place a value on such benefits in nonmarket terms. The President's Commission on America's Outdoors (1987) found natural beauty to be the single most important factor in choosing a tourist destination. In a related report, New England's governors recognized that open space is an important factor for the regional tourism industry (New England Governors' Conference, Inc., 1988). But since open fields, beautiful landscapes, and herds of livestock grazing in green meadows are, in most cases, nonmarket services, it is difficult to estimate their contribution to the total welfare of the economy. However, they can be looked upon as positive externalities of agricultural production (Hackl and Pruckner, 1995), and failing to account for these externalities may lead to an undersupply of farmland.

Researchers in European countries and the United States have tackled this issue mainly by using the contingent valuation method (CVM). In Sweden, agricultural landscape is used for tourism and recreation activities. However, the agricultural land is in a constant process of reverting back to a dense forest that inhibits access for tourist activities. From a survey of Swedish households, Drake (1992) estimated the parameter for the willingness to pay (WTP) for maintaining the agricultural landscape. He found the value of utility created by the agricultural landscape was about $130 per hectare. This is higher than the return from agriculture in many parts of Sweden.

In Austria, 80 percent of the landscape is agricultural (forests are included in the definition of agriculture). The farmers care for and preserve this landscape. Hackl and Pruckner (1995) conducted a survey among 4,000 tourists in 1991 using the CVM. The tourists were asked how much they were willing to pay for landscape-enhancing services. It was estimated that these services were worth $72 to $120 million (U.S.) to the tourists in the surveyed regions.

In Britain, the industrialization of agricultural production harmed the landscape in the countryside. The Environmental Sensitive Areas (ESA) Scheme was established to preserve the distinctive agricultural landscape. Garrod and Willis (1995) and Hanely et al. (1998) estimated the benefits derived from the ESA in the South Downs and Scotland respectively. Garrod and Willis (1995), using the CVM, determined that the benefits of the ESA Scheme surpass the public cost when the nonuse value is taken into consideration. Hanely et al. (1998) produced an estimate of the nonmarket value of the ESA Scheme while comparing the CVM to a choice experiment.

In the context of growing urban development, Halstead (1984) conducted a study in three counties in Massachusetts, where he estimated the nonmarket value of agricultural land using the WTP method. He found the mean annual bid to avoid low-density development ranged from $28 to $60, and to avoid high-density development, the figure ranged from $70 to $176. Bergstrom, et al. (1985) used the WTP method to measure the importance of protecting agricultural land in South Carolina. The numbers here were lower; the main bid to prevent development on all land was below $10.

Some areas in Israel that attract many tourists and visitors (Fleischer and Pizam, 1997) are mainly dominated by agricultural landscape. Between 50 percent to 80 percent of the land area is used for field crops, plantations,

Table 9.1. Distribution of Land use by Regions in 1993 (thousands of dunams)

Region	Uncultivated Land	Nature Preserves & Parks	Urban Use	Agricultural Land	Total
Hula Valley	14	21	35	276	346
	4%	6%	10%	80%	100%
Jezreel Valley	113	0	48	313	474
	24%	0%	10%	66%	100%
Yoav-Yehuda	287	2	88	473	850
	34%	0%	10%	56%	100%
All Israel	8,569	5,998	1,966	5,737	22,270
	41%	25%	9%	25%	100%

and natural meadows (table 9.1). The importance and contribution of the agricultural landscape to the tourism industry in these regions cannot be ignored. The major threat to this agricultural land, especially when close to urban centers, is urban development. The returns farmers receive from selling their agricultural produce cannot compete with the alternative value of selling the land for urban use. This could change if they were to receive the true returns on their land, that is, the value of the agricultural products they produce, together with the added returns for the welfare they create for the tourists and visitors in the region who enjoy the agricultural landscape and rural environment.

Some countries recognize this market failure and have developed different policies supporting the rural sector. In Austria, the owners of tourism businesses in rural areas that recognize the contribution of the landscape to their business make a payment directly to the farmer (Pruckner, 1995). In other countries in Europe, there are subsidy payments to farmers for their role as conservators of the landscape and protectors of natural resources (EU regulation 2078/92). In England, for example, farmers receive payment for permissive access to the farm landscape for recreational purposes. This payment is set up as part of a package of measures to meet the requirements of the above EU regulation (Cooke and Gough, 1997). In the state of Wisconsin in the United States, a land stewardship program was established (Bromley, 1994). In the 100 million dollars allocated to this program from 1990 to 1994, the state of Wisconsin bought agricultural land and converted it into parks, improved existing recreational facilities, and supported many other activities for preserving the natural habitat. By these actions, the state turned the agricultural and rural landscape into a public good, enhanced by the public sector and not by private farmers. Another support measure is to internalize the externalities by helping the farmers themselves establish tourism businesses. Many enterprises such as recreation farms, bed and breakfast enterprises, farm produce retail stores, special events, and more are based on the rural environment and are income generators for the farmers (Honadle, 1989; Moyer, 1989; Fox and Cox, 1992). Support schemes for rural tourism exist in Europe, the United States, and Israel (Fleischer and Pizam, 1997) and help the farmers to turn the nonmarket value of the landscape into market value via the tourism enterprises owned by the farmers.

The objective of this paper is to establish the importance of agriculture landscape for tourism in Israel and to estimate its nonmarket value for tourism in different regions by using the CVM.

The Contingent Valuation Method

The CVM was developed by environmental economists to estimate the value or cost of public goods, that is, parks, open space, and environmental externalities such as air and water pollution (Portney, 1994). It is also used to evaluate landscape (Price, 1994; Willis and Garrod, 1993). Since consuming public goods does not involve market transactions, the CVM uses surveys to simulate the nonexisting markets and to elicit from the relevant population its willingness to pay. This method has been hotly debated in the pertinent literature, especially since some landmark lawsuits have been based on it (e.g., the case of the Exxon Valdez oil spill). In 1993, a panel of experts appointed by the National Oceanic and Atmospheric Administration (NOAA) recognized the use of the CVM on the condition that it be used according to the panel's recommendations (Arrow et al., 1993).

Accordingly, a CVM survey should contain a very detailed description of the public good or environmental program at issue in order for the respondent to formulate a reliable answer. The second part of the survey should consist of questions eliciting the value of the respondents' WTP. There are different mechanisms to elicit such information, such as open-ended questions, discrete choice, bidding games, or referendum formats. There is an ongoing debate about the efficiency of the different mechanisms used and the reliability of the extracted information (see for example Boyle et al., 1996).

Most of the NOAA recommendations were adopted in the survey used in this paper. A discrete choice bid method was used for three different scenarios: the agricultural landscape is eliminated, it is replaced by urban land use, or it is replaced by any natural open space.

Data

Description of the Surveyed Regions

In order to estimate the nonmarket value of agricultural landscape in Israel, three rural peripheral regions were selected: the Hula Valley, the Jezreel Valley and the Yoav-Yehuda region. Each of these regions is dominated by agricultural landscape (table 9.1) and attracts many excursionists and tourists. The Hula Valley is located in the northern periphery of the country. It has the largest amount of agricultural land of the regions in this study and is also the most attractive for tourists who stay overnight in the region and take nature walks. Its agricultural landscape contains many orchards, open fields, and natural meadows. The Jezreel Valley is located south of the Hula Valley. Many people who travel from the urban centers in the center of the country to the north for tourism and recreational purposes pass through the valley and are exposed to its rural scenery. The Yoav-Yehuda region, which has the fewest agricultural features of the three regions in this study, is located south of the center of the country and is mostly used for day trips to the sites containing its various tourist attractions.

The Survey Method

During the spring season of 1997, which is the high season for domestic tourism in these three regions, 250 questionnaires were answered in each of the individual regions. The participants were chosen from a random sample of visitors to the different attractions in the regions. The questionnaire contains questions about the importance of agricultural landscape to the tourist experience and different bids for the WTP.

Findings

The Importance of the Agricultural Landscape

It was important to first establish the contribution of the agricultural space to the decision to visit the region. This was needed in order to assess my earlier assumption that agricultural landscape beautifies the region and thereby increases the number of visitors. The interviewees were asked how important the agricultural landscape was to their decision to visit the region. In each region, over one third of the respondents answered that the agricultural

Table 9.2. Distribution of Answers (in %) to the Question: Was the Agricultural Landscape an Important Factor in Your Decision to Visit the Region?

Region / Answer	Hula	Jezreel	Yoav-Yehuda	All Regions
Very important	35	44	36	38
Some importance	42	34	32	36
Not at all	23	22	32	26
Total	100	100	100	100

landscape was a very important factor in their decision to visit the region (table 9.2). About one-third said that it had some importance and the rest said that it was not an important factor. These findings show that the agricultural landscape of the surveyed regions is a significant factor in arriving at the decision to visit a region and contributes to the tourism attractiveness of the region.

For visitors having arrived to the destination region, it is then meaningful to assess the influence of the agricultural landscape on their tourism experience. Interviewees were asked to rank four statements according to their level of agreement. The statements in table 9.3 relate the importance of the

Table 9.3. Average of the Weights Given to Different Statements Concerning the Importance of the Agricultural Landscape (5 = Complete Agreement to 1 = Complete Disagreement with the Statement)

	Hula	Jezreel	Yoav-Yehuda	All Regions
Seeing open landscape is important to my well being	4.8	4.6	4.7	4.7
It is important for me to know that open agricultural landscape exists	4.7	4.6	4.7	4.7
The agricultural landscape improves my tourism experience	3.8	3.8	3.6	3.8
The agricultural landscape has no influence on me	2.1	2.3	2.1	2.2

agricultural landscape to their well being. It was found that there is almost full consensus that open landscape is important and improves the quality of the tourism experience. Although the regions differ in their agricultural nature and the type of tourist activities they offer, there is very little difference between the answers of the visitors to the three survey regions.

The WTP Estimates

The three regions differ in the intensity and characteristics of their agricultural landscape and in the available tourism amenities. The Hula Valley is the most rural region of the three, while the Yoav-Yehuda region is the least rural. The estimated value of the WTP for the agricultural landscape is different for each region. The Hula Valley is ranked the highest, with an average WTP of $15, the Jezreel Valley is ranked second, with an average WTP of $11, and the Yoav-Yehuda region, which has the least agricultural landscape, has the lowest WTP of $8. The regions are ranked differently when the average WTP is multiplied by the total number of visitors, since the Jezreel Valley has many more visitors than the Hula Valley.

Since the WTP values represent flows of benefits that are received each year for an infinite number of years, the present value of these flows of benefits can be calculated (fourth row in table 9.4). The total present value of the consumer surplus generated by the agricultural landscape in these three regions is $412 million U.S. This value represents the infinite flow of benefits from the agricultural landscape only, and not from the regions' other amenities.

Table 9.4. Distribution of WTP by Region

Region WTP	Hula	Jezreel	Yoav-Yehuda
Average per visitor($)	15	11	8
Number of visitors in the year preceding the survey[1]	490	749	648
Total for all visitors[2] (Million $)	7.3	8.2	5.1
Total present value[3] (Million $)	146	164	102

1. The number of visitors to the different regions in the year 1997 was estimated by a national survey in which representative random samples of adults were asked if they had visited the three regions in the past year.
2. Product of the multiplication of the average WTP by number of visitors.
3. Discounted at 5% interest rate.

Discussion and Conclusions

The agricultural landscape was found to be important to the visitors coming to the three surveyed regions for tourism and recreational activities. It generates benefits that are reflected in the consumer surplus. The benefits to the three regions total over $400 million U.S. and are supplied essentially free-of-charge by the farmers.

The average consumer surplus differs between the different regions. The region with the most agricultural rural landscape generates the highest values of consumer surplus. (There is an implied conclusion that the aesthetic value of a region increases with the area of agricultural landscapes.) That means that the benefits of the landscape are a function of aesthetic qualities that are not the same for all agricultural landscapes. The higher the aesthetic value, then the higher will be the benefits it generates.

In the Israeli case, the CVM gives lower estimates in comparison to the travel cost method. In the cases of both public park and agricultural landscape (Fleischer, Tsur, and Sidi 1996; 1997), the CVM estimates were lower. These findings negate the usual assumption that the CVM values are upwards biased (Kahneman and Knetch, 1992). In a survey measuring the value of open space in Israel (Fleischer and Tsur, 1999a), it was found that Israelis think that the government or other authorities should pay for such amenities. This finding may explain the differences.

The flow of benefits generated by the agricultural landscape is higher than the flow of profits from the agricultural activities in these three regions (Fleischer and Tsur, 1999b). However, the values of the land for urban use, especially where urban sprawl is already a reality, can be much higher. Even if the farmer were to receive the full compensation for the landscape values he provides, it would still be more profitable for him to sell the land for urban use. Thus, there are at least two possible ways for preserving agricultural landscape. One is by legislation that prohibits the net transfer of agricultural land to urban use. However, even when such laws are in force, experience has shown that it is possible to find ways to overcome and bypass such restrictions (Alterman, 1997). The second way is for the farmers to establish tourism enterprises that are based on the rural amenities of the region. The present value of the flow of profits from these enterprises, plus the present value of the profits from the agricultural activities, can surpass the value of the land for urban use. Thus, in the Israeli case, the best way to achieve market efficiency and overcome the market failure is to support nonagricultural activities that are based on the rural environment and agricultural landscape.

Acknowledgment

This paper is based on major research conducted jointly with Prof. Yacov Tsur from the Hebrew University and funded by the Israel Ministry of Agriculture and Rural Development.

References

Alterman, R. 1997. The challenge of farmland preservation: Lessons from a six-nation comparison. *Journal of the American Planning Association,* spring, 220–243.

Arrow, K., R. Solow, P. R. Portney, E. E. Leamer, R. Rander, and H. Schuman. 1993. Report of the NOAA panel on contingent valuation. Report to the National Oceanic and Atmospheric Administration. Federal Register, 58:4601–4614.

Bergstrom, J., B. L. Dillman, and J. Stoll. 1985. Public environmental amenity benefits of private land: The case of prime agricultural land. *Southern Journal of Agricultural Economics,* 17:139–149.

Boyle, K., F. Johnson, D. McCollum, W. Desvouges, R. Dunford, and S. Hudson. 1996. Valuing public goods: Discrete versus continuous contingent valuation responses. *Land Economics,* 18:243–253.

Bromley, D. W. 1994. Managing rural amenities in the United States. Paper prepared for the OECD Conference on Rural Amenities, Paris.

Cooke, R., and F. Gough. 1997. Permissive access to agricultural land provided through agri-environmental schemes: The current position in England. *Countryside Recreation,* 5(4):20–24.

Drake, L. 1992. The non-market value of the Swedish agricultural landscape. *European Review of Agricultural Economics,* 19:351–364.

Fleischer, A., and Y. Tsur. 1999a. Measuring the recreational value of agricultural landscape. Working Paper No. 9911. The Center for Agricultural Economic Research, Rehovot.

———. 1999b. The economic value of open space in Israel. A report to the Land Research Institute, Jerusalem.

Fleischer, A., Y. Tsur, and A. Sidi. 1996. The economic value of Park Goren. A report submitted to the Jewish National Fund, Jerusalem.

Fleischer, A., and A. Pizam. 1997. Rural tourism in Israel. *Tourism Management,* 18:367–372.

Fleischer, A., Y. Tsur, and A. Sidi. 1997. Estimating the economic value of agricultural landscape as a tourism resource. Jerusalem: Israel Ministry of Agriculture.

Fox, M., and L. J. Cox. 1992. Linkage between agriculture and tourism. In M.A. Khan, M. D. Olsen, and T. Var eds., *UNR's Encyclopedia of Hospitality and Tourism.* New York: Van Nostrand Reinhold.

Garrod, G. D., and K. G. Willis. 1995. Valuing the benefits of the South Downs environmentally sensitive areas. *Journal of Agricultural Economics,* 46: 160–173.

Hackl, F., and G. J. Pruckner. 1995. Environmental enhancement through agriculture. Proceedings of the Conference on Environmental Enhancement through Agriculture, Boston, MA: Center for Agriculture, Food and Environment, Tufts University.

Hackl, F., and G. J. Pruckner. 1997. Towards more efficient compensation programs for tourists' benefits from agriculture in Europe. *Environmental and Resource Economics,* 10:189–205.

Halstead, J. 1984. Measuring the non-market value of Massachusetts agricultural land: A case study. *Journal of Northeastern Agricultural Economic Council,* 13:12–19.

Hanely, N., D. MacMillan, R. E. Wright, C. Bullock, I. Simpson, D. Parisson, and B. Crabtree. 1998. Contingent valuation versus choice experiments: Estimating the benefits of environmentally sensitive areas in Scotland. *Journal of Agricultural Economics,* 49:1–15.

Honadle, B. W. 1989. Cooperative extension and tourism development. *Proceedings of the National Extension Workshop.* Minneapolis, MN.

Kahneman, D., and J. L. Knetsch. 1992. Valuing public goods: The purchase of moral satisfaction. *Journal of Environmental Economics and Management,* 22:57–70.

Moyer, H. 1989. Ag-tourism—How to get started in your state: Using tourism and travel as a commodity and rural revitalization strategy. *Proceedings of the National Extension Workshop.* Minneapolis, MN.

New England Governors' Conference, Inc. 1988. Report of the Committee on the Environment. Boston, MA.

OECD. 1993. *What Future for Our Countryside? A Rural Development Policy.* Paris: OECD.

Portney, P. R. 1994. The contingent valuation debate: Why economists should care. *Journal of Economic Perspectives,* 8:3–17.

President's Commission on American Outdoors. 1987. Americans and the Outdoors. Washington, D.C.: U.S. Government Printing Office.

Price, C., ed. 1994. Economic value of landscape (whole issue). *Landscape Research,* spring.

Willis, K. G., and G. D. Garrod. 1993. Valuing landscape: A contingent valuation approach. *Journal of Environmental Management,* 37:1–22.

Part 4

Tourism Frontiers in Urban Areas

Chapter 10

Tourism Development and Environmental Implications for the Indian Frontier Region: A Study of Himachal Himalaya

R. B. Singh

In recent years tourism has gained importance because it has become a major activity contributing to economic development and employment generation with numerous forward and backward linkages within the national and regional economies. Since most tourism products are in the rural and interior hinterlands, tourism can provide the impetus for regional development of these areas leading to employment for people in the traditional and service sectors. The Indian environment, with its scenic, climatic, and ecological attributes, is the primary resource on which the tourist industry is based. Apart from the environment, cultural and historical factors may add to the attraction of the place. Many states of India have declared tourism as an important industry. This industry provides substantial foreign exchange to the country.

Though tourism has become important both from social and economic considerations, great concerns are now being expressed on the sustainability of its development in terms of environment, ecology, and culture. A lot of work has been going on in studies of sustainable development, not only in the context of tourism but in the context of large and small scale industries, and the setting up of large infrastructure projects and commercial complexes and organizations in most countries. However, many regions experience increasing risks as a result of a rapid and largely unplanned growth of tourism. It is very important to understand the impact of tourism on sustainable development. Natural hazards, man-made catastrophes, anthropogenic activities, and unethical tourism—which may entail the vast destruction of the quality of human life and increase environmental damage (as witnessed in many mountain regions)—are a matter of great concern. Therefore, it is essential to develop environmentally friendly ecotourism in the hills of Himalaya for the conservation of this biological heritage to ensure its sustenance and help the people understand the dynamics of the environment (Singh, 1992; Singh and Haigh, 1995).

It is rightly stated that tourism and environment do not need to confront each other but can develop a harmonious, complementary nexus between them. The tourism-carrying capacity of a place has to be determined, first by taking proper care of its existing infrastructure and second, by ensuring participation of local communities. Such an approach will help the tourism sector to integrate into a diversified viable economy and to establish a symbiotic relationship with natural resources and tourism support systems. It is high time for a more integrated and streamlined approach to tourism and the environment, which should be evolved at a global level. A report on the impact of tourism on the environment by the Organization for Economic Cooperation and Development (OECD, 1994) stated, "A high quality of environment is essential for tourism. On the other hand, the quality of the environ-

Table 10.1. Growth of International Tourist Traffic at World Level

Year	Tourist Arrivals (Million)	Annual Growth (%)
1950	25.28	—
1960	69.32	10.6
1970	165.79	9.1
1980	287.77	5.7
1990	456.59	2.3
1997	612.00	4.3

Source: W.T.O. Compendium of Tourism Statistics, 1997.

Table 10.2. Domestic Tourists

Year	No. of Domestic Tourists	Percentage Change (%)
1991	85,864,892	—
1992	102,465,705	19.3
1993	109,237,566	6.6
1994	127,116,655	16.4
1995	136,643,600	7.5
1996	140,119,672	2.5
1997	156,222,311	11.5

Source: Ministry of Tourism, Indian Tourism Statistics, 1997.

ment is threatened by tourist development itself which is promoted ... because of its economic importance" (p. 236). Or, to put it briefly, "tourism destroys tourism." Despite this paradox, worldwide experience shows the growing importance of the tourist sector with continuous growth of tourists, both international and domestic.

State of Tourism Development in India:
Emerging Scenarios

Over the years, tourism has emerged as a major segment of the Indian economy, contributing substantially to the foreign exchange earnings, which have increased from Rs.320 million in 1974–75 to more than Rs.30,000 million in 1991–92. Domestic tourism too plays an important role in the integration of people, employment generation, and economic development of the country. The foreign tourist arrivals in India increased from about 17,000 in 1951 to 1.17 million in 1990. However, a share in the total world arrivals has only ranged between 0.28 percent and 0.32 percent in the last ten years. However, it is anticipated that tourist traffic will grow at the rate of 9 percent to 10 percent per annum (Government of India, 1992).

The Seventh Plan was a watershed in the development of tourism in the country. Several new policy initiatives were taken to develop the tourism sector along an accelerated growth path and tourism was accorded the status of an industry. At present, fifteen states and three union territories have done so. The government set up the Tourism Finance Corporation in 1989 to provide financial assistance for setting up or for development of tourist-related activities and services, which include inter alia, hotels, restaurants, amusement parks, resorts and complexes for entertainment, education, and sports (table 10.3).

Table 10.3. Allocation on Tourism in Different Plan Periods

Plan Period	Allocation amount in millions (Rs.)	Including allocation for State sector amount in millions (Rs.)
Second Five Year Plan	33.63	17.84
Third Five Year Plan (1961–66)	80.00	40.00
Fourth Five Year Plan (1969–74)	485.88	—
Fifth Five Year Plan (1974–80)	592.82	285.23
Sixth Five Year Plan (1980–85)	1,799.60	1,129.60
Seventh Five Year Plan (1985–90)	3,261.50	1,874.70
Eighth Five Year Plan (1992–97)	8,041.00	5,051.80

Source: Different Plan Document.

In 1992, the government of India released a new Action Plan for Tourism based on the Tourism Policy of 1982 and the Report of the National Committee on Tourism in 1982. The Action Plan emphasized the socio-economic development benefits to the community that would derive from the program and improve the quality of life of the people, the employment opportunities provided by tourism, preservation of national heritage and environment, developing domestic and international tourism, and diversification of tourism products (Misra, 1999). The strategy laid out for achieving the above objectives were the following:

1. Improvement of tourism infrastructure.
2. Developing areas on a selective basis for integrated growth, along with marketing of destinations to ensure optimal use of existing infrastructure.
3. Restructuring and strengthening the institutions for development of human resources.
4. Evolving a suitable policy for increasing foreign tourist arrivals and foreign exchange earnings.

The Action Plan Components

1. The state governments should consider development of special tourism areas (STA) in consultation with the Indian government Ministry of Tourism.
2. In each special tourism area, a special area development authority would be constituted by the state government. The state government should provide basic infrastructure in terms of roads, transport network, bus

terminals, wayside amenities, electrical grids, water supply, law and order, and municipal services.

3. The state governments should freeze the rates on water and electricity supply for at least ten years in such areas.

4. The state governments should exempt all projects connected with hotels and tourism related industry being set up in the STAs from all state and local taxes for a period of at least ten years.

5. The central government should provide infrastructure support as required for development of STAs, such as airports and airline services, railway stations, communication networks, and so on.

6. The central government should consider granting exemption from specific central taxes, and providing fiscal incentives in the shape of capital subsidies, interest subsidies, and so on for development of capital-intensive tourism projects.

7. The central government should set up a Tourism Development Fund for providing equity support to investors in such areas for capital intensive projects.

8. The central government should provide special clearance from the environmental angle for all projects being set up in STAs.

9. India investment center/embassies/government of India tourist offices should give wide publicity to such areas for foreign investors.

10. At the national level, a coordination committee should be set up with representatives from the state governments, private trade, and the government of India for coordinating all matters related to the STAs.

The aim of these developments was to activate tourist activities so that a proper and well-coordinated tourism sector would become functional. India, as compared to other Asian countries, has lagged behind, and to attain their level the country needs a coordinated development of tourism, both sectorally and spatially. It is very important to implement an integrated and unified strategy in coordinating development plans for various Indian states.

Tourism in an Indian Frontier Region

Tourism in the Kullu Valley of the Himachal Himalaya is a relatively new phenomenon. It began in earnest in the 1980s, when the Kashmir Valley was totally closed down to tourists due to insurgency and border strife and tourists were increasingly diverted to Manali. Since then, tourism has been the most potent factor of the last decade as an agent of physical and socio-economic change. Manali came of age during the 1980s as an important tourism destination. By then, television travel programs and the travel sections of newspapers and magazines were regularly featuring Manali, while game shows were offering sports packages in skiing, paragliding, and trekking as prizes. At the same time, the government came to recognize that tourism can have a role in economic development. Slowly, funding for tourism increased and tourism-related projects began to appear in economic strategies.

Effect of Urbanization and Tourism

The high influx of tourists and the high rate of urbanization have disturbed the ecohydrology. With the increase in tourism, urbanization has also increased (table 10.4). The months showing the maximum concentration of tourist population are June (12.84 percent), July (11.62 percent), and May (11.38 percent), while October (10.78 percent) and September (9.91 percent) stand in between the summer and winter seasons. During the winter season, February (4.85 percent) and January (6.4 percent) are the two months when tourist flow is weakest. The trend of increase in tourists for both Kullu and Manali showed a significant sixfold increase in the tourist flow from 1985 to 1993 (tables 10.5 and 10.6).

Many tourists come from countries like Great Britain and United States. Other than these, tourists also come from countries like France, Finland, Germany and Canada. Quite a few tourists are also Israeli; some of them are distinguished by the use of noisy motorbikes to travel around. This loud unnecessary sound spoils the peace of the area, according to the natives and the other tourists.

Table 10.4. Population of Kullu Valley

Towns and Regions	Total Population (1991)
Banjar	1,037
Bhuntar	2,972
Kullu	14,569
Manali	2,433
Kullu Valley	157,018
Kullu District	301,729

Source: Census of India, Kullu District.

Table 10.5. Growth of Tourism in Kullu Valley

Year	Number of Tourist	Growth Rate (%)
1965	118	—
1975	32570	275
1985	135109	315
1995	439734	225

Source: Himachal Pradesh Tourism, Manali.

Table 10.6. Changing Traffic Flow at Manali, April–May 1991–1999

Days	April		May		June	
	1991	1999	1991	1999	1991	1999
1–10	2,312	4,069	2,627	6,929	4,280	11,752
10–20	1,206	5,048	3,290	9,444	5,945	11,733
21–30,31	1,340	5,698	3,388	13,138	4,389	11,162
Total	4,858	14,815	9,305	29,511	14,614	34,649

Source: Office of the Nagar Panchayat Manali, Kullu.

The average duration of stay for the tourists was four to six days, although there are some who have stayed in Manali for a month and plan to come again for a longer duration. These are the kind of tourists who stay in villages and Ashrams and practice Yoga, meditation, and other things. They adopt completely the culture of the place and are blended into the general milieu. However, the main aim of most tourists is purely recreational. Indian tourists consist mainly of students on fieldtrips and excursions or newly wedded couples. The duration of stay normally does not extend beyond one week (table 10.7).

Earlier the majority of tourists were domestic but the trend of foreign tourists is gradually increasing in the upper Kullu Valley. The total number of foreign tourists increased from 9,757 in 1989 to 12,910 in 1991–92. This figure is projected to go up to 52,204 by 2001. The growth of tourism and the process of urbanization goes hand in hand. The infrastructure required to provide basic amenities to the tourists leads to acceleration in the process of urbanization, which has caused a significant change in trends in consumption, supply, and management of mountain water resources in the area. Among the positive indicators, the distribution of pipelines, storage tanks, and sewerage lines are important, while pollution, open garbage dumped into streams, and storage of water through privatization of sources are important negative effects of the urbanization process (Gardner, 1996). The rapid increase in numbers of hotels and guest houses to provide infra-

Table 10.7. Preferences of Tourist Places (1992)

Spots/ Places	# Visitors	Total (%)
Hidimba Temple	105	100
Van Vihar	30	28
Buddhist Monastery	30	28
Club House	45	42
Nehru Kund	73	70
Vashist	105	100
Jagat Sukh	65	62
Manu Temple	60	57
Naggar	40	30
Solang Valley	63	60
Rothang	90	85
Rahla Water Fall	62	60

Source: J. K. Associates, 1992, SPA, N. Delhi.

structures for tourism has led to water shortages in the region. The springs, which were earlier managed and utilized by the community, are now being managed by hotel owners, creating crisis situations for the villagers.

Tourism Infrastructure and Environmental Implications

Studies have shown that landscape is a most important motivation in the choice of holiday location (Chetwode, 1972). The ecology of any region has only a certain capacity for sustaining a limited number of people and no more. During the tourist season, there is a sharp increase in population numbers, which has to draw sustenance from the life-support system of the area. Although the settlement pattern in the valley is scattered in clusters along the slopes of the Beas basin, the headwater location of Manali has become an epicenter for the growth of tourism-induced urbanization in the Kullu Valley. There has been a great increase in the number of hotels and guest houses in these decades, such as, between 1985–1996, their number rose from 2 to 640 hotels/guest houses (table 10.8).

In this context, it is important to mention that in the course of this survey, most of the tourists revealed a preference for staying in the village as paying guests with a family rather than living in a hotel. The daily expenditure of most of the tourists was between Rs.200–300. Hence, the budgetary requirements of a large number of tourists were suited to this mode of accommodation. Due to the sudden spurt in the number of hotels/guest houses, as

Table 10.8. Growth of Hotels/Guest Houses in Upper Kullu Valley

Year	No. of Hotels/Guest houses
1975	2
1980	5
1985	10
1988	100
1990	200
1993	400
1995	550
1996	640

Source: Tourist Information Center, Manali.

well as temporary seasonal housing, the area under nonagricultural activities is increasing rapidly. The urban data of Kullu Valley available from the last two decades indicate that there is a change in the urban-occupied area.

Another important factor has been the shift from traditional paper bags and jute bags to polythene, which is one of the most widely manifested impacts of tourism. In the tourist regions, this menace is more widespread, because the tourist population is mobile and the practice of eating out of packets is more prevalent. During our survey, we found that the tourist area of Manali was badly littered with polythene and plastic mineral water bottles. Such nonbiodegradable waste keeps increasing with the increasing number of tourists, thus affecting adversely the environment of the area. Shortly after this survey, though, the Himachal government banned the use of polythene bags in the area. Such a positive measure is welcome and is a step in the right direction.

Transport Growth and Environmental Pollution

Another change that has occurred in the area is the growing number of private vehicles. During the season, a number of tourists arrive in their own vehicles, leading to overcrowding. Since Manali is located on the National Highway (No. 21), it also receives much traffic passing through Manali on its way to Leh and Ladakh as well as Lahaul and Spiti. However, the maximum concentration of vehicles is due to tourist influx.

Consequently, as in any other commercial city, traffic jams in the main market area of Manali are frequent. Apart from private automobiles, the number of buses has also increased. In fact, transport was one of the amenities the improvement of which was agreed upon by a majority of the respondents

Table 10.9. pH Value of Various Stations along the Beas River

Time Period	Manali Upstream	Kullu Down Stream	Bhuntar Up stream (Parvati)	Aut Down Stream	Largi Down Stream	Pandoh Upstream
Jun. 94	7.42	7.40	8.22	7.16	7.08	7.20
Sep. 94	7.21	7.08	6.98	7.36	7.83	7.32
Dec. 94	7.75	7.89	7.41	7.93	7.75	8.24
Mar. 95	7.30	6.90	6.60	7.00	6.90	7.60
Jun. 95	8.10	8.50	8.50	7.70	8.40	7.90
Sep. 95	8.70	8.10	8.50	8.10	8.40	8.20
Dec. 95	8.70	8.50	8.70	8.50	8.70	8.20
Jun. 96	8.60	7.50	6.90	8.40	8.50	8.50
Sep. 96	6.90	7.80	7.40	7.60	7.80	6.80
Dec. 96	8.34	8.12	8.36	8.24	7.69	7.97
Mar. 97	8.33	7.44	7.33	7.78	7.80	7.74

Source: District Pollution Control Board, Kullu.

surveyed. This has affected the peace and tranquillity of the area and, to some extent, the quality of air. This may not be so true of the hamlets, but the main area of Manali certainly suffers from this problem. A large number of tourists who realized this problem put forward the suggestion that the bus station should be shifted five kilometers away from the main market center to avoid noise, crowding, and pollution in the central area.

With the pressure of population increasing, the sewage facilities also need to be revamped. There are signs of pollution in the Beas river (table 10.9). According to the survey, the situation is not very objectionable now, but care definitely needs to be taken. Tourists mostly rated the sewage facility as being of an average quality, but a sizable number were also of the view that it needed attention and was not satisfactory. This was that segment of the tourists that stayed in the village as paying guests and thus had a closer interaction with the mode of living of the residents and the problems affecting them.

Tourism Impact and Extreme Events

In the study of the upper Beas basin, natural hazards do occur and some forms of it are more frequent than others. To what extent these hazards are induced by human activity is open to discussion, but that human interference does seem to have some kind of an impact is certain (Singh and Pandey, 1998). With the development of the region, new hill roads have been created quickly and cheaply across uncharted geology, ancient landslide zones, and active scree slopes. In the survey, people from the hamlets of Vashisht, Goshal, and Chichoga felt that tourism had served to induce landslides due to its resultant population growth and other factors. The incidence of landslides has increased, according to the respondents.

The survey showed that of all problems, increased runoff is the most serious. A great many people felt this in Goshal, Palchan, Chichoga, and Old Manali. Increased runoff affects the fertility of soil and also has an impact on agriculture, as the top layer of the soil is washed off. The respondents felt that the soil quality has been affected and the soil no longer gives proper yield unless liberal doses of chemical fertilizers are applied. This is not to say that production levels have gone down. On the contrary, they have increased, and now crops are very largely dependent on fertilizer usage. Increased runoff is also a nuisance for the people residing in the lower reaches of the hills. Due to the steep slopes, the water flows rapidly down and collects in the lower parts, thus creating a problem for those staying there.

There is one more aspect that needs to be looked into. The inhabitants of the area feel that floods are on the rise (especially the instances of flash-floods). Of all the hamlets surveyed, a majority of people in the hamlets of Chichoga and Vashisht felt that this was the case. These two hamlets have a continuous ravine running in the lower reaches, and during the monsoon season, the ravine floods. The increase in flooding can be somewhat related to the increase in runoff. As the soil particles are loosened and are washed off in the rain, they are in the end taken by the flow of the river into the ravine. This has resulted in the increase in siltation and has thus raised the river bed. The same can be said of the boulders that fall into the flow. This results in a quicker raising of the water level, so flooding occurs even when the water quantity is not increased remarkably.

There can be another dimension to the problem when looked at from a different angle. With an increase in population, areas that were earlier vacant are now inhabited. Therefore, when flooding occurs, there is more loss of life and property. This may have induced the perception among villagers that the number of such incidents has risen.

Sociocultural and Economic Issues in Tourism Development

The inhabitants of the area are of the opinion that there has been a tremendous spurt in the incidents of crime and petty theft, but such incidents are seldom reported. There is a spatial pattern associated with the crime rate. Villages that are close to the main area of Manali and that have more interaction with visitors report a higher percentage of crime in their area. According to the village elders, increasing aspirations of the youth who seek to imitate the modern and luxurious lifestyles of the tourists are, to some extent, responsible for the increased crime rate.

According to data from the Kullu superintendent of police, crime against women is negligible, that is, less than 5percent, but when weighed against an almost complete lack of crime against women earlier, the statistic is not very welcome. With tourism has also been a steady rise in the prevalence of drug addiction among youth. Plantations of "Charas" (a kind of narcotic grass) are common in most of the villages, and while some respondents are of the view that it was always there and isn't a new phenomenon, many feel that tourists and particularly "hippies" have contributed heavily to the increasing drug addiction amongst youth. Even though the contention that Charas is not a new introduction to the area may be true, the knowledge of its importance as an attractive tourist consumer item is certainly recent. Once again, a spatial trend was observed—old Manali led in the number of respondents who attributed increase in drug addiction to tourism, followed closely by Vashisht, Chichoga, and Palchan. This trend is deepening in these three villages, as villagers have now started the practice of keeping paying guests, and this may sometimes inculcate drug addiction amongst members of the family.

A change in the manner of dressing among the youth is evident. Gone are the traditional "pattus," caps, and so on. Instead, there is an assault of modern wear on village culture. Even though the older population holds on to a tenuous link with its old attire and language, the younger folk increasingly aspire to modernize.

Turning to education, in the areas that were surveyed, there was an almost total school enrollment of children at the primary level. Parents are also sending their children to the city for higher studies. Female education has received a boost and girls are gradually taking up employment, a trend that has been facilitated by the provision of job opportunities made available by tourism.

In the case of employment opportunities, even though the job prospects have risen, the local inhabitants have not benefited as much as could have been possible. The local administration does not seem to have made enough effort to incorporate local people, particularly the interior village people, into the mainstream. Although tourism is called the "money crop" of the region, the number of people actually gaining a livelihood from it is not very high as of now. This form of earning may escalate as awareness of tourism increases in the future and knowledge of how to make use of it for their economic benefit spreads among the locals. In the villages that were surveyed, only those villages that were in the close vicinity of Manali benefited from the tourism industry. Old Manali village has the greatest benefit from tourism, followed by Palchan, Solang, and Vashisht.

Tourism also provides a wider market for the goods that the inhabitants of the area manufacture. Tourists buy such goods to take back as souvenirs and are prepared to pay a decent price. But the major problem is that as the growth of tourism has been unplanned and haphazard, a suitable infrastructure does not exist. The village people need to exhibit their culture more. Tourism has not been able to provide enough benefits for the people of the area because of the lack of publicity about the villages' culture and way of life. The marketability of the region's culture ought to be increased.

No studies have been carried out ascribing the effects relating to the change in special diversity, their growth rates, and age structure specifically to tourism development. Some conclusions can be made on the basis of limited data regarding recreational use of vegetation. The greatest damage to vegetation cover has been witnessed in the initial stage of development.

Sustainable Tourism Development Strategy: Policy Issues

After the Rio Earth Summit, the World Tourism Organization (WTO), in cooperation with the World Travel and Tourism Council (WTTC), has been trying to summarize and to distill from AGENDA 21 the main postulates arising from the 1992 Earth Summit that should be applicable to tourism. The guiding principles, based on the Rio Declaration on Environment and Development, have been identified and are as follows:

1. Travel and tourism assist people in leading healthy and productive lives in harmony with nature.
2. Tourism should contribute to the conservation, protection, and restoration of the earth's ecosystem.
3. Travel and tourism should be based upon sustainable patterns of production and consumption.
4. Tourism, peace, development, and environmental protection are interdependent.
5. In order to achieve sustainable development, environmental protection shall constitute an integral part of the tourism development process.
6. Tourism development issues should be handled with the participation of concerned citizens, with planning decisions being adopted at local levels.

7. Tourism development should recognize and should support the identity, culture, and interests of indigenous peoples.
8. International laws protecting the environment should be respected by the worldwide travel industry.

Carrying Capacity and Ecosystem Evaluation Approach

The ecosystem should be considered as a holistic unit, integrating and grouping plants and animals interacting within a particular physical environment. Environmental impact assessment relating to tourism is emerging, where planners attempt to predict what effects a set of activities will have and try to determine how to enhance benefits of the activities and reduce their negative impacts. This is supplemented by carrying capacity utilization, where the planners attempt to determine the biophysical limits of productivity of various natural resources. The measurement of carrying capacity and ecosystem evaluation approach should reflect:

1. the range of biophysical capacities of the environment;
2. the range of values supported by each environment;
3. the sensitivity of each part of the environment to our actions;
4. the impacts of our actions on the capacities of the ecosystem;
5. the resulting effects on the sustainability of the environment;
6. the sensitivity of the key values to change.

An environmental monitoring mechanism is further needed, where planners and managers seek to test how accurate their predictions have been and use the results to determine what changes are required to achieve better results (Misra, 1999). Successful tourism can be developed only by careful market research to assess the potential. Development of national tourist services and infrastructure on a planned basis, well-designed and truthful publicity about the attractions of a country, an awareness on the part of nations of the importance of welcoming tourists, and reducing entry and exit formalities to the necessary minimum are some of the measures that can be implemented.

There is a need to encourage collaborative economic efforts such as the regionalization of businesses, government-to-government cooperation in promoting tourism, joint private or private-public investments in tourism projects, and the possibilities opened up by gateways. New projects and programs should be discussed along with cultural and heritage issues, particularly the construction of heritage sites, awareness about heritage programs, and the sharing of heritage management experience for tourism development (table 10.10).

Table 10.10. Government Financial Support for Tourism Development in Manali

Year	Amount in (Rs.)	Work
1992–93	50,000	Toilet at Manali
	100,000	Fountain at Rambagh, Manali
1993–94	250,000	Toilet at Manali
1994–95	2,124,200	Toilet at Marhi, Kothi, Rohtang, and Solang Nalla
	500,000	Flood lights at Hadimba Devi Temple, Manali
1995–96	64,300	Pacca path up to Hadimba Devi Temple
	160,617	VIP vehicle parking at Solang Nalla
	92,950	Car parking near Manu Temple, Manali
1996–97	379,000	Civil works of musical fountain at Manali
	254,000	Pacca path from Hadimba Temple to Van Vihar
	100,000	Pacca path at Vashist

Source: Department of Tourism, Shimla, Himachal Pradesh.

Concepts of ecotourism include activities such as employment genera-tion and use of natural resources, conservation of biological diversity, and the sustainable growth of adventure games. This approach provides an ex-change of ideas, formulation of a viable strategy for conservation, and motivation for the programs (Singh, 1996).

Steps have been taken for development of permanent camping sites, with basic facilities such as public conveniences, cafeterias, and so on along the routes frequently used by tourists in the interior parts of the region. A comprehensive plan has to be formulated for improving the water supply, sewage system, and garbage management arrangements. Balanced infra-structural development and preservation of rich cultural heritage is of critical importance (Kuniyal et al., 1995). To achieve this objective, it is necessary to formulate master plans for all states highlighting their tourism potential.

Conclusion

The Himalayas are a unique and priceless treasure of India. The flora, fauna, and water resources of this region must be carefully preserved. At the same time, an imaginative strategy should be developed to enable tourists to visit the region in large numbers to marvel at the grandeur of the Himalayas, thereby contributing to the economic development of the region. Tourism has resulted in rapid growth of urbanization and increased cost of living for the locals, changes in the pattern of agricultural production, and alienation from traditional values. Tourism has also brought about a negative impact on the local environment, and this trend is on the increase. Therefore, an integrated long-term perspective plan for development and promotion of tourism in the region has to be drawn up in consultation with the local self-governments and community organizations.

The present pattern of tourist flow to the Kullu region is seasonal and uneven. Much of the bulk of the tourist flow is concentrated during April-June and October, when tourist facilities are under pressure, whereas during the remaining months of the year, there is underutilization of the existing facilities. It is necessary to take steps to spread the inflow of tourists during the lean months to optimize the utilization of the infrastructure facilities. The valley is an ecologically sensitive region sustaining a variety of unique flora and fauna. Therefore, it has to be promoted as a destination for eco-tourism, in addition to the traditional activities such as adventure, pilgrimage, and cultural tourism. Since heritage constitutes the major tourist attraction of the region, special incentives have to be conceived and offered to develop the Manikaran region. There is an urgent need to initiate a concept of controlled tourism, fixing a ceiling for tourist traffic to the area, so that the traffic load is related to the existing carrying capacity and infrastructure services. In recent years, the region has also been attracting a sizable number of domestic tourists. It is advisable to target the more serious domestic tourists in the promotional campaigns.

One of the major attractions for tourists is the region's cultural heritage and traditional knowledge. Steps have to be taken for the maintenance and conservation of historical buildings and heritage sites, such as the Hidimba temple. The role of government in development of tourism has to be restricted to the creation of basic infrastructural support with minimum interference in the commercial aspects of the industry. The *Manali Tourist*, with complete tourist information and interpretation of culture, flora and fauna, heritage and cultural assets, and so on, has to be improved. In order to promote conference and convention tourism, dissemination of information is needed about the Manali Wildlife education, awareness, and information. For mobilization of resources from the private sector, for development of cultural tourism, an autonomous organization has to be set up.

The guidelines of the Environmental Protection Act of 1986 and National Forest Policy 1988, with reference to maintenance of ecological balance and environmental management, have to be considered while formulating tourism development plans.

References

Census of India. 1981. H. P. Series 7, Part X–A., Kullu District. Shimla: Government of India Publication.

Chetwode, P. 1972. *Kullu: The End of the Habitable World.* London: Murray Publishing.

Gardner, J. S. 1996. Tourism and risk from natural hazards—Manali, Himachal Pardesh, India. In R. B. Singh ed., *Disasters Environment and Development.* New Delhi: Oxford & IBH Publishing Co. Pvt. Ltd.

Government of India. 1992. *Eighth Five Year Plan (1992–97),* Vol. II. New Delhi: Planning Commission.

Kuniyal, J. C., S. C. Ram, G. S. Singh, and A. P. Jain. 1995. Environmental assessment of Kullu Dussehra in Himachal Himlaya, India. In R. B. Singh and M. J. Haigh eds., *Sustainable Reconstruction of Highland and Headwater Regions.* New Delhi: Oxford & IBH Publishing Co. Pvt. Ltd.

Misra, C. T. 1999. Impact of tourism on sustainable development, Asian perspective. Unpublished Ph.D. thesis submitted to the Jawaharlal Nehru University, New Delhi.

Organization for Economic Cooperation and Development (OECD). 1994. Tourism policy and international tourism in OECD countries, 1991–1992. Special Feature: Tourism Strategies and Rural Development. Paris: OECD.

Singh, R. B., ed. 1992. *Dynamics of Mountain Geosystem.* New Delhi: Ashish Publications.

Singh, R. B., and M. J. Haigh, eds. 1995. *Sustainable Reconstruction of Highland and Headwater Regions.* New Delhi: Oxford & IBH Publishing Co. Pvt. Ltd.

Singh, R. B. 1996. Environmental, economic and social sustainability through human development initiatives: A case study of an Indian marginal region—Upper Kullu Valley. *Proceedings of the I.G.U. Study Group on Development Issues in Marginal Regions.* Glasgow: University of Strathclyde.

Singh, R. B., and B. W. Pandey. 1998. Impact of tourism on ecohydrology in headwater region of Beas, Himachal Pradesh. In S. R. Chalise and A. R. Herman eds., *Ecohydrology of High Himalayas.* Kathmandu: ICIMOD-UNESCO Publishers.

Chapter 11

Tourism Development in a Desert Frontier Town

Arie Reichel and Natan Uriely

The purpose of this chapter is to present a conceptual strategic approach for tourism development in remote, isolated areas in the desert. Focusing on a case study of tourism development in the town of Yeruham in the Negev desert, the chapter presents a postmodern concept that combines the natural resources of the area with man-made "contrived" attractions. In addition, it is suggested that a two-tier development process be implemented, where central planning provides the basis for entrepreneurial profit-making activities.

The trigger for the present study was the significant growth of rural tourism in northern *kibbutzim* and peripheral *moshavim* (collective farming settlements and villages) in Israel during the 1990s. This success indicates the paramount role of nature-oriented tourism as a contemporary solution for social and economic development in peripheral areas (Fleischer and Pizam, 1997). In light both of the success of these northern sites and of the global trend toward nature-oriented tourism, the chapter proposes a conceptual strategy for tourism development on the Negev desert frontier in southern Israel. In taking an active approach to tourism development, the plan calls for suggestions for specific actions. Thus, this chapter emphasizes the active role of individual entrepreneurs in the development of nature-oriented tourism in the Negev. Clearly the "green version" of nature-oriented tourism is not an appropriate image for the development of tourism in the "yellow" environment of the desert. The development of nature-oriented tourism in this area, therefore, requires a different approach to the concept of nature and sustainable tourism in desert environments. In line with this premise, the chapter calls for a postmodern approach to remote desert locations that combines the authentic with the man-made, stimulated, or contrived, as well as the central planning approach with the individual entrepreneur.

Tourism Development in the Desert: The Current State

The common notion of frontier desert tourism is usually distinct from contrived attractions. It is often associated with concepts such as nature, "eco," sustainable, and adventure tourism. However, it is clear that the "contrived" has penetrated the desert environment. For example, the city of Las Vegas, where gambling takes place in the stimulated environments of theme-related hotels/casinos, is currently one of the most impressive illustrations of mass tourism based on contrived attractions. With more than 30 million visitors annually and over 120,000 hotel rooms, Las Vegas is probably the most successful desert location for tourists (www.vegasfreedom.com/learn-5.asp).

The nature-oriented approach considers the desert as a potential environment for the development of the "other" postmodern tourism, rather than one of contrived mass tourism. This approach seems to be more compatible with the periphery of the Israeli Negev desert and has long been the mainstream attitude to the development of the Negev region. Specifically, the Israeli government created an incentive system that was intended to encourage tourism entrepreneurial investment in the Negev. It was assumed that these tourist ventures would primarily be small-scale and appropriate for nature or ecotourism, that is, a concept that is the complete opposite of that of contrived tourist attractions.

This traditional approach is here challenged in light of the current situation of tourism development in the Negev and experience gained in other locations. With the exception of the frontier city of Eilat, on Israel's Red Sea coast, most of the Negev region tourism ventures suffered a severe recession during the late 1990s. Foreign tourists, who arrived in Israel despite the perception of risk and instability, preferred to follow the routes of Christianity and Judaism and not to visit the unspoiled natural sites of the Negev. The government agency for tourism development in the Negev did encourage domestic visitors to fill the void left by foreign tourists, but most of the promotion was directed toward special events and vacation offers that did not reverse the effects of the recession.

Despite limited economic prospects during the years 1995–1999, several entrepreneurs started their ecotourism ventures in the Negev region. A study by Haber and Lerner (2001; chapter 8 in this volume) randomly sampled fifty-three businesses in the region. It is interesting to note that out of the total sample, eleven were classified as lodging ventures, developed by families in order to augment their income. This reflects the growing Israeli trend toward rural tourism.

In our context, we refer to "rural desert tourism" rather than the green, luscious image associated with rural tourism in northern Israel (Fleischer and Pizam, 1997; Reichel, Lowengart and Milman, 2000). Since the decline of agriculture, numerous farmers have turned to lodging tourists as a source of income. In addition, Israeli Bedouin, in an attempt to conserve their rich desert lifestyle and traditions, have established their own ventures. Others are devoted to desert wildlife, enabling visitors to interact with animals.

According to Haber and Lerner's (2001) study (chapter 8 in this volume), governmental assistance is made available for all such business ventures. This assistance is given in two forms: financial and advisory. Specifically, most ventures qualify for governmental loans at preferred rates and also for the assistance of specially appointed small business administration consultants. It is interesting to note that thirty-two (more than half) of these business ventures did not apply for any assistance from governmental tourism incubator agencies. However, the tourism ventures that are financially supported by external sources performed better than did those without financial support. On the other hand, in the case of advisory support from a tourism incubator, the nonassisted ventures exhibited better performance. Obtaining financial support from external sources is evidence of the entrepreneur's success in persuading these external sources that the venture is sound, well planned, and economically viable. Thus, one can conclude that it is the entrepreneurs and their business acumen that account for the success and survival of business ventures in the Negev region.

The distribution of the ventures indicates no "grand plan" or obvious local municipality planning priorities, but rather entrepreneurial attempts to take advantage of the unique conditions that are characteristic of the Negev frontier by adopting an authentic, ecotourism approach.

Note that, for most entrepreneurs, it was obvious that development must be defined in terms of ecosustainable tourism that is compatible with the Zionist ethos of desert development. Unlike the case of the city of Eilat, their approach constituted the very antithesis to Boorstin's (1964) notion of tourism as a superficial activity that is based on "pseudoevents." One might ask, however, what would have happened had the entrepreneurial efforts been a part of a regional planning policy that did not limit its scope to the "authentic" alone? Our main premise is that, had the motivation and ability in evidence among these entrepreneurs been adapted to a more comprehensive plan entailing postmodern concepts, they would have achieved better results.

The Postmodern Approach to Tourism

This chapter emphasizes the need to market remote, isolated desert locations by combining them with man-made themes and attractions. In addition, it presents the option of combining nature-oriented tourism with contrived attractions. This emphasis, which links together ostensibly separate dimensions of tourism experience, is derived from the theoretical framework of postmodern tourism. In this context, it is significant that up until the late 1970s, most students of tourism were united in their perception of tourism as a modern phenomenon. During those early days of tourism studies, the field was dominated by two opposing viewpoints regarding the nature and meaning of tourist experience. One side of the debate was represented by Boorstin (1964), who perceived the tourist experience as trivial and superficial, as an activity that involves a quest for contrived experiences and "pseudoevents." On the other hand, MacCannell (1973) conceptualized the tourist experience as a meaningful, modern ritual that involves a quest for authentic experiences. This debate contributed to a process of distinguishing between contrived and nature-oriented experiences. Nevertheless, the conceptual distinction between nature-oriented experiences and contrived attractions was challenged by the postmodern perspective.

Since the late 1970s, a growing number of scholars have addressed various tourist activities as expressions of postmodernist culture. Contemporary trends in tourism, such as the rise of small and specialized agencies, the growing attraction of nostalgia and "heritage tourism," the flourishing of nature-oriented tourism, and the increase of simulated tourism environments, are all labeled as aspects of postmodern tourism. Indeed, scholarly discourse in this field consists of two theoretical perspectives of postmodern tourism—the "simulational" and the "other" (Munt, 1994). The "simulational" line of scholarship focuses on the analysis of "hyper-real" experiences and refers to simulated theme parks and other contrived attractions as typical postmodern environments (Baudrillard, 1983; Eco, 1986; Featherston, 1991; Gottdiner, 1995; Lash and Urry, 1994; Pretes, 1995). Conceptualizations of the "other" postmodern tourism stress the search for the "real" and indicate the growing appeal of the "natural" and the countryside as postmodern expressions (Barrett, 1989; Munt, 1994; Poon, 1989; Urry, 1990).

The distinction between the "simulational" and the "other" postmodern tourism appears to follow the polarity observed, as previously mentioned, in earlier theories of modern tourism. While "simulational" postmodern tourism follows Boorstin's notion of "pseudoevents" (1964), the "other" concept of postmodern tourism follows MacCannell's (1973) argument with regard to the quest for authenticity. However, unlike the earlier notion of modern tourism, the "simulational" and the "other" dimensions of postmodern tourism do not derive from two opposing conceptual realms. On the contrary, some of the important scholars of postmodern tourism include both "simulational" and "other" dimensions in their complete portrayal of postmodern tourism (Urry, 1990). Furthermore, unlike former theories, both dimensions of postmodern tourism generate complementary rather than contradictory proposals with regard to the nature of tourism. For instance, Munt's article on the "other" postmodern tourism begins with the following statement regarding the "simulational" trend of postmodern tourism: "I do not set out to challenge these but to consider figuratively the 'other' possibilities of postmodern tourism" (1994:101). According to Uriely (1997), this statement reflects the compromising nature of postmodern theories that entails what Denzin (1991:27) calls "both-and" rather than "either-or" scientific attitudes. This chapter adopts the "both-and" postmodern premise while taking an active approach for frontier tourism development in the Negev. In order to substantiate this premise, a specific tourism plan for the Negev town of Yeruham is presented below.

Postmodern Tourism Planning: The Case of Yeruham, Israel

The notion of postmodern tourism that combines nature-oriented as well as contrived attractions has been incorporated in a master plan for tourism development in the economically depressed, isolated town of Yeruham, which is located above the "Grand Crater" in the Negev area. The object of this plan (designed by the Department of Hotel and Tourism Management at Ben-Gurion University of the Negev) was to emphasize the open landscapes of the desert as a potential environment for frontier tourism development based on nature-oriented themes. The strategy was to strive for competitive advantage based on an attempt to distinguish the town of Yeruham from other nature-oriented tourism locations in the Negev. In order to achieve this strategic goal, the plan set out to adopt a wide concept of "nature" that included geology, ecology, and astronomy-related themes. Furthermore, these themes were actualized by relying on simulated attractions and interactive experiences.

This plan focuses on a three-floor center and museum located on the edge of the Grand Crater, and its goal is to combine natural elements with contrived, staged attractions dealing with concepts and themes such as the strata of the earth, the story of the Creation, outer space, and unidentified flying objects (UFOs). The center's three levels are to include these attractions: the basement accommodates geology-related themes, the ground floor is designated for ecological concepts, and the top floor houses astronomy-related attractions. In line with postmodern experiences, the proposed center also encourages interactive encounters between visitors and the site's attractions and personnel. In this context, the center will incorporate creativity corners primarily devoted to activities for children. The center's personnel will include actors in costume, similar to Disneyland or other conventional theme parks. In addition, the nearby Crater is ideal for accommodating outdoor activities such as hiking, hot air ballooning, jeep trips, and horse or donkey riding. Independent entrepreneurs, who are expected to conform to the general plan, would manage these tourist activities. Some ventures specifically planned for typical ecotourism will involve minimum interference with the unique natural gifts of the area (hiking, horse riding, etc.). On the other hand, the plan calls for staged experiences in nature, such as the landing and taking off of UFOs and similar simulations using hot air balloons and other Disney-style mechanisms, such as "the City of Ants," "the Black Hole," the "UFO Highway," the "Milky Way." Obviously, these staged attractions would have to be developed in accordance with the general plan while leaving enough latitude for entrepreneurial creativity and acumen.

Discussion

As noted above, the two main possible approaches of economically viable tourism development in the Negev are (a) sporadic entrepreneurial ventures and (b) central regional or city planning. An initial glance seems to indicate that all city/regional plans have hitherto failed. The only exception might be the frontier city of Eilat, where major businesses dominate the development scene in accordance with a broadly defined central development scheme.

Eilat's tourist area is isolated from the rest of the city, located on prime land, and blocks the view of the Red Sea from the city's inhabitants. Moreover, the acceleration in development is clearly an antithesis of ecotourism, often resembling the spirit prevalent in Las Vegas, Acapulco, or Kuta Beach (Bali). At the same time, a survey of entrepreneurial tourist ventures in the Negev indicates a lack of specific direction, although the common trend is toward small ecotourism ventures. No clear patterns can be found in terms of government support. In sum, we are left with two seemingly major tourism development alternatives: a central plan that incorporates local municipality investment along with entrepreneurial investment or the current situation of sporadic, modest attempts by Negev entrepreneurs. At the same time, the "overdevelopment" of Eilat serves as a warning against overzealous efforts.

As already mentioned, however, the development of nature-oriented tourism in the Negev requires a new approach. For instance, the open landscapes and the Craters of the Negev desert may be perceived as a potential environment for tourism development encompassing geology and astronomy-oriented themes such as "earth and outer space." Figure 11.1 presents the dilemma in clear terms, illustrating four available options.

	Type of Nature Tourism	
Central Planning	Authentic	Simulational
Yes	A	B
No	C	D

A – Central planning that allows for only "authentic" tourism development.
B – Central planning that calls for tourism development based on simulations.
C – Entrepreneurial development without central planning; dominant authentic nature-tourism ventures.
D - Entrepreneurial development without central planning; dominant simulated ventures.

Figure 11.1. Type of Tourism and the Central Planning Dilemma

This chapter clearly advocates cells A and B—central planning that combines simulated as well as authentic nature-oriented tourist ventures (i.e., a "both-and" approach). Moreover, this combination calls for the integration of entrepreneurs within a general framework. As such, the approach presented here is postmodernist, not only in terms of the compatibility of both authentic and simulated nature-development and tourism schemes, but also in terms of the compatibility of regional and local intervention with entrepreneurial ventures. The suggested plan for the development of the depressed Negev frontier town of Yeruham illustrates this approach. Again, the premise of this chapter is that successful tourism development requires a balance between entrepreneurial ventures and a well-defined central plan.

Lacking the capacity for global industrial competition, most isolated frontier towns in the Negev are facing severe unemployment. The panacea most cited is high-tech industry, followed by tourism development. Since there is little likelihood of a high-technology industry influx into the Negev, tourism development seems the most viable option. Given this need and the government policy of supporting tourist entrepreneurs, the postmodern proposal for Yeruham seems appropriate for the needs of all parties involved. From the viewpoint of the entrepreneur, it is important to provide the possibility for guidance and support from local municipalities. Therefore, the simplest, most obvious solution would be for local authorities and entrepreneurs to join together in an effort to develop postmodern tourism. Accumulated global experience indicates that controlled planning accompanied by specific investment incentives and benefits seems to be the most effective model of cooperation. The regional and local planners can define the required balance between the "good" of the citizens and the appropriate trend of development. Consequently, they should design not only a physical plan but also a financially sound business plan that would include incentives and benefits and specify the boundaries of development both in terms of the authentic and the contrived. Within such a framework, postmodern entrepreneurs can function and thrive while respecting the unique features of the Negev frontier.

Finally, through the combined efforts of the Israel Government Office of Regional Cooperation and its Jordanian counterparts, the same approach is currently being used in the planning of "the Spice Route." Following the footsteps of ancient caravans, their goal is to design a route with attractions and lodging facilities that combines the aforementioned postmodern elements and maintains the balance between a central plan and entrepreneurial projects.

References

Barrett, F. 1989. *The Independent Guide to Real Holidays Abroad.* London: The Independent.

Baudrillard, J. 1983. *Simulation.* New York: Semiotext.

Boorstin, D. 1964. *The Image: A Guide to Pseudo-Events in America.* New York: Harper.

Denzin, N. K. 1991. *Images of Postmodern Society: Social Theory and Contemporary Cinema.* London: Sage.

Eco, U. 1986. *Travels in Hyper-Reality.* London: Picador.

Featherston, M. 1991. *Consumer Culture and Postmodernism.* London: Sage.

Fleischer, A., and A. Pizam. 1997. Rural tourism in Israel. *Tourism Management,* 18:367–372.

Gottdiner, M. 1995. *Postmodern Semiotics: Material Culture and the Form of Postmodern Life.* Cambridge: Blackwell.

Haber, S., and M. Lerner. 2001. Small tourism ventures in peripheral areas: The impact of environmental factors on performance. In S. Krakover, and Y. Gradus eds., *Tourism in Frontier Areas,* Lanham, Maryland: Lexington Books.

Lash, S., and J. Urry. 1994. *Economies of Signs and Space.* London: Sage.

MacCannell, D. 1973. Staged authenticity: Arrangements of social space in tourist settings. *American Sociological Review,* 79:589–603.

Munt, I. 1994. The "other" postmodern tourism: Culture, travel and the new middle class. *Theory, Culture, and Society,* 11:101–123.

Poon, A. 1989. Competitive strategies for a "new tourism". In C. P. Cooper ed., *Progress in Tourism, Recreation and Hospitality Management* (Vol. 1). London: Belhaven Press.

Pretes, M. 1995. Postmodern tourism: The Santa Claus industry. *Annals of Tourism Research,* 22:1–15.

Reichel, A., O. Lowengart, and A. Milman. 2000. Rural tourism in Israel: Service quality and orientation. *Tourism Management,* 21:451–459.

Uriely, N. 1997. Theories of modern and postmodern tourism. *Annals of Tourism Research,* 24:982–984.

Urry, J. 1990. *The Tourist Gaze: Leisure and Travel in Contemporary Societies.* London: Sage.

Chapter 12

Tourism Infrastructure in Frontier Regions: An Analytical Framework of the Public, Social, and Political Context

Naomi Moreno

This chapter examines the role of professional, social, and political discourse in raising issues for public discussion and the impact of this discourse on tourism development in peripheral regions.

Theoretical Background

Such discourse will be examined against the background of its broader context, in keeping with Goffman's (1961) theory, which argues that any comprehensive institution exists within a broader context than the organization constituting its social dimensions. Accordingly, in order to understand developments in the selected research domain (the microcosm to be examined, or the development of tourism infrastructure in the city of Beer Sheva), it is necessary to take a step back, so as to examine a much broader range of issues: the political, social, and tourism systems as the macro within which the micro operates.

Conceptual Framework

In order to reflect the multidimensional nature of the examination process, the conceptual starting point is the developmental-structural approach, which emphasizes processes that are common to the development of all systems, from simple conditions to conditions of specialization, differentiation, and renewed integration. According to this approach, the political character of a given social unit is the direct product of the action of political processes, examples being intergroup conflicts or governmental decentralization. The unit's development reflects political values and ideas, becoming simultaneously a source of both inputs and outputs (Cohen, 1987).

By way of analogy, the developmental-structural approach has been adopted in order to analyze political processes as factors influencing social structure and shaping the development of new tourism products. Through a process of feedback, these products, in turn, influence the organization of sociopolitical processes so that an ongoing cycle exists involving all parts of the system. I shall refer to this entire process as "the sociopolitical construction of reality" (fig. 12.1).

As shown in figure 12.1, while the developmental-structural approach prioritizes overt sociopolitical variables as a motivating source for the entire process, it also attributes considerable importance to the other variables/

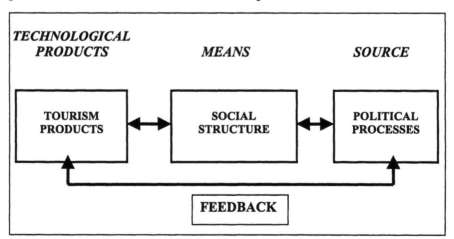

Figure 12.1. The Process of Structuring the Sociopolitical Construction of Reality Based on the Developmental-Structural Approach

spheres included in the dynamics of the realpolitik. These dynamics create the interrelationship between the variables, whose characterization and clarification in the course of this study will be based upon these interrelationships.

Thus, the realpolitik is viewed not as an autonomous reality but rather as a stage in the emergence and development of renewed political discourse, fueling changes in the field of tourism development. Accordingly, the foci of this theoretical review will include the following spheres:

1. *Political processes*—the concept of politics and the related concept of power on both the overt and covert levels, as well as their sources of legitimacy.

2. *Social structure*—the communal basis of social structure, the social rifts within this structure, and accordingly, social values and dilemmas that influence development trends.

3. *The construction of reality*—the processes of constructing the meaning of sociopolitical reality and the role of politics, the development of tourism services and products, and the role of various consumer groups in this process. This construction takes place within the context of clarification of the connection between the construction of meaning on various levels by individuals, groups, and the overall social fabric.

After presenting the theoretical background, I shall describe the situation that was examined relating to tourism development in the city of Beer Sheva, Israel. This situation was selected due to its suitability for yielding broad social meanings from the arguments made therein, as will be shown in this section and clarified in the description of the content categories and prominent themes in the process of tourism development in Beer Sheva.

Political Processes: Politics, Power, and Legitimacy

Politics and Power

A basic assumption underlying this chapter is that politics is the key to creating conditions that promote or impede changes in the overall sociopolitical fabric. Shapira (1996) argues that this assumption is particularly valid in Israel, where politics is absolute and controls important fields of social activity.

Giddens (1976) defines politics as "a mutual human activity during which collective goals, their meaning in the social order, and the means required for their achievement are determined, through an overt/covert struggle between the different interests in society." The title of Laswell's (1958) book, *Politics: Who Gets What, When and How* depicts politics as relating to the sources and dispersal of power in society as well as the mechanisms of power and collective goals.

In any society, ongoing bargaining processes take place regarding the determination of joint social goals. This bargaining is due largely to a lack of adequate resources as well as to the perception that benefits accruing to one party must necessarily come at the expense of another. This bargaining is the sociopolitical process, which incorporates the following elements:

1. A definition of the identity boundaries and chief components of a given society—the boundaries of a society determine who belongs to the collective and who does not. Boundaries both determine and are influenced by collective conscience, and they are generally the product of a bargaining process among social power brokers.

2. A definition of common goals and priorities—since it is impossible to realize all goals simultaneously, goals must be prioritized by means of the sociopolitical process.

3. Establishing the rules of the game—the norms and laws used to regulate the manner in which the boundaries of a society are established, and the means used to achieve the society's goals.

4. Determining patterns for the mobilization and allocation of resources— social order and government determine the ownership of resources and the principles guiding their distribution.

5. Establishing social organizations and institutions—formalizing the institutions and organizations responsible for realizing goals and maintaining the social order. These organizations are often subject to pressure from those who seek to change existing patterns. These demands for change may lead to the disintegration of existing institutions (Kimmerling and Koffman, 1995).

The Struggle for Legitimacy

At the center of interwoven relationships among the various interest groups in a society lies negotiation of various messages, as each group struggles to gain the legitimacy conferred by the existing sociopolitical order. This ongoing negotiation influences the character of political culture and the discourse that takes place therein. Equally, however, the negotiation is conditional on this political culture and on the modalities it uses to channel and construct information, since political participation itself is premised on the bidirectional flow of information from government to citizens and vice-versa. The struggle for legitimacy is characterized by the following:

1. *Takes place between powers and counter-powers*—since the seeds of counter-ideas lie in the sociopolitical center itself, in which hegemony develops and is applied, the struggle for legitimacy forms the actual basis for the dilemmas occurring in the center itself (Gramsci, 1978).

2. *Includes overt and covert expressions*—the overt aspect of power is expressed by the capacity of groups and individuals to shape the decision-making process, while the covert aspect relates to the delegitimization of certain political issues and the ability to remove these issues from the public agenda (Lukes, 1974; Schattschneider, 1960). Removal of issues is achieved by the manipulation of values, myths, institutions, and political processes (Bacharach and Baratz, 1963).

3. *Creates secondary power relations*—according to Blaw's (1964) exchange approach, power relations are not a given, but determine the changing bargaining positions of the parties engaged in political discourse.

Acquiring legitimacy forms a substantive part of the sociopolitical process per se, which is an object of constant struggle among opposing forces in the sociopolitical arena. In general, bargaining and power positions are based on diverse and opposing sources of legitimacy (Weber, 1968; Kimmerlink and Koffman, 1995; and Shapira, 1996).

Assumption No. 1: Based on the aforementioned conceptual background it is argued that the development of tourism entities and products in Israel forms a part of Israeli sociopolitical dynamics, which allocate resources and centralize or decentralize power by means of the sociopolitical bargaining process. This process includes a struggle for the legitimacy of power and its sources and the development of mechanisms of varying accessibility to power foci and resources.

Social Structure: Social Rifts and Dilemmas

Social Rifts

The sociopolitical process regarding the use of power and the means by which it is distributed in society varies from place to place. The internal contradictions inherent in a democracy emphasize the need to discuss either the extent to which democratic components dominate given social arrangements or the extent to which a tendency toward democratization applies in a given arrangement. Social rifts in society are an impediment to the exertion of maximum power by government regarding the distinguishing characteristics of various social groups that correspond to economic, religious, linguistic, geographical, ideological, political, and other variables.

Social rifts in general, and those typical of Israeli society in particular, help to distinguish various social currents within a society. Whether the variance between the social groups is the result of the way messages are mediated through "opinion leaders" who create the "multi-staged flow of information" (Katz and Lazarsfeld, 1956), or whether the variance is due to unequal participation in the social system (Churchman, 1988; Katan, 1980; Bernstein, 1979), sociopolitical discourse in Israel is tainted by this variance.

The Dilemmas

Sociopolitical discourse is tantamount to a competition between differing positions that aim to respond to a range of value-based dilemmas addressed by the reigning political culture. The social dilemmas and the balance between the responses to them can be examined by means of sociopolitical symbols and codes representing an entire system of meanings. The balance between these various responses creates the reigning political culture in any society at a given time (Kimmerlink and Koffman, 1995). As shown by Hazan (1988), and as outlined in the literature relating to Israel, sociopolitical discourse in Israel is based on the following central dilemmas:

1. The geographical and symbolic borders constituting the Jewish nation-state (Newman, 1985; Shavit, 1987; Kimmerlink and Koffman, 1995).
2. The modalities by which various social resources are mobilized and allocated; the various social rifts involved in the struggle over the modalities of mobilization and allocation of resources.
3. The continuity of the community in the temporal dimension, or the political determination as to who is "friend" and who is "foe" (Schmitt, 1976; Kimmerling, 1989).

Assumption No. 2: Based on these rifts and dilemmas, it is argued that the analysis of a given sociopolitical reality requires a combination of the cultural approach (which assumes that political decisions are shaped by values, norms, and symbols) and the structural approach (which assumes that political institutions and the division of power between the various social groups dictate the nature of political behavior and its dominant values).

Understanding the analytical process also constitutes the basis for locating and analyzing existing trends at any given point in time in the development of tourism infrastructure in outlying regions.

The Construction of the Meaning of Reality

In their book *The Social Construction of Reality* (1967), Berger and Luckmann emphasize that reality is not objective but is defined and constructed by people in a manner that serves the interests of a given group. The social construction of reality takes place through the development of unique terms that make up a language, which in turn reflects the values and myths of the political culture in a given society.

Each group with political interests has an interest in the construction of reality regarding both subgroups and the entire collective. Accordingly, part of the process of the construction of reality is the creation of differences in power and social boundaries while offering a subjective interpretation of the resources of various social groups. This process creates artificial definitions as to the capabilities, resources, and skills required in order to participate in the social foci of power and activity. As a result, a paucity of capabilities, resources, and skills is defined in artificial terms, and individuals, groups, and issues are thus distanced from foci of power. The question is: why do individuals and groups comply with the charged messages created by this process and cooperate with it?

An examination of this question must address the affinity between various levels and aspects of the existence of the individual, creating a subjective process experienced by and consolidating on the social structure level to form constructs of meaning. The theory of logotherapy developed by Victor Frankl (1963) emphasizes our search for a higher meaning to life, which itself becomes a web of significance and responsibility for the individual.

Antonovsky (1987) argues further that the motivation to find meaning in one's life is the main component in creating a "sense of coherence," a metaconcept he uses to relate to the individual's overall orientation and reflecting the extent to which one's existence embodies a dynamic, constant, and stable sense of the following elements:

1. An overall perception regarding the extent to which stimuli in one's external and internal world are comprehensible and predictable.

2. An ability to manage one's personal resources in coping with the challenges raised by environmental stimuli.

3. The meaningfulness of the challenges one faces in life, and the extent to which one finds purpose in investing in and committing to these challenges.

It is therefore the need for a sense of coherence that forms the foundation of one's social construction of reality.

Assumption No. 3: Accordingly, the construction of reality, political processes, and the development of tourism products are interrelated in the following ways:

1. On the macro level of the sociopolitical entity, the roots of the process of the social construction of reality lie in the symbolic systems of the sociopolitical fabric.

2. Again on the macro level, the development of tourism in Beer Sheva in particular and in the Negev in general is the product of deliberate efforts by at least two parties with vested interests: politicians, and the members of organizations and institutions involved in tourism who are participating in this process.

3. The role of the tourism industry, as a consumer and developer of tourism products, is dependent on its access to and participation in determining and shaping the manner in which various resources are allocated for such development.

Due to the dynamic nature of this participation process, the potential for promoting regional interests exists. However, there is an "equal and opposite" potential for covert and overt failure on the path to implementation.

In conclusion, professional sociopolitical discourse regarding the development of a tourism infrastructure in Beer Sheva is marked by the creation and exchange of meanings in the social context of parties to sociopolitical discourse. It is possible to unravel the discourse and decode its messages by extending the scope of analysis to include the social fabric within which the messages' meanings are created, attributing importance to the constant interaction and negotiation between this fabric's various components. In turn, this examination parallels the sociopolitical approach, which examines the aspect of power in the discourse process as well as both the external (political and social) and internal constraints—both inter- and intraorganizational within the tourism industry—within which the discourse is engaged.

Methodology

Approach

Based on the assumption that it is possible to use the micro of a given research field with "intentional" boundaries to produce broader social insights, and that interrelationships exist between the components and levels of sociopolitical discourse, the study process ranges from the analyzed micro (the development of tourism infrastructures in Beer Sheva) to the macro (social processes of innovation and development in outlying regions in Israel).

At the same time, a semiotic perspective that focuses on study of the message is introduced, arguing that decoding given messages is facilitated by extending the range of data to include the social context in which the messages are transmitted. According to the semiotic method, I shall characterize the format and verbal statements constituting discourse regarding the issue of tourism development in Beer Sheva according to the following thematic questions:

A. With respect to format, what characteristics of the tourism picture in the Beer Sheva vicinity are expressed?

B. With respect to the semantic components, what are the verbal and conceptual forms of expression reflected in the public discourse on tourism? The encoding and analysis of the various semantic categories will illustrate the dilemmas that underlie development in outlying regions.

C. The construction of reality is a metaquestion relating to the dynamics between the various interested parties, who construct a sociopolitical reality around the development of the tourism industry in the field examined.

The answers to the above questions will allow an examination of the components of the reality construction process and of the political culture within whose constraints tourism development trends in Beer Sheva in particular, and in the Negev in general, are either enabled or impeded.

Research Method

Because the process of reality construction is both multifaceted and long-term in nature, this study does not claim to determine causal relationships between the variables. Employing theoretical and empirical evidence, I assume the existence of mutual relationships but do not empirically examine their existence. Rather, I examine the manner in which these relationships are expressed in public discourse on tourism development in Beer Sheva.

The data in this study are based on a variety of documents, such as minutes of meetings and conferences, position papers, publications, and work plans available to the author in her official capacity as tourism and information director for the city of Beer Sheva.

The data collection technique made use of broad analytical categories enabling the collection of a range of responses. This broad-based approach encompassed not only verbal statements regarding the characteristics of Beer Sheva's tourism situation but also the dynamic quality of the interaction between the discourse participants, capturing its unique phraseology and subjective orientation.

Table 12.1. Where the Negev Begins: Locating the "Gateway" to the Negev

Location	Percent of Respondents
Dead Sea	2%
Dimona	2%
Ashkelon	2%
Kiryat Gat	3%
Beit Kama	3%
Beer-Sheva	66%

Source: Municipality of Beer Sheva, Israel. 1997. Tourism potential of the Negev. Survey conducted by the Mutagim Company.

However, the benefits of this method also define its inherent limitations. An initial examination of the sociopolitical aspect of tourism development in Beer Sheva exposes the need for additional structured studies based on the thematic categories of its findings.

Findings

Background Data: Tourism Trends

During certain periods, Beer Sheva played an important role in the history of Israel, as it is one of the few ancient cities in Israel that remain from the period of Ottoman rule, as reflected in its unique planning and in the architecture of its Old City. Beer Sheva's history dates back to biblical times when Abraham, the father of monotheism, and his son Isaac lived in the area and forged peace treaties with the peoples of the region.

Beer Sheva is located in the center of the Negev, at the junction leading south to Eilat. It lies in convenient proximity to the Negev mountains, the Ramon crater, and other tourism routes and attractions in the Negev region (see table 12.1).

In a survey examining common perceptions regarding the point where the Negev begins, 66 percent of the respondents perceived Beer Sheva as the "Gateway to the Negev." It seems that the potential inherent in this perception of Beer Sheva has not been fully exploited. In addition, Beer Sheva is only ninety minutes by car from Jerusalem and could potentially serve as the base for exploring biblical routes running across the entire region.

Planned Local Impact of Tourism

Tourism could have a positive long-term impact on Beer Sheva's image as well as potentially contribute to the local economy by realizing investments on various levels of initiatives and stimulating the development of cultural offerings in the city for residents as well as visitors.

Unfortunately, this positive perception of Beer Sheva's potential is not reflected in practice, due to the lack of locally attractive sites that would encourage visitors to plan stays of a significant length. However, at the time of the writing of this study, efforts to realize this potential may be turning a corner, as the following examples testify:

1. The drafting of an urban outline plan positioning Beer Sheva as Israel's "fourth metropolis." Development of the tourism industry is included in the plan, with an emphasis on the southern entrance to the city as a venue for tourism development.

2. Plans to renovate and rehabilitate the Beer Sheva Wadi and surrounding area, transforming it from an ecological hazard to a park and a promenade.

3. An attempt to renovate and develop historical sites in Beer Sheva's Old City, where a visitors' center has already been established

4. Developing tours and unique tourism packages designed for specific target populations (at present, mainly groups) and staging tourism-oriented events

5. Accelerated development of urban amenities such as quality shopping, which improve Beer Sheva both as a tourist and an urban base

6. Establishing a special unit in city hall responsible for both tourism development and for regional tourism coordination, with an eye toward development of an overall region-wide marketing plan.

Tourism planners and practitioners in the region assume that efficient exploitation of tourism potential—particularly emphasizing Beer Sheva's marketability and its positioning as a tourism product—will create added value in economic, image, and cultural terms, in turn improving a product promoting the Negev in particular and Israel in general in both the domestic and global tourism market.

Thematic Categories

The starting point for examining tourism development in the Beer Sheva region is the diverse range of attitudes toward the region and the interaction among them. Following are the identified thematic categories relating to the southern tourism situation and the broader context in which it operates, with their various subissues and the attitudes toward them:

Tourism Prominence

The tourism industry is usually accorded a secondary status in public discourse, both on the national level—where security-related issues are central—and on the local level. This low position on the agenda is reflected both by the absence of tourism from the agendas of most local politicians and the meager resources allocated to it on the municipal and local levels. The disparate attitudes of special interest groups, as well as failed efforts and appeals to advance the industry, are further evidence of tourism's low priority. The secondary status of tourism is further reflected in the fact that it is usually paired with other issues perceived as more central, such as:

1. *The peace process*—usually in the context of open borders and tours/packages including the entire region
2. *Un/employment in the Negev*—in the context of the proposed development of a casino in the Negev
3. *Transportation*—the Beer Sheva railway, a regional airport, and other proposed projects

There is, however, a perceptible rise in the prominence of the tourism issue, which may partly be attributed to regional efforts to promote tourism, including the establishment of new tourism associations and services in the region, such as Ben-Gurion University's Department of Tourism and Hotel Management, the first five-star hotel in the region, and plans and preliminary activities for tourism projects created through public investment, all of which have generated renewed interest on the part of tourism promoters.

What Issues Are Raised?

1. *Tourism development as a component in the overall promotion of the Negev*—As an alternative to Israel's overcrowded center in order to efficiently utilize Israel's land resources. This was David Ben-Gurion's vision, Israel's first prime minister, who settled in the region toward the end of his life and encouraged his fellow citizens to "go south" in order to create a fair balance in Israel's investment in the various parts of the country.
2. *Beer Sheva as the "Gateway to the Negev"*—The advantage of regional organization as opposed to separate activity engaged in by the individual local governments in the region is an issue that is continually raised.
3. *"Tourism 2000"*—Current timing has led to a reexamination of the millennium angle on both national and local levels. In general, the new millennium is regarded as a window of opportunity for a tourism breakthrough.

4. *Tourism and peace*—Tourism as an industry is dependent on the appropriate political and security atmosphere, which can generate economic growth as well.

5. *Welcoming tourists*—A recurrent theme is that of Israel falling short as a "quality tourism destination," with perennial complaints of lack of cleanliness in public places and even at classic tourist sites. Education toward tourism among the general public and for those working with tourists in particular is viewed as an area where improvement is needed.

6. *The "social gap"*—The social rift in Israel is often mentioned in the context of the general neglect of Beer Sheva and the Negev under governments headed by both main parties.

7. *The ethnic rift*—This is cited regarding relations between Jews and Bedouins in the region, as well as regarding the region's multiethnic character, as a potential selling point for tourism products. The ethnic issue is also mentioned in terms of its historical context, in that Beer Sheva is presented as the "City of Abraham" belonging to all faiths, and the city of he who made peace treaties with the inhabitants of the region (referring to the biblical story of Avimelech and Abraham). Thus, Beer Sheva is cast as a city of peace and reconciliation and as a relatively safer place than some other areas in Israel.

8. *The rift between the center of Israel and the periphery*—This is raised repeatedly in the context of allocation of resources, enforcement of the Capital Investments Encouragement Law, and incentives to encourage business initiatives in the region.

9. *Social dilemmas*—These are mentioned mainly in the context of allocation of resources and the demand that large government allocations be made to the region, emphasizing its social and historical importance as well as its place within the Zionist ethos. Tourism, a business that by definition is based on open physical and cultural borders, is mentioned in both positive and negative contexts from the standpoint of maintaining the region's unique identity as well as its cultural and religious norms.

The Tourism Situation

1. *The positioning of the region*—While the actual borders of the Beer Sheva region as a tourism product remain elusive, a clear picture does emerge regarding the overall effort to reinforce Beer Sheva's centrality as a tourism base for the region as a whole.

2. *Establishing rules*—The rules and forums for tourism development in Israel are in a state of flux. The Tourism Development Administration,

a department of the tourism ministry that had been active in the region and then closed in the summer of 1999, changed the rules of the game and the relations between the players. Representatives of the region's tourism industry wish to work directly with the tourism ministry and the resources that it offers, but the tourism ministry conditions this arrangement on regional reorganization. Other public bodies, agencies, and publicly owned companies also seek to concentrate resources.

3. *The consumers*—An examination of attitudes prevalent among travel agents, tourism promoters, and end consumers is perceived as crucial to influencing the tourism situation. Resources have been and are being invested in surveys and plans based on the surveys' findings. The entity known as the "consumer public" is perceived to be one of the key mechanisms in the process.

4. *Defining the situation*—Israel's unpredictable conditions have been cited as posing an objective and subjective threat to the entire tourism industry, while the general economic inferiority of the south of Israel is perceived as creating hypersensitivity to economic fluctuations.

5. *Coping resources*—Mention is made of the physical amenities lacking in the region and the need to develop a "regional product." The following are perceived as necessary resources for industry players:
   (a) Experience in the industry
   (b) Professionalism
   (c) Networking with foci of power and state resources
   (d) Authenticity
   (e) Knowledge of the area on the part of regional representatives, as opposed to operating according to the decisions of national agencies or using professionals from outside the region

The Players

6. *Public tourism entities in the region*—Each interest group attempts to gain the relative advantage, though there is a prominent trend toward uniting interests on the regional level. This process is naturally dynamic and affected by external changes. In addition, each entity competes for prominence on the regional level, with the goal of channeling resources to its organization and to improving its status in the region as a whole.

7. *National tourism entities*—They are responsible for allocating state resources and for reinforcing the publicly perceived legitimacy of Beer

Sheva as a regional leader of development in general. In most cases, these entities also determine the opening parameters for the game as well as its rules.

8. *Local and national politicians*—Although the tourism industry is not perceived as prestigious relative to other issues, the habitual linking of tourism to other issues encourages undue political and administrative manipulation.

9. *Professionals in other areas vie with tourism for various resources*—This includes budgets, the prominence of their issues on the public agenda, legitimacy and priorities in promoting local projects, and personal and professional prominence.

10. *Local tourism businesses*—This includes all businesses that potentially profit from tourism, such as restaurants, transportation services, retail outlets, and so forth.

11. *Promoters, industry professionals, and tourism consultants*—All of these players have an interest in influencing and securing their piece of the pie, including developing expertise in a new tourism niche and/or gaining professional or economic prominence.

12. *Tourism consumers*—These include the individual consumer, decision-makers in the industry, travel agents, and tour guides.

13. *Local residents*—Residents naturally constitute the sociocultural milieu within which the tourism product operates. Residents traditionally oppose the tourism product due to their priorities or cultural sensitivities.

14. *The media*—Local, national, and international media are important by virtue of their ability to place the region and its issues on the public agenda. Media coverage includes manner of presentation, the prominence and frequency with which reporting occurs, and the "spin" put on the various issues.

15. *Historical figures*—Abraham and other biblical figures are used to emphasize the unique history of the region; Ben-Gurion and others are used to bring to life the recent history of the region.

All of the above-named players may act to promote or to impede Beer Sheva's tourism product, according to their motivating interests.

The Dynamics of Power: Interaction between the Players

The instrumentalist aspects: The players generally responded to questions regarding tourism in essentially instrumentalist terms: "to promote projects," "to recruit resources," and so forth. The common denominator of the public discourse studied shows that the participants draw on one or more types of instrumentalist power arguments, including:

(a) Legitimizing that entity's power.

(b) Using increased power as a response to loss of control.

(c) Achieving power by reducing the power of another player.

(d) Linking interests or impairing existing couplings of interests in order to achieve a common instrumentalist goal.

The Legitimization of Power

The legitimization of one's own power, or challenging the legitimacy of another player, draws on the following types of legitimacy:

1. affiliative basis, wherein the spokesperson or organization is part of an existing and familiar tourism tradition or institution;

2. public support, including support from the various players' systems (power as derived from a democratic source—public opinion, majority opinion, and so forth);

3. capabilities and professional skills;

4. authenticity or direct representation of the region;

5. connections to and affinity with foci of power and decision makers;

6. access to use of existing and promised resources.

Regulation and/or Acceleration of Conflicts

In this respect, methods mentioned repeatedly included the following:

1. *Regional organization*—This creates regional coalitions or seeks to dismantle existing alliances in the industry.

2. *Competitiveness*—This was described as one or more players competing for prominence within a single tourism niche. Competition was also reflected in the media and in the presentation of similar brands by various individuals or organizations, all of whom present themselves as the brand's progenitor.

3. *Coopting of tourism*—This is defined as a redistribution of resources and attention to the player network in order to exert control over tourism products and human resources region wide.

In conclusion, the four thematic categories dealt with here are: the issues raised, the situation and its characteristics, the players network, and the dynamics of power involved in the interactions between them.

The next section will attempt to cast light on the relationship between these four categories, analyze them, and use them to respond to the meta-issue addressed in this study: the process of the construction of a sociopolitical reality, and the manner in which this impacts on the development of new tourism products.

Discussion

Discussion of the findings requires the conversion of the identified thematic categories into a social review, the scope of which extends beyond these concrete data. The data emphasize the democratic aspect of tourism in terms of discourse regarding the development of tourism infrastructures and products in Beer Sheva in particular and in the Negev in general. However, as Kimmerling and Koffman (1995) argue, democracy is not only institutions, elections, and protected liberties, it is also the democratic way of life.

Democracy is, among other things, a social agreement to resolve differences by peaceful means. It entails a willingness to accept gradual change without violent rebellion in accordance with the accepted rules of the game. Nonviolent democratic approaches are rooted in the recognition of the right of differing opinions and opposing parties to coexist as well as in an emotional and intellectual willingness to lose and to accept a situation where the rival perception and/or party gains the upper hand.

This willingness is also reflected in free debate based on the agreement that disagreements are permitted and proper. According to Shamir and Sullivan (1985), opposition is an essential foundation for political tolerance, since without opposition to a group or idea, it is impossible to speak of either tolerance or intolerance but only of apathy.

However, as this study shows, the conceptual world and arguments revealed in the analyzed discourse are replete with terms drawn from the thematic world of struggle. As is the case with any struggle, this sociopolitical struggle also revolves around existing and needed resources. However, in the process of examining the issue of the construction of a reality, an additional variable emerges: the dynamics of power.

The dynamics of power inherent in conflicts and overt struggles over tourism are reflected in the issues involved, in the tourism situation, and in the mutual relations between the players. Figure 12.2 summarizes the categories of the findings, presenting the component of conflict on both the micro level of the analyzed situation and on the overall macro (social) level.

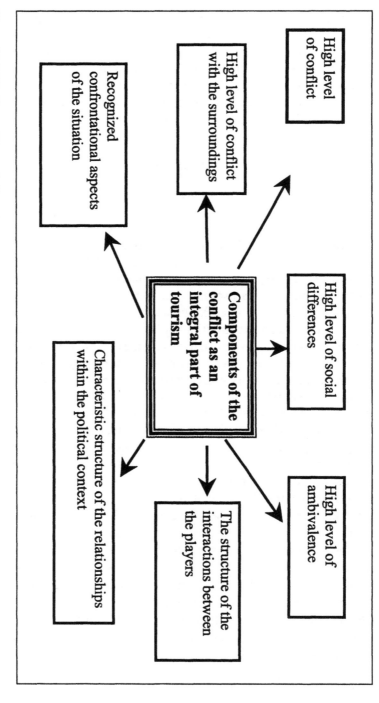

Figure 12.2. The Power Dynamic Structure

In total, seven variables were identified in the dynamics of tourism-related conflicts, presenting the conflict component as an integral part both of media presentation and the broader sociopolitical context:

1. A high level of social variance
2. A high level of conflict
3. A high level of external/security conflict
4. A high level of ambivalence
5. Patterns of political interpersonal relations
6. The presence of normative violent behavior
7. Patterns of interaction between the players

The above-mentioned seven variables are expressed at the mere mention of the subject of tourism development and the related issues that arise in the course of discussion, and/or in perceptions and definitions of the tourism situation, and/or in interaction between the players, both present and absent.

The conflict component on the micro level stems from the basic fact that the tourism situation constitutes a competition for resources. The resources in turn relate to the abilities of the various players to compete while playing by the rules and to influence the formulation of these rules. The success of each player is measured neither by position nor by behavior but rather by degree of control regarding the setting of the public agenda and the channeling of public resources in favor of that player's interests.

Accordingly, the competition between the players may be defined as a struggle for control and acquisition of power. Examples of this struggle may be seen in the types of arguments raised by the players as well as in common modalities for regulating and/or accelerating conflicts.

In the same way, the conceptual mindset of center/periphery enables an examination of the political struggle for social priorities as reflected in the position of the Negev in general and the status of the tourism industry in particular. The struggle breaks down into the agenda of the tourism industry nationally and the limits on the Negev's proportional power in the industry over time.

The tourism situation, as described in the section on thematic categories, would seem to define some of the rules of the game and norms according to which the sociopolitical process occurs. Tourism also defines the functions of the players and the functional and normative behavior expected of them within this structure, which they may either choose to reinforce or attempt to change.

The macrolevel conflict is presented in the context of Israel's constant state of struggle, wherein its considerable security restraints make it prone to pressure. Emphasis on the social context also presents Israel as a collective subject to cultural, religious, historical, economic, developmental, and other pressures, forced to cope with unique dilemmas relating to its borders—both geographical and symbolic—and the delicate relationships that it must maintain. The vulnerability of the entire system to conflict lies in its intense and highly charged nature, in the historical resentments between various groups, and in its cultural diversity (as reflected in the fact that Israel is an immigrant society), as well as in the rapid changes that Israel has undergone since its establishment.

It should be noted that the importance attached to issues on Israel's overall agenda influence both the level of prominence of the tourism industry and the issues raised within the discourse on the development of this industry.

What are the characteristics of Israeli political culture as reflected in the findings? In Shapira's terms (1996), the findings reflect the development of the components of civilian culture in Israel, as distinct from the political and ideological culture that formerly characterized Israel. The dynamics of power described above present a range of players, principles, and issues; the arguments for the legitimacy of power draw on a diverse range of types of legitimacy, including legitimacy on an affiliative basis, according to capabilities and skills, authentic representation of a region, connections, existing resources, and so forth.

In concluding this section, I shall present the connection between all of the key variables of this study in light of the various findings reflected therein. Numerous mentions of the conflict and struggle component have led me to search for a social model that could be used to summarize the web of variables connected to the tourism situation. The perception that conflict and struggle may be explained by pressure—expressed both regarding tourism and the social fabric in general—led to an analysis of the conflict/struggle component as pressure situations. Figure 12.3 illustrates the key components in the process of the construction of a reality, drawing on the classic conceptual structure proposed by Hill (1949) for analyzing pressure situations.

It appears that the principal categories of the research findings may be presented using an adaptation of the study's concepts to those of Hill's (1949) ABC-X Model. The ABC-X Model has served since its inception as the accepted conceptual structure for analyzing pressure situations (McKenry and Price, 1994). Hill, as well as others, defines pressure situations as being characterized by the following components:

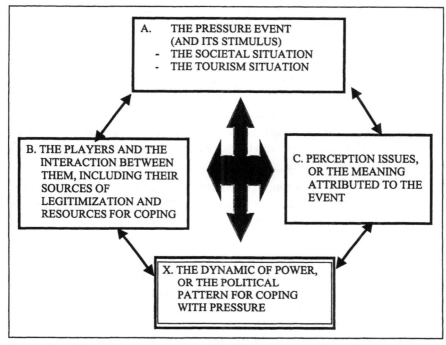

Figure 12.3. The Process of a Sociopolitical Construction of Reality in Israel

A = *The pressure event*—an event creating an objective and/or subjective threat and the need for its removal

B = *The resources available to cope with the pressure event,* including the qualities and capabilities of individuals and the social groups to which they belong (in this context, political, economic, and professional entities in the tourism industry) and of the broader social fabric within which they operate (both people and institutions).

C = *The perception of the event,* or the meaning attributed to the event by those involved. This is significant, since people respond to *their perception* of events, which may not necessarily be the objective facts of the situation.

X = *The level of pressure experienced*—A pressure event becomes problematic when the pressure reaches a level that impairs the ability of the players to function effectively.

Figure 12.3 shows the process of the sociopolitical construction of reality in terms of this conceptual structure, as follows:

A. *The pressure event,* defined in figure 12.3 according to the terms specified in the data categories as the tourism situation, both regarding the situation and its constraints, as well as the existential situation of Israel and its stimuli.

B. *The resources available for coping with the event,* defined in figure 12.3 according to the terms specified in the data categories as the interrelationships of the players and the interaction between them, including the characteristics and capabilities of the parties involved in the conflicts, of the social groups to which they belong, and of the broader sociopolitical fabric of Israel.

C. *The perception of the event,* defined in figure 12.3 according to the terms specified in the data categories as "perception issues," or the meaning attributed to the various aspects of the situation as reflected in Israeli society and the various dilemmas that characterize it

X. *The level of ancillary pressure,* defined in figure 12.3 according to the terms specified in the data categories as "the dynamic of power," or the power relations between the players both as parties to conflict and as politicians, as well as power relations in the broader social context. Power relations are effectively a political pattern for coping with pressure. This coping pattern describes the outline of Israeli political culture, which both influences and is influenced by the process of the construction of a reality.

To summarize, the situation, the network of players and the interactions between them, the issues raised, and the dynamics of power are the four categories of the research findings, as outlined above. The arrows depicted in figure 12.3 symbolize a circular process that does not grant preference to any one variable but rather is composed of the interactions between them.

Conclusions and Recommendations

The findings of the study confirm the basic assumption that the development process of tourism organizations and products in Israel actually constitutes (in part) the sociopolitical dynamics of the country. It is this dynamic that allocates opportunities and distributes and/or concentrates power through the process of sociopolitical bargaining, including the struggle over legitimacy and sources of power as well as the development of differential and varying access mechanisms to power foci and their resources.

In addition, the research findings confirm the assumption that alongside the structural distribution of power in society, decisions are fashioned by way of a cultural discourse based on values, norms, and symbols characteristic of the society and its various rifts (see the detailed discussion of the thematic categories and the arguments). In addition, the centrality of the parties engaging in tourism discourse, and the interaction between them, was confirmed.

The application of innovations and opportunities for development must be filtered through social conditions, along with the various players that take part in the filtering. Considering this "filtering requirement," in order to create systemic balance in tourism development in outlying regions in general and in Beer Sheva in particular, it is proposed that the four following guiding principles be adopted:

1. *The Integrated Tools Principle:* Tourism has ramifications for the quality of life in the host city, which in turn influences the host city's ability to develop tourism. Accordingly, the Integrated Tools Principle emphasizes the creation of an affinity between tourism and local cultural development.

    The tourism industry potentially offers employment opportunities, the realization of high-investment initiatives, contributions to the local economy, improvement in the local quality of life, and expansion of cultural options for the host city's residents. Accordingly, the realization of this potential requires a joint effort with the local population to maintain development, nurture the host city's appearance, and welcome tourists, all of which have significant impact on the host city's image.

2. *The Self-Evidence Principles:* The following two principles are self-evident—the requirements of the local population and the tourists, on the one hand, and the image and marketing of the city/region, on the other. First, the population of the host city and its surrounding region should be considered the economic backdrop for commercial tourism initiatives. Accordingly, investments should be channeled to cultural and tourism projects that meet the needs of the local population while at the same time meeting the needs of both domestic and foreign visitors.

    Second, creating a distinct brand entails presenting Beer Sheva as both the "City of the Patriarchs" and as the "City of Tomorrow" in the heart of the desert, the perfect urban jumping-off point for exploring the entire Negev.

3. *The Traveling Wagon Principle:* The Traveling Wagon Principle requires the cooperation of tourism and commercial and cultural interests, creating synergy and positive interactions between the various foci and recruiting them to new activities.

4. *The Comprehensive Planning Principle:* The Comprehensive Planning Principle forges connections between various development plans from

the strategic to the operational level in addition to coordinating physical development plans with marketing themes and networks.

These four principles complement one another, jointly forming the basis of the recommended policy for tourism development in Beer Sheva in particular, and with modification, in outlying areas in general.

References

Antonovsky, A. 1987. *Unraveling the Mystery of Health: How People Manage Stress and Stay Well.* San Francisco: Josses-Bass Publishers.

Bacharach, P., and S. M. Baratz. 1963. Decision and nondecision: An analytical framework. *American Political Science Review,* 56:623–642.

Berger, P., and T. Luckmann. 1967. *The Social Construction of Reality.* New York: Anchor Books.

Bernstein, D. 1979. The Black Panthers: Conflict and protest in Israeli society. *Megamot,* 25:65–80. (Hebrew)

Blaw, P. M. 1964. *Exchange and Power in Social Life.* New York: John Wiley and Sons.

Churchman, A. 1988. Involving residents in project renewal: Goals and achievements. *Megamot,* 31:342–362. (Hebrew)

Cohen, S. B. 1987. Structural-developmental approach in the study of the political landscape of rural communities in Israel. In S. B. Cohen, A. Shmueli, and N. Kliot eds., *City and Region,* 17:32–61. (Hebrew)

Frankl, V. E. 1963. *Man's Search for Meaning.* New York: Washington Square Press.

Giddens, A. 1976. *New Rules of Sociological Method: A Positive Critique of Interpretative Sociology.* London: Hutchinson.

Goffman, E. 1961. *Asylums.* New York: Doubleday.

Gramsci, A. 1978. *Selections from the Prison Notebooks.* Edited and translated by Q. Hoare and G. Nowell-Smith. London: Lawrence and Wishart.

Hazan, H. 1988. The renewal neighborhood as a community: An anthropological analysis from the perspective of the social world. *Megamot,* 31:286–298. (Hebrew)

Hill, R. 1949. *Families Under Stress.* New York: Harper and Row.

Katan, Y. 1980. The practical involvement of clients, methods in community work. Jerusalem: Ministry of Labor and Social Affairs, Community Work Service report. (Hebrew).

Katz, E., and P. F. Lazasfeld. 1956. *Personal Influence.* New York: Free Press.

Kimmerling, B. 1989. Boundaries and frontiers of the Israeli control systems. In B. Kimmerling ed., *The Israeli State and Society.* Albany: SUNY Press.

Kimmerling, B., and E. Koffman. 1995. State and Society: *The Sociology of Politics,* Units 1–3. Tel Aviv: Open University. (Hebrew)

Laswell, H. D. 1958. *Who Gets What, When, How?* New York: Meridian Books.

Lukes, S. 1974. *Power: A Radical View.* London: Macmillan.

McKenry P. C., and S. J. Price, eds. 1994. *Families and Change: Coping with Stressful Events.* Thousand Oaks, CA: Sage Publications.

Newman, D., ed. 1985. *The Impact of Gush Emunim: Politics and Settlement in the West Bank.* London: Croom Helm.

Schattschneider, E. E. 1960. *The Semi-Sovereign People.* New York: Holt, Reinhart, and Winston.

Schmitt, C. 1976. *The Concept of the Political.* Piscataway, NJ: Rutgers University Press.

Shamir, M., and J. L. Sullivan. 1985. Jews and Arabs in Israel: Everybody hates somebody, sometimes. *Journal of Conflict Resolution,* 29:283–305.

Shapira, Y. 1996. *Society Imprisoned by Politicians.* Tel Aviv: Sifriyat Hapoalim. (Hebrew)

Shavit, Y., ed. 1987. *The Canaanite Group: Literature and Ideology.* Tel Aviv: Open University. (Hebrew)

Weber, M. 1968. The theory of social and economic organization. In G. Roth, and C. Wittich eds., *Economics and Society.* New York: Bedminster Press.

Part 5

Tourism Frontiers in Borderlands

Chapter 13

Tourism in Borderlands: Competition, Complementarity, and Cross-Frontier Cooperation

Dallen J. Timothy

Since many of today's tourists require pristine environments and off-the-beaten-path destinations, much of the growth of tourism has occurred in the peripheral and isolated parts of the world. This fact was examined early on by Christaller (1963:95), who recognized that in the context of Europe, tourism "avoids central places and the agglomerations of industry" and that "tourism is drawn to the periphery of settlement districts as it searches for a position on the highest mountain, in the most lonely woods, along the remotest beaches." Christaller argued that most economic forces are drawn toward population centers, while with tourism, the opposite is true—there is a propensity to develop toward the periphery, "away from the familiar scene toward distant places" (von Böventer, 1969:118).

In a national or regional sense, the periphery generally comprises areas of physical isolation or the territory immediately adjacent to international boundaries. Peripheries are often isolated and inaccessible—physically inaccessible owing to harsh climates and rough topography and less accessible to markets because of distance from population centers and the resultant high cost of travel. Wanhill (1997:48) identified several properties of peripheral regions that are particularly influential in the context of tourism. These include: (1) distance from the core and high cost of access; (2) limited local economic control; (3) low GDP per capita; (4) sparse populations in small, isolated towns and villages; and (5) an economic structure that is based largely on primary and tertiary industries with little secondary production. Additionally, peripheral areas are commonly characterized by some degree of neglect by national governments and core-area residents. Many of these conditions constitute a significant attraction base for tourists and give some destinations their appeal. More often, though, they are deterrents to the growth and development of tourism.

With exceptions such as Canada, border regions demonstrate most of the characteristics described above because they are on the national periphery. However, they also demonstrate features that are unique to boundary zones. First, borders affect the nature of human behavior on both sides. They often act as barriers to human interaction so that in some cases, border residents' action space may be skewed only to one side. However, where boundaries represent less of an obstacle, local economies and societies are often more closely linked to adjacent areas across a border than they are to the interior of their own countries. Second, two sets of administrative structures and policies come together at international frontiers, a situation which can create conditions of incompatibility and misunderstanding. Third, borders often mark differences in economic systems and levels of development, which can mean that residents on one side have a much higher standard of living than their neighbors. Fourth, sovereignty is jealously guarded by individual nations and border formalities are established to limit or monitor the flow of people and goods into and out of the country. Finally, border fortifications can disrupt the holistic functioning of ecosystems and constitute a major eyesore in the human landscape.

While most borderland characteristics described above are viewed as challenges by administrators and residents on a daily basis, many are also opportunities. For example, the barrier effects and differences in administrative structures and levels of development can produce contrasts that appeal to tourists. As Leimgruber (1989) and Ryden (1993) suggest, it is for many people the feeling of going beyond their familiar environment to visit a place that is culturally, politically, and economically different that motivates them to cross borders. Examples also exist where methods of boundary demarcation are themselves significant tourist attractions, such as the Berlin Wall (before and after its collapse in 1989) and the Peace Arch between Canada and the United States. Additionally, different economic and political systems create situations where traveling to neighboring countries is cost-effective for activities such as shopping and sightseeing. All of these opportunities can grow if the border is sufficiently permeable to allow the free flow of people and goods between neighboring countries.

The purpose of this chapter is to review the primary types of tourism in border regions. It also examines how changing geopolitical conditions are beginning to allow partnerships in tourism development and planning across political boundaries, which results in a decrease in competition between sides and increases complementary relations.

Tourism in Border Regions

Although in many instances the boundary itself acts as a tourist attraction, most borderland tourism occurs beyond the actual boundary line in regions adjacent to the frontier, where the economic and social life is directly affected by proximity to a border (Hansen, 1983; Timothy, 2001). When political conditions are right, the existence of an international boundary in a region creates an economic and sociocultural environment that is conducive to the development of certain types of tourism, including shopping, vices (e.g., prostitution, gambling, and drinking), exclaves, and international parks. Some of these activities/attractions are complementary in that both sides benefit in some way from their existence and can work together to develop and manage a joint tourism industry. Others, however, create a competitive environment in the borderlands where one side benefits much more than the other and little can be done to cooperate in developing tourism. The following sections describe the main types of tourism that exist in border regions, after which complementarity, competition, and cooperation are examined.

Cross-Border Shopping

One of the most common forms of borderlands tourism is cross-border shopping. This activity, known in the traditional marketing literature as out-shopping, refers to people who live in one political jurisdiction traveling to neighboring regions to shop. Leimgruber (1988) argued that certain conditions must exist before cross-frontier shopping can develop. First, there must be enough contrast between the home environment and that on the other side to attract people across the border. Differences in price, product quality, and selection are the most common contrasts. Second, there must be an awareness of what lies on the other side. Residents of one country must have sufficient information about the products for sale beyond the border, usually by means of personal visits, friends and relatives who have visited before, and advertising. Third, potential consumers must be able and willing to make the trip, particularly in terms of exchange rates and personal mobility. Finally, the border has to be open enough to allow the flow of people across it.

Transfrontier shopping has probably existed as long as political boundaries have existed and is a common phenomenon throughout the world. Where borders have historically been relatively easy to cross, this activity has occurred for many years, and many communities in the borderlands of North America and Western Europe have become highly dependent on spending by their cross-border neighbors. In regions where borders were once difficult or in some cases nearly impossible to cross (e.g., much of Eastern Europe), this form of international travel is booming. Most research attention has been devoted to its existence in North America (Asgary et al., 1997; Di Matteo and Di Matteo, 1996; Timothy, 1999b; Timothy and Butler, 1995) and Europe (Leimgruber, 1988; Minghi, 1999; Weigand, 1990), although it is prominent in Asia, South America, and Africa as well (Mikus, 1994; Ngamsom, 1998).

Several push and pull factors have been identified that contribute to the growth of cross-border shopping. Typically, favorable exchange rates appear to be the most influential factor (Asgary et al., 1997; Patrick and Renforth, 1996; Timothy, 1999b), although lower sales taxes, wider selections of products, lower prices owing to more efficient distribution systems, and better customer service are viewed as major motivators as well. Media coverage and advertising (Lewis, 1990), per capita incomes, seasonal determinants, and gasoline prices also influence people's decisions to cross the boundary to shop (Di Matteo, 1999; Di Matteo and Di Matteo, 1996).

While some of the reasons associated with transfrontier shopping are economics-based, it is also clear that many people are motivated in large part by pleasure and enjoyment, and many participate in other tourism and recreational activities while abroad, such as watching a movie, dining in a restaurant, staying in hotels, and visiting historic sites and museums (Timothy and Butler, 1995). One study found that between one-third and one-half of the cross-border consumers surveyed were motivated by pleasure

(Ritchie, 1993), and another study by the Canadian Chamber of Commerce (1992) shows that one of the primary reasons Canadians shopped in the United States was that it allowed them to escape from their home environment and experience something new.

By way of example, until the late 1980s, cross-border shopping in the U.S.-Canada borderlands was a fairly consistent activity in both directions, although most traffic was composed of Canadians shopping in the United States. In 1987, the number of Canadian shopping trips began to soar (31 million), finally reaching its zenith in 1991 (nearly 60 million) (see table 13.1). Most of the push and pull factors described above were present in the Canadian situation, and the increased value of the Canadian dollar was believed to be the primary cause of this extraordinary growth (Di Matteo and Di Matteo, 1996). This phenomenon became so worrisome to Canadian officials that they initiated anti–cross-border shopping campaigns to try to keep their citizens at home. They also made special efforts to devalue the Canadian dollar and tighten border controls by enforcing tax laws more strictly against returning residents. Canadian spending in the United States was estimated during this period to have caused the loss of millions of dollars in tax revenue, thousands of Canadian jobs, and billions of dollars in lost sales (Timothy, 1999b). American border towns, on the other hand, were thriving.

Table 13.1. Cross-Border Shopping in the U.S.-Canada Borderlands

Year	Canadians to the United States	Americans to Canada
1985	25,247,446	20,522,103
1986	25,894,260	22,555,457
1987	30,977,958	22,278,161
1988	36,184,815	21,465,298
1989	43,299,657	20,795,542
1990	51,829,338	20,691,693
1991	59,074,151	19,808,659
1992	56,985,648	19,019,020
1993	48,312,821	19,012,837
1994	38,223,022	20,667,063
1995	36,413,934	22,745,610
1996	36,267,422	23,803,557
1997	34,757,520	25,252,250

Source: Statistics Canada, 1986–1998.

In 1992, as the Canadian currency began to decline in value against the U.S. dollar, numbers of Canadian shopping trips fell dramatically. For American communities, this became a major turning point—Americans began shopping in Canada (see table 13.1). Since 1992, Canadian border towns have seen a rapid rise in American consumerism, and it is now common for Americans to cross for items such as appliances, food, CDs, and clothes. As of 1999, the tide has turned, as American businesses are closing their doors and Canadian communities are flourishing.

This is only one example of the importance of shopping as a form of tourism in border regions. Along the southern U.S. border, it is estimated that in 1995, Mexican consumers spent around USD $20–22 billion in the United States and supported more than one million American jobs (Timothy, 1999b). Millions of tourists from the United States also visit Mexican border towns every year, spending millions of dollars primarily on souvenirs and medical services (Arreola and Madsen, 1999; Patrick and Renforth, 1996).

Tourism of Vice

Vices, such as prostitution, underage and excessive drinking, and gambling, are commonly located in borderlands, because they thrive on foreign patronage when they are located near an international boundary adjacent to countries where they are not permitted. This is largely owing to the fact that when people travel from their home environments, they are escaping the "puritanical bonds of normal living, anonymity is assured away from home, and money is available to spend hedonistically" (Mathieson and Wall, 1982:149).

Like shopping, gambling, which is viewed by many community groups as negative, often develops at border crossings when one jurisdiction that allows activities of this nature meets another where they are prohibited. The convergence of two systems provides opportunities for communities within the gaming country to attract large numbers of people from nearby areas by establishing casinos and other gaming halls just inside their boundaries. The importance of this phenomenon on an international level is remarkable. Countless examples exist of one nation attracting people from adjacent countries to participate in gaming activities. For years, Monaco has attracted tourists from France and other European countries. Like Monaco, Macau's economy has also been dependent on Hong Kong gamblers who have regularly visited the Portuguese colony to play at its casinos and betting establishments. This provides an important venue for day trippers from a crowded city where casinos are not permitted (Leiper, 1989). Likewise, on the island of St. Martin, casinos have been built on the Dutch side, luring tourists and residents from the French side, and over 90 percent of the patronage of the casino at Taba, just inside Egypt, is Israeli (Felsenstein and Freeman, 1998).

Prostitution often follows large-scale tourism development, and border regions are particularly vulnerable to the growth of sex tourism for many of the same reasons as those described above for gambling—visitors from a neighboring country do not have to venture far into unknown territory to find their pleasures. Also, many frontiers are becoming heavily industrialized, such as in Eastern Europe and northern Mexico. Nonetheless, they are unable to provide adequate employment for the masses of people who flock there from the national interior. This results in many people being driven into menial service occupations, including prostitution. For a variety of reasons, sex tourism along Mexico's northern frontier had become such a popular activity for American visitors by the 1970s that guides were published to direct them (mostly men) to pleasure spots all along the border. In discussing the red light district of Nuevo Loredo, Mexico, one 1973 publication claimed that

> The one entrance and exit is carefully supervised by Nuevo Loredo's finest. Girls come from all over Mexico to work in the four or five nicest places. This is the best on the border ... Most unique and pleasing structurally, both in building and clientele, is the Tamyko, a huge Japanese pagoda with outside patio and fishponds spanned by arched bridges, surrounded on two levels by bedrooms. The girls are almost all between 14 and 18 years old. (West, 1973:73)

Although prostitution is still extant in Mexican border towns, it does not exist to the degree it did between World War II and the 1970s. The activity plays a much smaller part in the frontier economy as more *maquiladoras* (foreign-owned assembly plants) have been built and begun employing a larger portion of the local population. In addition, the emergence of topless bars, increased sexual permissiveness, increased availability of pornographic videos, the fear of AIDS, and the spread of pornography shops and escort services in the United States has decreased the unique selling proposition that the Mexican border towns once possessed (Curtis and Arreola, 1991: 343).

In common with prostitution and gambling, drinking establishments are commonly located at international boundaries. People cross borders to purchase liquor for home use or to spend time drinking in bars and taverns elsewhere. Lower drinking ages, lower liquor taxes, cheaper alcoholic drinks, and longer opening hours all encourage the growth of this borderland activity. Matley (1977:25) termed this phenomenon "alcohol tourism" and argued that, like prostitution, it is of questionable value, since it attracts the worst types of tourists, resulting in drunkenness, public disturbances, violence, and vandalism.

Alcohol tourism becomes a major concern when underage youths travel across borders in search of cheap drinks and bartenders who do not bother to check for identification. All along the U.S.-Mexico border, American teenagers regularly cross to drink, and until quite recently, radio stations in Tucson, Arizona, advertised for Mexican clubs that targeted Arizona teens. Public concern for youth has forced the stations to stop running ads from teen-targeting clubs south of the border, but the bars have learned to sidestep this obstacle by paying students to distribute brochures at school (Bowman, 1994:62).

International Exclaves

Exclaves, or enclaves, are small parts of one country completely surrounded by a neighboring country. Therefore, they can only be accessed from the homeland by traveling over foreign territory. Pene-exclaves are similar but are not completely surrounded by a different state. Nevertheless, they can generally be accessed by wheeled traffic only through foreign territory (figure 13.1). These unusual political outliers are generally located within one or two kilometers of the boundary between home and host states, are usually very small in size, and normally have a small population base. More than 100 of these unique communities exist throughout the world in Western Europe, North America, Asia, and the Middle East (Catudal, 1979). Most enclaves in Western Europe and North America have become reliant on tourism as a primary form of economic development. Table 13.2 provides key characteristics of seven exclaves and the types of tourism that have developed.

Regardless of the specific attraction bases described in table 13.2, the primary charm of all enclaves is their unique political situations and small size. With the exception of Point Roberts, most exclaves have been traditionally known for their open frontiers and lack of border formalities. These conditions have led to the development of activities such as shopping and gambling where laws are less restrictive or taxes and prices are lower in the home country than in the host country. According to official sources from within the enclaves, with the exception of the Northwest Angle, the large majority of visitors are from the host countries, which appears to imply that the association of traveling abroad with intrigue can be realized for residents

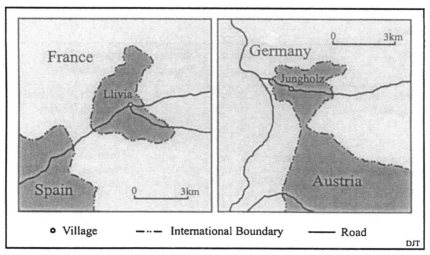

Source: Timothy, 2001.

Figure 13.1. Examples of an Exclave (Llivia, Spain) and Pene-Exclave (Jungholz, Austria)

of the host country without having to pass through the intimidating frontier formalities that are typically required when traveling abroad (Timothy, 1996).

Tens of thousands of people visit the enclaves of Europe and North America every year and have a significant economic impact. In fact, tourism accounts for between 25 and 95 percent of the workforce and a significant proportion of the infrastructure of each community (Catudal, 1979; Timothy, 1996). However, despite the apparent successes, developing tourism has not been easy. These communities face several unique obstacles that are not commonly confronted by most destinations; these include physical inaccessibility, political isolation, small size, and irregular provision of services. Physical inaccessibility, owing to high mountains or large water bodies, has created difficult conditions in several enclaves such as Campione, Llivia, Jungholz, and the Northwest Angle. Political isolation means that the outliers are politically dependent upon the will of the enclaving state in allowing public services, transport of goods, and flow of people between the home state and enclave over host state territory. Small size hinders the growth of transportation centers and other infrastructure developments and limits the range of natural and cultural resources that can be utilized for tourism. Difficulties also arise in the provision of public services. Agreements have to be reached between home and host states regarding which of them will provide utilities, roads, and postal services. In some cases, it is the host state that provides

Table 13.2. Characteristics of Tourism-Oriented Exclaves in Europe and North America

Exclave	Enclaving Country	Size in Area	Approx. Population	Primary Tourist Attraction(s)
Baarle Hertog (Belgium)	Netherlands	7.25 km^2	8,000	Small size, political situation, historic buildings, market
Büsingen (Germany)	Switzerland	7.62 km^2	900	Small size, political situation, historic church, restaurants
Campione (Italy)	Switzerland	2.60 km^2	2,400	Small size, political situation, gambling, historic buildings, art
Jungholz (Austria)	Germany	6.89 km^2	1,000	Small size, political situation, skiing, mountain hiking
Llivia (Spain)	France	12.87 km^2	900	Small size, political situation, skiing, museums, festivals, spas
Northwest Angle (U.S.A.)	Canada	83.00 km^2	70	Small size, political situation, fishing, hunting, winter sports
Point Roberts (U.S.A.)	Canada	39.50 km^2	450	Small size, political situation, shopping, boating, summer homes

Source: Catudal, 1979; Timothy, 1996.

most services, while in others, the home state is responsible but must seek permission from the enclaving nation to divert electricity and water through its sovereign territory (Timothy, 1996).

International Parks

Owing to improvements in international relations, there has been a significant growth in numbers of international parks that lie across or adjacent to political boundaries. In borderlands where natural and cultural heritage are worthy of conservation, international parks have been established since the early 1900s. Most have been designated international by virtue of the fact that two or sometimes three national parks or other protected areas meet at an international boundary. Denisiuk et al. (1997) and Thorsell and Harrison (1990) identified over seventy borderland parks and nature reserves throughout the world.

Poland and Czechoslovakia originated the concept of international cooperation for the development of frontier parks. In 1925, the two countries signed an agreement that eventually cleared the way for the establishment of three international parks between 1948 and 1967. In 1932, legislation in the United States and Canada established the Waterton-Glacier International Peace Park. This connected Waterton Lakes National Park, Canada, to Glacier National Park, U.S.A., with the goal of promoting peace between neighbors and conserving the natural environment on both sides of the border. These early endeavors set the precedence for the establishment of dozens more international parks during the twentieth century, and many more are currently in the creation process or still in the negotiation phases (Timothy, 2000) (figure 13.2).

International borders are ideal locations for parks and protected lands because their attributes, being on the national periphery, are in most cases remote, sparsely populated, and underdeveloped. According to Young and Rabb (1992), the old frontier zones of Eastern Europe contain some of Europe's most fascinating and undisturbed natural scenery and wildlife, and efforts are underway to create international parks in that region. Many of Central and Eastern Europe's parks already exist along national frontiers (Denisiuk et al., 1997), and according to Westing (1993), several hundred of the nearly 7,000 protected natural areas that existed in the mid-1990s worldwide are either adjacent to, or very near, national boundaries.

Just as national parks are one of the most important types of tourist destination in the world, by extension, international parks have become important global destinations. Places such as Waterton-Glacier, Iguazu Falls, and Maasai Mara-Serengeti attract millions of tourists every year on their own accord (Timothy, 2000). Other lesser-known international parks are more prominent as destinations for domestic tourists and foreign visitors from countries within a region, or as ancillary attractions for global tourists who are already visiting an area for other purposes. This second type is the most common, as only a few have major international acclaim.

To demonstrate the magnitude of tourism, table 13.3 shows annual visitor numbers at three international parks in North America. Waterton-Glacier is one of the most important tourist destinations in the North American

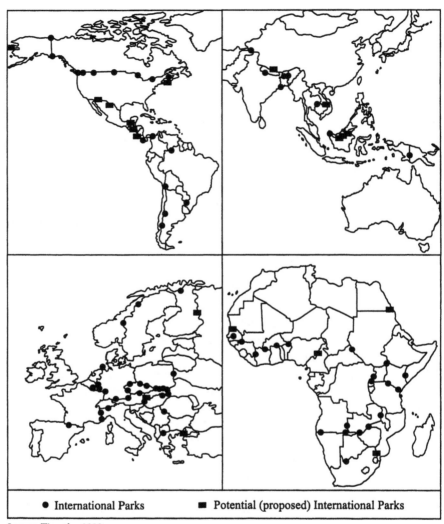

● International Parks   ■ Potential (proposed) International Parks

Source: Timothy, 2000

Figure 13.2. Locations of International Parks

mountain west, attracting around two million visitors per year to the U.S. side and nearly 400,000 to the Canadian side each year. Consistently, more than 200,000 people visit the International Peace Garden each year, primarily from the American Midwest and Canadian prairies. The Garden is especially popular among young people for its music and athletic camps, which attract

Table 13.3. Tourist Numbers at Three International Parks

Year	Number of Tourists	Year	Number of Tourists
Waterton-Glacier International Peace Park*			
Waterton		Glacier	
1985	n/a**	1985	1,580,620
1986	n/a	1986	1,579,191
1987	n/a	1987	1,660,737
1988	n/a	1988	1,817,733
1989	338,157	1989	1,821,523
1990	353,908	1990	1,987,000
1991	344,028	1991	2,096,966
1992	345,662	1992	2,199,767
1993	344,453	1993	2,141,704
1994	389,510	1994	2,152,989
1995	364,740	1995	1,839,518
1996	346,574	1996	1,720,576
1997	370,733	1997	1,708,877
International Peace Garden			
1985	177,300	1992	209,345
1986	183,600	1993	215,625
1987	187,400	1994	222,093
1988	186,000	1995	218,036
1989	191,580	1996	211,495
1990	197,327	1997	205,151
1991	203,247		
Roosevelt Campobello International Park			
1985	131,477	1992	138,950
1986	148,678	1993	135,842
1987	153,939	1994	132,551
1988	160,369	1995	122,682
1989	162,881	1996	111,431
1990	144,678	1997	121,530
1991	151,327		

* Each park enumerates visitors separately and some people are counted twice since they visit both sides of the park.
** Prior to 1989, a different counting system was used in Waterton Lakes N.P.
Source: Personal communication with superintendents at Waterton Lakes National Park, Glacier National Park, International Peace Garden, and Roosevelt Campobello International Park.

youth from many countries every summer. Visitor numbers at Roosevelt Campobello International Park range from 110,000 to 150,000 annually. Most visitors are from the eastern United States and Canada, although many come from other parts of North America and overseas.

When relations are good between neighbors, crossing from one side of an international park to the other can generally be accomplished rather easily. This has the potential to bring economic benefits to both sides of the border and allow visitors to view the local ecosystem more holistically. For some tourists, seeing the attraction from both sides of the border, and even experiencing the border itself can be a highlight of the visit (Timothy, 1995). Usually, passage between sides requires frontier formalities, but in some cases, crossing the border goes unhindered and unregulated within the parks (e.g., the International Peace Garden).

Other Attractions

As mentioned earlier, border markers are themselves very often primary tourist attractions. Examples include the border gate between Macau and China and the Berlin Wall, parts of which are still being conserved in several forms for tourism purposes. Additionally, many other types of tourist attractions that are not directly a consequence of the existence of a border are also present in border regions (Butler, 1996; Boyd, 1999; Timothy, 1995, 2001; Paasi and Raivo, 1998).

Several well-known beaches are bisected by international boundaries, including the eastern end of the Gulf of Aqaba, where a 20 kilometer stretch of attractive seashore is divided between Egypt, Israel, and Jordan (*Economist*, 1995). Historic sites also exist in several borderland locations. Preah Vihear, for instance, is an ancient temple complex located just a few hundred meters inside Cambodia near the border with Thailand. It is one of the best examples of Khmer architecture and one of the most impressive temples in Southeast Asia. It is also a significant tourist attraction, although visitation levels vary dramatically according to the intensity of political unrest in the region (St. John, 1994). Likewise, nature-based tourism is common in border regions, largely due to their typically peripheral locations. Rain forests along the Costa Rica-Panama and Uganda-Democratic Republic of Congo borders are acclaimed areas for ecotourism and various other forms of nature travel. While these tourism types are not necessarily a result of their proximity to an international border, they are influenced by it.

Competition, Complementarity, and Cooperation

Rapid geopolitical changes during the past two decades have created borders that are easier to cross and regions that are more integrated economically and politically, thus allowing the development of the types of tourism described above. Owing to these changes, borders are becoming viewed more as lines of integration and harmony than lines of military defense and contention (Gradus, 1994; Krakover, 1997; Minghi, 1991). The European Union (EU) is an excellent example of this, where frontiers can be traversed easily without formalities and without the trade restrictions typically associated with border crossings.

These political changes have facilitated the growth of local-level international regions, where cooperation exists between communities on two sides of a boundary in matters of social exchanges, environmental protection, and economic development, including tourism. Such local endeavors are important because, as Hansen (1983:260) suggested, it is "local and regional cooperative efforts that typically have led, rather than followed, those between national governments." Likewise, Leimgruber (1989:57) recognized that "cooperation on a local scale on matters such as touristic promotion or public services . . . effectively contributes to reduce the separative role of the boundary; the common problems in a peripheral region prevail over nationalist considerations."

Perhaps one of the best illustrations of this phenomenon is the establishment of cross-border regions within the European Union since the late 1980s, the aims of which have been to solve the traditional problems of border areas, such as underdevelopment, and to contribute to the decrease in regional disparities (Bertram, 1998:215) in preparation for EU integration. These areas, known as Euroregions, are voluntary associations of border region governments that base their transboundary activities on specific technical, economic, and sociopolitical issues (Scott, 1998:608).

Similarly, the European Commission's "Interreg" programs have been instrumental in boosting the economic development of Europe's borderlands, based on concepts of local-level international cooperation. These programs aim to prepare border regions for the introduction of the single market, terminate economic and social isolation of border regions through direct problem-solving measures, and promote transboundary cooperation and networking (Scott, 1998:607). Some of the objectives of the Interreg programs have included tourism initiatives, such as in the Swiss-French and Swiss-Italian borderlands (Leimgruber, 1998).

Competitiveness in economic development on a broad regional level has traditionally referred to situations where neighboring countries or partners offer similar goods and services so that they are thus competing for the same market base (Imada et al., 1991). On the other hand, complementarity usually refers to conditions where neighboring states or regions offer different products and services, creating a symbiotic or complementary trade relationship (Perry, 1991).

In terms of regional tourism, similar conditions exist when political boundaries function primarily as barriers, usually resulting in a lack of cooperative arrangements. Regional tourism tends to be competitive rather than complementary because the industry in each country is essentially self-contained, and each functions as an individual destination (Hussey, 1991). However, it is argued here that, for some types of borderlands tourism, this view of tourism and trade is economically inadequate, for these regions are unique in this regard, and the concepts are sometimes reversed. Two principal variables determine whether border tourism is competitive or complementary—the nature of the primary attraction and the level of cooperation that exists between sides.

In the case of enclaves and international parks, complementarity exists because the attraction base is similar on both sides of the frontier—complementary because the two sides, working together, can create a local-level international destination, much in the same way that Euroregions have developed in Europe. Competition dominates when borders create distinct differences in political and social systems that spur activities such as shopping, gambling, and prostitution. This situation is competitive in the sense that communities on one side lure visitors across the border, while the other side battles to keep them from crossing. However, competition can also increase when one side becomes aggressive by adding the same type of attraction that already exists beyond the border, particularly in the case of gambling and shopping. For example, in an effort to provide employment and tax dollars in economically depressed Canadian border towns, strict Ontario anti-gaming laws were relaxed in 1994 to allow the development of casinos adjacent to popular American border crossings in important gateway and tourist communities such as Windsor and Niagara Falls (Smith and Hinch, 1996). Their primary purpose is, of course, to attract American spending across the border. These efforts have so far been successful, thus increasing pressure on their U.S. urban counterparts to respond by opening up comparable establishments on their side of the border to keep Americans home and bring Canadians in (Eadington, 1996; Nieves, 1996).

The second factor in determining levels of competition and complementarity is cross-border partnership. Private and public cross-border initiatives have become more commonplace today than ever before (Church and Reid, 1996; Hussey, 1991; Leimgruber, 1998; Scott, 1998), and several benefits have been identified in the realm of tourism (Timothy, 2000). Cross-boundary partnership is particularly important when natural and cultural resources lie across or adjacent to national frontiers, because it can help prevent the overutilization of resources and eliminate some of the economic, social, and environmental inequities that are common on opposite sides of a border. It also helps decrease the costly and unnecessary duplication of facilities, services, and infrastructure. Marketing and promotion can benefit in terms of efficiency with jointly published promotional materials and broadcast media that are cost effective and reach a wider audience. Finally, tolerance and understanding between administrative personnel and business people may be improved through transfrontier networking. While several authors have highlighted some of the potential negative effects of cross-border cooperation, such as political opportunism, bureaucratization of partnership processes, and reinforcement of existing power structures (Church and Reid, 1996; Scott, 1998), the potential benefits are numerous.

However, these kinds of joint efforts do not go unchallenged. Cultural and administrative differences can produce significant divisions between neighboring regions and it can be difficult to produce results that are agreeable to both parties (Blatter, 1997; Saint-Germain, 1995), primarily because participating nations may feel that they have to give up some degree of sovereignty to compromise in a cooperative agreement (Blake, 1994). Border formalities can hinder the free flow of goods, services, and people between countries, thus dampening personnel exchange efforts and collaborative agreements (Steffens, 1994). Additionally, different levels of development on opposite sides of a border also make negotiations on an equal footing difficult, especially when many less-developed countries are more concerned with domestic problems, such as poverty and unemployment, than they are with international collaborative issues (Timothy, 2000). Finally, peripherality leads to the marginalization of border regions as well as of residents' concerns during policy development. Sometimes, national polices are completely at odds with border needs and priorities (Ingram et al., 1994).

Based on the foundations of Martinez's (1994) work, Timothy (1999a) introduced a five-part typology of levels of cross-border partnerships in tourism that exist in various situations throughout the world: *alienation, coexistence, cooperation, collaboration,* and *integration.* Alienation, he sug-

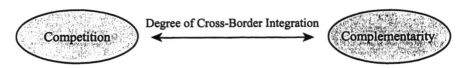

Figure 13.3. Competition-Complementarity in the Borderlands

gests, means that no partnerships exist between contiguous nations, because political relations are so strained and cultural differences so vast that joint efforts are neither feasible nor possible. Coexistence denotes minimal levels of partnership. In this case, neighboring nations tolerate each other but exist without much harmony. Cooperation is characterized by nascent efforts to solve common problems, primarily in terms of illegal migration and resource use. Collaboration is found in regions where transnational relations are stable and joint efforts are well established. Partners actively seek to effect changes together on issues of development and agree to some level of equity in their relationship. Finally, integration exists when border-related impediments are eliminated and both sides are functionally united.

Figure 13.3 highlights a dynamic relationship between complementarity and competition. As the degree of transfrontier partnership increases along the alienation-integration continuum, so will the level of complementarity to the extent that even the competitive activities mentioned above could potentially become integrated if both sides adopt them, or dissolved if the activity is disallowed altogether, on both sides. While few examples exist of integration where vices and shopping dominate the tourism base, several cases that illustrate a shift from competitive to complementary have been documented.

For example, with the normalization of relations between the Soviet Union and China after years of hostilities, their common boundary was opened up to trade in 1988—an action that permitted the growth of cross-border tourism. That same year, the cities of Heihe (China) and Blagoveshchensk (USSR, now Russia), located on opposite banks of the Amur River, began to establish local-level international relations. As a result, an exchange of tourists for one-day excursions was initiated giving residents on both sides the opportunity to travel abroad for the first time (Vardomsky, 1992; Zhao, 1994). To avoid problems related to foreign currency exchange, which was still strictly controlled by both governments, special arrangements were made allowing each side to receive the same number of tourists as its counterpart, usually in the range of 200 people a day, and provided the same services of comparable quality, including sightseeing, food, and accommodations (Zhao, 1994). Each party charged the participants from its own country for the cost of hosting groups from across the border, thereby eliminating the need for travelers to deal with foreign currencies (Zhenge, 1993). In 1988, each city sent 520 people across the border. In 1989, this increased to 8,000, and in 1992, the number had grown to 49,000 (Zhao, 1994).

Initially, tourists from both countries only did sightseeing on these day trips, involving a small amount of shopping using goods from their own countries as the medium of exchange. However, with the collapse of the USSR, civilian trade between Russia and China developed rapidly. Cheaper prices south of the river began attracting larger numbers of Russian shoppers and an influx of western products began luring more Heihe residents to Blagoveshchensk (Zhenge, 1993). As the phenomenon developed, tourism began to center less on sightseeing than on the exchange of goods, although sightseeing was still important, because the curiosity factor still existed. Chinese travelers carried their goods across to trade for Russian commodities, and vice versa.

As news of the two cities' success spread, several other twin border towns in the region began to institute similar exchanges, and tourists from the interior also became involved (Zhao, 1994). On the Heihe side of the river, Chinese travelers from further inland purchased cigarette lighters, cosmetics, jackets, clothing, and other goods that were popular among Russians. These things were then exchanged for Russian goods, such as furs, watches, and leather products, when they went sightseeing in Blagoveshchensk the next day (Zhenge, 1993:71). Although this unique form of tourism has seen its share of challenges in the mid and late 1990s, it is still important in the region (Gengxin, 1997), and it has changed the image of China's Heilongjiang Province from that of an underdeveloped and peripheral region to one of growing prosperity and international cooperation.

Another example of similar success is found between Israel and Jordan, where a 1994 peace treaty has stimulated the growth of extensive cross-border cooperation, much of which focuses on tourism. Partnership between the two countries is increasing, and dozens of programs for joint efforts have been recommended for tourism development (Government of Israel, 1996; Gradus, 1994). These projects, when implemented, will increase complementarity in a region that has heretofore been notorious for its contentious and competitive history. Recommendations include the expansion of the existing Aqaba airport into a common airport serving both countries, since there is more available land on the Jordanian side of the border. New terminals, a new runway, and dual customs facilities are under consideration (Roberts,

1995), and plans are underway to promote the Israeli-Jordanian borderlands as a joint tourist destination (Kliot, 1996).

Similar conditions exist along the U.S.-Mexico border, where there is talk of building a new airport astride the international border where San Diego and Tijuana meet (Christian Science Monitor, 1991). Furthermore, the two cities are so interconnected and such an integral part of the same region that promotional efforts in each community are usually carried out with the other city in mind. For example, much of the tourism literature for San Diego includes information about, and tries to promote visits to, Tijuana (Modler and Boisclair, 1995).

Figure 13.3 also suggests that the journey from competition to complementarity is a dynamic process, that must take into account the possibility of regression toward alienation, as has happened recently along the U.S.-Canada border. Despite years of negotiations between the United States, Canada, and Mexico to establish the North American Free Trade Agreement (NAFTA)—supposed to improve trade relations and allow for freer passage of citizens between member nations—the United States recently enacted a new law that has hurt U.S.-Canadian relations.

The 1997 Illegal Immigration Reform and Immigrant Responsibility Act, which is part of a crackdown on illegal entry into the United States, will, among other things, require the documentation of every non-U.S. citizen entering and leaving the country. To the dismay of its neighbors to the north, the U.S. law in its present form will apply to the nearly 100 million annual trips made by Canadians to the United States as well. Considerations are under way to install an automated system that can check travel documents of every person entering and leaving the country, and separate lanes are being planned for U.S. and non-U.S. citizens. Canadians fear that this will require them to obtain visas, and observers predict that the new measures will create massive traffic jams stretching for tens of kilometers at the busiest border crossings (McKenna, 1997). This action on the part of the U.S. Congress will most likely result in fewer Canadians crossing the border for all types of travel, and the border, which was supposed to become a line of integration under the tenets of NAFTA, will clearly become even more of a barrier if and when the legislation is operationalized. Members of congress from U.S. border states and Canadian diplomats are fighting the new law and are seeking an exemption for Canadians.

Conclusion

From a regional economic perspective, complementarity applies to situations where countries or regions provide products and services different from those of their neighbors. Competition refers to the provision of similar products and services by neighboring regions so that they are both competing for the same market base. However, this chapter has argued that such a traditional approach to regional economics is inadequate for some types of borderlands tourism. Instead, the nature of the attraction base and the level of cooperation between sides determine whether or not a specific border region is complementary or competitive.

The nature of political boundaries and the relationships between neighboring countries usually determine the types of tourist attractions that exist in border regions. Tourism types and tourist attractions such as gambling, drinking, prostitution, and shopping are, by nature, competitive, because they compete for potential visitors from the other side, while the other side attempts to dissuade its people from crossing. Borderlands tourism, based on international parks, enclaves, beaches, rain forests, and historic sites, has a greater tendency to be complementary because both sides are more often viewed holistically as one attraction and, where conditions are right, can be planned and developed through bilateral coordinated efforts.

As political changes have swept the planet in recent years, the role of international borders has become more a zone of integration and amity than traditional outposts of military defense and lines of separation between nations. In the realm of tourism, these changes have facilitated an increase in transboundary interaction in information sharing, planning, and development, contributing to greater levels of complementarity in tourism in some border regions. Thus, it is argued that frontier regions can progress from zones of alienation and competition to zones of integration and complementarity as the level of cross-border cooperation increases. Unfortunately, the possibility also exists that relations can sour and result in regression from complementary toward competition.

A symbiotic relationship appears to exist between cross-border cooperation and the change of borders to zones of harmony. While cross-boundary partnership requires some degree of goodwill between neighbors, it can also be a precursor to it. As McNeil (1990:25) argues in the context of parklands, binational cooperation does not have to wait for peaceful conditions, rather it can "precede, lead to, and result in, as well as help to maintain, peace among nations and communities." Tourism is often referred to as the world's peace industry, and since frontier regions are so commonly the venues of contention and wars, tourism in the borderlands has the potential to contribute to peace and harmony between nations.

References

Arreola, D. D., and K. Madsen. 1999. Variability of tourist attraction on an international boundary: Sonora, Mexico border towns. *Visions in Leisure and Business*, 17:19–31.

Asgary, N., G. de Los Santo, V. Vincent, and V. Davila. 1997. The determinants of expenditures by Mexican visitors to the border cities of Texas. *Tourism Economics*, 3:319–328.

Bertram, H. 1998. Double transformation at the eastern border of the EU: The case of the Euroregion pro Europa Viadrina. *GeoJournal*, 44:215–224.

Blake, G. H. 1994. International transboundary collaborative ventures. In W.A. Gallusser ed., *Political Boundaries and Coexistence*. Berne: Peter Lang.

Blatter, J. 1997. Explaining crossborder cooperation: A border-focused and border-external approach. *Journal of Borderlands Studies*, 12:151–174.

Bowman, K. S. 1994. The border as locator and innovator of vice. *Journal of Borderlands Studies*, 9:51–67.

Boyd, S. W. 1999. North-South divide: The role of the border in tourism to Northern Ireland. *Visions in Leisure and Business*, 17:50–71.

Butler, R. W. 1996. The development of tourism in frontier regions: Issues and approaches. In Y. Gradus, and H. Lithwick eds., *Frontiers in Regional Development*. Lanham, MD: Rowman & Littlefield.

Canadian Chamber of Commerce. 1992. *The Cross-Border Shopping Issue*. Ottawa: The Canadian Chamber of Commerce.

Catudal, H. M. 1979. *The Exclave Problem of Western Europe*. Tuscaloosa: University of Alabama Press.

Christaller, W. 1963. Some considerations of tourism in Europe: The peripheral regions-underdeveloped countries—Recreation areas. *Papers of the Regional Science Association*, 12:95–105.

Christian Science Monitor. 1991. US, Mexico propose airport astride border. *Christian Science Monitor*, 2 July, p. 4.

Church, A., and P. Reid. 1996. Urban power, international networks and competition: The example of cross-border cooperation. *Urban Studies*, 33:1297–1318.

Curtis, J. R., and D. D. Arreola. 1991. Zonas de tolerancia on the northern Mexican border. *Geographical Review*, 81:333–346.

Denisiuk, Z., S. Stoyko, and J. Terray. 1997. Experience in cross-border cooperation for national parks and protected areas in Central Europe. In J. G. Nelson, and R. Serafin eds., *National Parks and Protected Areas:*

Keystones to Conservation and Sustainable Development. Berlin: Springer.

Di Matteo, L. 1999. Cross-border trips by Canadians and Americans and the differential impact of the border. *Visions in Leisure and Business,* 17:72–92.

Di Matteo, L., and R. Di Matteo. 1996. An analysis of Canadian cross-border travel. *Annals of Tourism Research,* 23:103–122.

Eadington, W. R. 1996. The legalization of casinos: Policy objectives, regulatory alternatives, and cost/benefit considerations. *Journal of Travel Research,* 34:3–8.

Economist. 1995. X marks our border post. *The Economist,* 16 December, p. 42.

Felsenstein, D., and D. Freeman. 1998. Simulating the impacts of gambling in a tourist location: Some evidence from Israel. *Journal of Travel Research,* 37:145–155.

Gengxin, J. 1997. Heilongjiang achieves gratifying results in border trade. *Heilongjiang Ribao,* 15 May, p. 2.

Government of Israel. 1996. *Programs for Regional Cooperation.* Tel Aviv: Prime Minister's Office.

Gradus, Y. 1994. The Israel-Jordan Rift Valley: A border of cooperation and productive coexistence. In W. A. Gallusser ed., *Political Boundaries and Coexistence.* Bern: Peter Lang.

Hansen, N. 1983. International cooperation in border regions: An overview and research agenda. *International Regional Science Review,* 8:255–270.

Hussey, A. 1991. Regional development and cooperation through ASEAN. *Geographical Review,* 81:87–98.

Imada, P., M. Montes, and S. Naya. 1991. *A Free Trade Area: Implications for ASEAN.* Singapore: Institute of Southeast Asian Studies.

Ingram, H., L. Milich, and R. G. Varady. 1994. Managing transboundary resources: Lessons from Ambos Nogales. *Environment,* 36:6–38.

Kliot, N. 1996. Turning desert into bloom: Israeli-Jordanian peace proposals for the Jordan Rift Valley. *Journal of Borderlands Studies,* 11:1–24.

Krakover, S. 1997. Boundary permeability model applied to Israel, Egypt, and Gaza Strip tri-border area. *Journal of Geopolitics,* 2:28–42.

Leimgruber, W. 1988. Border trade: The boundary as an incentive and an obstacle to shopping trips. *Nordia,* 22:53–60.

Leimgruber, W. 1989. The perception of boundaries: Barriers or invitation to interaction? *Regio Basiliensis,* 30:49–59.

Leimgruber, W. 1998. Defying political boundaries: Transborder tourism in a regional context. *Visions in Leisure and Business,* 17:8–29.

Leiper, N. 1989. Tourism and gambling. *GeoJournal,* 19:269–275.

Lewis, K. 1990. Buying across the border. *Canadian Consumer,* 20:9–14.

Martinez, O. 1994. The dynamics of border interaction: New approaches to border analysis. In C. H. Schofield ed., *World Boundaries, Vol. 1, Global Boundaries.* London: Routledge.

Mathieson, A., and G. Wall. 1982. *Tourism: Economic, Physical and Social Impacts.* London: Longman.

Matley, I. M. 1977. Physical and cultural factors influencing the location of tourism. In E. M. Kelly ed. *Domestic and International Tourism.* Welles-ley, MA: The Institute of Certified Travel Agents.

McKenna, B. 1997. U.S. border law attacked. *The Globe and Mail* (Toronto) 15 October, p. 12.

McNeil, R. J. 1990. International parks for peace. In J. Thorsell ed., *Parks on the Borderline: Experience in Transfrontier Conservation.* Gland, Switzerland: International Union for the Conservation of Nature.

Mikus, W. 1994. Research methods in border studies: Results for Latin America. In W. A. Gallusser ed., *Political Boundaries and Coexistence.* Bern: Peter Lang.

Minghi, J. V. 1999. Borderland "day tourists" from the East: Trieste's transitory shopping fair. *Visions in Leisure and Business,* 17:32–49.

Minghi, J. V. 1991. From conflict to harmony in border landscapes. In D. Rumley and J. V. Minghi eds. *The Geography of Border Landscapes.* London: Routledge.

Modler, H., and M. Boisclair. 1995. Destination guide: San Diego. *Meetings & Conventions,* 30:104–108.

Nieves, E. 1996. Casino envy gnaws at Falls on U.S. side. *New York Times,* 15 December.

Ngamsom, B. 1998. Shopping tourism: A case study of Thailand. In K. S. Chon ed., *Proceedings, Tourism and Hotel Industry in Indo-China and Southeast Asia: Development, Marketing, and Sustainability.* Houston, TX: University of Houston.

Paasi, A., and P. J. Raivo. 1998. Boundaries as barriers and promoters: Con-structing the tourist landscapes of Finnish Karelia. *Visions in Leisure and Business,* 17:30–45.

Patrick, J. M., and W. Renforth. 1996. The effects of the peso devaluation on cross-border retailing. *Journal of Borderlands Studies,* 11:25–41.

Perry, M. 1991. The Singapore growth triangle: State, capital and labour at a new frontier in the world economy. *Singapore Journal of Tropical Geography,* 12:138–151.

Ritchie, K. D. 1993. A spatial analysis of cross-border shopping in southern Ontario. Unpublished undergraduate honor's thesis, Department of Geography, University of Waterloo.

Roberts, J. 1995. Israel and Jordan: Bridges over the borderlands. *Boundary and Security Bulletin*, 2:81–84.

Ryden, K. C. 1993. *Mapping the Invisible Landscape: Folklore, Writing and the Sense of Place*. Iowa City: University of Iowa Press.

Saint-Germain, M. A. 1995. Problems and opportunities for cooperation among public managers on the U.S.-Mexico border. *American Review of Public Administration*, 25:93–117.

Scott, J. W. 1998. Planning cooperation and transboundary regionalism: Implementing policies for European border regions in the German-Polish context. *Environment and Planning C: Government and Policy*, 16:605–624.

Smith, G. J., and T. D. Hinch. 1996. Canadian casinos as tourist attractions: Chasing the pot of gold. *Journal of Travel Research*, 34:37–45.

St John, R. B. 1994. Preah Vihear and the Cambodia-Thailand borderland. *Boundary and Security Bulletin*, 1:64–68.

Statistics Canada. 1986–1998. *Touriscope: International Travel*. Ottawa: Statistic Canada.

Steffens, R. 1994. Bridging the border. *National Parks*, 68: 36–41.

Thorsell, J., and J. Harrison. 1990. Parks that promote peace: A global inventory of transfrontier nature reserves. In J. Thorsell ed., *Parks on the Borderline: Experience in Transfrontier Conservation*. Gland: IUCN.

Timothy, D. J. 1995. Political boundaries and tourism: Borders as tourist attractions. *Tourism Management*, 16:525–532.

———. 1996. Small and isolated: The politics of tourism in international exclaves. *Acta Turistica*, 8:99–115.

———. 1999a. Cross-border partnership in tourism resource management: International parks along the US-Canada border. *Journal of Sustainable Tourism*, 7:182–205.

———. 1999b. Cross-border shopping: Tourism in the Canada-United States borderlands. *Visions in Leisure and Business*, 17:4–18.

———. 2000. Tourism and international parks. In R. W. Butler and S. W. Boyd eds., *Tourism and National Parks: Issues and Implications*. Chichester: Wiley.

———. 2001. *Tourism and Political Boundaries*. London: Routledge.

Timothy, D. J., and R. W. Butler. 1995. Cross-border shopping: A North American perspective. *Annals of Tourism Research*, 22:16–34.

Vardomsky, L. 1992. Blagoveshchensk and Heihe engage in across-the-border cooperation. *Far Eastern Affairs,* 2:81–86.

von Böventer, E. 1969. Walter Christaller's central places and peripheral areas: The central place theory in retrospect. *Journal of Regional Science,* 9:117–124.

Wanhill, S. 1997. Peripheral area tourism: A European perspective. *Progress in Tourism and Hospitality Research,* 3:47–70.

Weigand, K. 1990. Drei Jahrzehnte Einkaufstourismus über die deutsch-dänische Grenze. *Geographische Rundschau,* 42:286–290.

West, R. 1973. Border towns: What to do and where to do it. *Texas Monthly,* 1:62–73.

Westing, A. H. 1993. Building confidence with transfrontier reserves: The global potential. In A. H. Westing ed., *Transfrontier Reserves for Peace and Nature: A Contribution to Human Society.* Nairobi: UNEP.

Young, L., and M. Rabb. 1992. New park on the bloc. *National Parks,* 66:35–40.

Zhao, X. 1994. Barter tourism along the China-Russia border. *Annals of Tourism Research,* 21:401–403.

Zhenge, P. 1993. Trade at the Sino-Russian border. *China Tourism,* 159:70–73.

Chapter 14

Tourism and Culture Clash
in Indian Country

Alan A. Lew and Christina B. Kennedy

> When every effort was made to wipe out our culture and religion, we made
> adjustments to insure that there was an outward showing of compliance.
> We managed to keep our religion and culture going (underground, as it
> were) so we were able to survive the Spaniards. So too are we able to survive
> the tourists and culture they represent.
>
> A member of the Taos Pueblo (Luhan, 1998:145)

For most of the history of European settlement in North America, the frontier has been defined as the border between Anglo-American property ownership and the vast communal lands (often perceived as "unowned") of Native
Americans. The flood of European migrants into what today is the United
States relentlessly pushed the American frontier westward, until, at the end
of the nineteenth century, the American frontier was officially declared no
longer to exist and Native Americans were confined to small tracts of reser-

vation land. Today, however, Native Americans' reservation lands still form a frontier between the dominant American society and nominally sovereign, communally managed Indian nations. This sense of the "old frontier" is especially strong on larger reservations of the American West, which have become popular twentieth century tourist destinations. The major attraction is that many aspects of traditional Native American values and identities have persisted despite five centuries of European efforts to acculturate and assimilate tribes into the conquering society.

The history of Native American relations with Europeans has been characterized by misunderstanding and suffering on both sides. Throughout most of this history, however, the European settler society has dominated and controlled the dialogue between the two groups. Consequently, Native American societies have continually had to respond to initiatives coming from the dominant society. A pattern of dominance, response and frequent misunderstanding continues today.

Although tourism is not often perceived as a means of forced assimilation, it has many of the same affects (Lew, 1999). Native Americans have been an American tourist attraction since the late 1700s, because they *represented* the antithesis of industrializing Euro-American culture. Throughout the years, Native Americans have, at best, tolerated the tourists, since benefits received from tourism were seldom seen to outweigh its negative impacts on Indian culture and traditions. This attitude often has been perceived as one of hostility or ambivalence toward tourists. To understand this situation, it is necessary to examine the relationship between Native American cultures in general and mainstream United States society. The cultural difference between these two groups and how each perceives and treats the other plays a fundamental role in shaping tourism and tourist-related development on Indian reservations.

American Indian Reservations

Whereas the Spanish settlers, in what is today Mexico, Central and South America, tended to intermarry with the native peoples they encountered, the northern European settlers on the eastern seaboard of the United States preferred to keep their distance and form distinct lines of separation. At the time of United States independence from British rule (1776), this line ran approximately down the center of the Appalachian Mountain Range. In 1830, President Andrew Jackson, a former Indian fighter, signed the Indian Removal Act to relocate the eastern tribes to designated Indian Territory west of the Mississippi River (primarily in present-day Oklahoma and North and

South Dakota) (Cohen, 1988:72; Waldman, 1985:183). The relocation originally was supposed to be voluntary. Soon thereafter, however, the U.S. Army
was ordered to force the removal of tribes who stood in the way of non-
Indian settlement (Cadwalader, 1996). The Indian Wars in the mid-1800s
resulted in the near genocide of many native groups (Wishart, 1979). The
official justification for these actions of the U.S. military against Native
Americans, which were denounced by the U.S. Supreme Court, was that force
was necessary to protect non-Indian settlers from the threat of Indian inva-
sions (Snipp, 1994). From the Native American perspective, however, settlers were invading the tribes' traditional homelands, that they were trying
to defend.

The first true reservations were established by the state of California
shortly after the discovery of gold in 1848 brought a huge influx of non-
Indian fortune seekers to the state (Findlay, 1992). These lands were called
"reservations" because they were set aside, or reserved, for exclusive use of
Native Americans. Therefore, they were not available for settlement, as was
the rest of the country. The California solution to the "Indian problem" quickly spread throughout the western United States The mid-1800s was a period
in which, under the self-proclaimed Doctrine of Manifest Destiny, the United
States subjugated Native Americans in the name of westward migration and
the exploitation of the continent's resources (Sears, 1989:125). Through various acts of the U.S. Congress from 1830 to 1960, Indian territories were reduced to isolated reservations. Reservations were then further reduced in size
and number through sale of "surplus land" on reservations to non-Indians
and termination of others (Waldman, 1985; Wilkinson, 1992).

Native American culture was under attack, not only through military
action and reduction of tribal land bases but also through an extensive government policy of forced assimilation as reservations became unofficial "internal colonies" (Snipp, 1994). Indian children were forced to attend
government and church operated boarding schools to "become civilized and
Christianized" (Cadwalader, 1996:26; Waldman, 1985:192). This attempt at
overt acculturation was, however, far from successful. By the 1920s, Native
Americans were the most poverty-stricken culture group in the United States
(Meriam, 1928). By the 1960s, they had the lowest educational levels, the highest unemployment, and the lowest life expectancy of any minority group in
the United States (Brophy and Aberle, 1966). Since the late 1960s, federal
programs have increasingly emphasized administrative independence and
economic self-sufficiency for Native American nations (Smith and Hardy,
1984). Yet even these policies are difficult to implement on reservations.
This is largely the result of inadequate infrastructure on many reservations

(Alcoze, 1999) and a history of exploitation of natural resources by economic interests in the dominant society (Henderson, 1992; Wilkinson, 1992; Churchill, 1994). However, the difficulty of achieving economic self-sufficiency in the terms of mainstream society is also due to continuing cultural differences (Striner, 1968).

Culture Clash on the Reservation Frontier

Indian history and culture have been largely ignored by mainstream American society, except when Native Americans play roles allotted to them by popular culture (Hoxie, 1988; Nilsen, 1999). Most roles considered appropriate for Native Americans have been heavily biased by European perspectives. Assessment of Native American cultures in terms of "economic success" and other off-reservation values uses measures stemming from the dominant American cultural system. Using these measures creates false images of Native Americans, due to the tremendous cultural differences that exist between Native Americans and the dominant society. Some even argue that Indian culture simply can not be understood in Western terms (Martin, 1987:219–20). As an example, the conflicting cultural values between dominant American society and Native American traditional societies in one re-

Table 14.1. Some Competing Values on American Indian Reservations

Traditional American	Dominant American
Indian Values	Cultural Values
Cooperation	Competition
Prestige and Authority Based upon Family, Age, and Religion	Prestige and Authority based upon Political Position, Education, and Economic Wealth
Education from Elders	Education in Schools
Animist Religious Beliefs	Scientific Rationalism
Morality based upon Social Conformity	Morality Based upon Legal Definitions of Good and Bad
Life Organized around Ceremonial Activities	Life Organized around Work Activities
Communal Land Tenure and Management/Development	Fee Simple Land Tenure and Private Property Rights

Source: Lew, Alan A., 1990.

gion of the United States the Southwest are generalized and summarized below.

Table 14.1 reflects an attempt to understand the distinctiveness of American Indian culture in general as it exists within the dominant American system. One should be cautious of stereotyping individuals based on these values as there are many successful American Indian entrepreneurs who have managed to bridge both cultures. For others, however, these cultural differences cause problems. For example, Vogt (1951) found that Navajo veterans of World War II who more successfully adopted Western values were less able to readjust to traditional reservation life than less acculturated veterans. Readjustment was even more difficult for Pueblo Indian veterans from tribes such as the Hopi and Zuni who lacked the warfare tradition of the Navajo and Apache (Adair and Vogt, 1949).

Traditional Native American relationships were egalitarian and land ownership was communal (Spicer, 1940; Thomas, 1950). Formal ownership of property and complex social hierarchies were rare (Vogt, 1951). A parcel of land that was continuously worked and improved by an individual or group was considered to belong to that individual or group (Ezell, 1961:27–8.). If work on the land ceased, it would return to the public domain. Life was closely tied to seasonal agriculture and hunting. These characteristics were shared by all of the tribal groups in the Southwest, despite differences in lifestyle between seminomadic herding tribes and settled agriculturalists. Traditional values continue to play a major role in reservation politics and development experiences. Today, many traditional tribal members tenaciously preserve their language and culture despite continuing pressure to assimilate that comes from the non-Indian controlled mass media and the economic and legal systems of the dominant society (Schoepfle et al., 1984).

Egalitarian and communal relationships minimize interpersonal conflicts. They can also result, however, in a reluctance to enter into competitive situations. It is generally considered improper to be, or to appear to be, more prosperous than one's neighbors or relatives on the reservation. This attitude has a leveling affect on the relative status of family and tribal members. Elders often caution the young to maintain their humility and to share generously with those around them. Prosperous individuals share their wealth freely with other family members. While some may maintain elaborate households in off-reservation cities such as Tuscon or Phoenix, their reservation home is often humble, at least on the outside.

Within the traditional Native American cultural system, behavior oriented toward creating harmony in the present is valued over future intentions. There is a general belief that if the present is in harmony and balance, both socially and spiritually, then the future will correspond accordingly. Problems are seldom addressed with a demonstrated sense of urgency. Tribal meeting agendas move slowly and decisions are unhurried. Enough time is allowed for consideration of viewpoints from each individual in the group. Discussions continue until a consensus is reached, or until the opposition feels it is no longer worthwhile to press its point of view (Kluckohn and Leighton, 1946; Trosper, 1998*)*. Strategic planning models are avoided, because they often require long-term commitments of time and resources that may not demonstrate an immediate benefit. Instead, traditional religious and social practices are relied upon to provide guidance in how to manage natural and community resources for long-term sustainability. In contrast to this approach, the dominant American cultural system is very time conscious—time is money. The efficient use of time and the compartmentalization of time are considered important to successful management. To traditional Native Americans, this sense of urgency and compartmentalization interrupts natural flow, is insensitive, and can be insulting. Decisions that might require a few weeks of deliberation in non-Indian communities may require years of consideration in a traditional American Indian setting.

The family is the basic unit of Southwest Native American society (Joseph et al., 1949). In many instances, families or clans are more important than the tribe. Indeed, family ties have been shown to be more resistant to change than other aspects of tribal culture. Traditionally, actions or changes would not occur until representatives from each family agreed. Beyond the kinship ties, male and female religious societies and clans existed. These were responsible for ceremonial activities (Spicer, 1940; Thompson, 1950). These societies cut across familial lines and acted to integrate the tribal group. Traditionally, each village usually had a designated leader, and many had additional individuals who served on a tribal council of elders (Ezell, 1961:124–127). For the most part, however, Native American social structure was traditionally decentralized (Thompson, 1950). Law was a matter of mutual understanding, with moral persuasion and ostracism serving as dominant sources of social control.

The traditional Native American calendar was organized in keeping with the practices and ceremonies of their religion (Spicer, 1940; Wishart, 1979). Failure to observe religious practices was an extremely serious offense. Despite the loss of many traditional ceremonies in recent decades, ceremonies remain a dominant force that sometimes call off-reservation Indians back to their home for a week or more at a time. Religion provides a deep sense of identity that directly ties the culture to the land and plays a major role in on-reservation business and development decision making. The secular and highly competitive world of American business is often offensive to more traditional Native Americans (Van Otten, 1985; Paul and Van Otten, 1992).

Establishing modern business ventures on reservations inevitably causes some individuals to adopt the classical economic model of competition and materialism. For others, however, the transition from the cooperative, un-hurried lifestyle of reservation to the competitive, high-stress life of modern American society has been extremely difficult. Job training has been one instance where reservations have had to accommodate themselves to federal government programs and the dominant cultural system because of limited alternatives that exist on reservation lands. These training opportunities frequently focus on integrating American Indians into the economic system of the larger U.S. society. Aggressive training programs attempt to overcome the traditional cultural system barriers discussed above. These programs are not always successful and even when they are, the lack of job opportunities forces trainees to seek employment off the reservation.

Frequently, business opportunities are also hindered by tribal political systems. To the outsider, tribal politics may seem cumbersome and compli-cated. This is because of an often less than successful adaptation to secular political institutions imposed by the federal government. These federally imposed tribal governments often compete with traditional, religious institu-tions. Economic development efforts require consideration and approval by several committees and agencies of tribal and federal government. This approach is the antithesis of the relaxed, informal ways of traditionally ordered societies. Many traditional Native Americans are not comfortable with formal government processes characteristic of mainstream American culture. At the same time, non-Indians are often confused by a perceived lack of structure in tribal governance. Today, tribal governance may be characterized as being a blend between the informal, traditional, consen-sual framework and an imposed, secular, representative model. Inherent conflicting values leave much of the political process ill-defined by either system.

In the past, geographic isolation, language barriers, and traditional pat-terns of intercultural contact lessened the acculturation pressures for some tribal groups. While this is changing, it is still true that few American Indians living on reservations regularly work with the non-Indian business commu-nity. Because of their lack of experience and their history of semiisolation, they can be vulnerable to exploitation and manipulation. In some cases, developers and individuals who wish to sell land or partnerships to a tribe have promised them future wealth beyond their dreams if the tribe makes substantial financial investments (Van Otten et al., 1988).

Nonetheless, reservations are less isolated today than they were at any time in the past. Linkages with off-reservation street and utility networks have decreased both isolation and traveling distance from major urban centers. Many tribes have good access to nearby rail lines and interstate freeways that bring large quantities of goods and people both to and from the reservation. This greater accessibility can enhance the economic value of traditional cultural resources as developed through cottage industries and traveler services.

However, American Indian reservations will probably always be the frontiers of American settlement and cultural influence. The existing reservation system in the United States is the result of a long and torturous relationship between American Indians and northern European settlers. Reservations served to isolate Native Americans because the cultural gap between them and European settlers was seen as too great to overcome (Tyler, 1973). The Indian wars of the nineteenth century were essentially ethnic conflicts between the dominant European culture group and the minority American Indian society. Most Indian tribes were relegated to reservations located on land that was considered too isolated or of only marginal use to be of interest to settlers. Indian reservations, therefore, continue to be the last frontier of the dominant American culture that has spread to every remote corner of the forty-eight coterminous states. They are the last place where a distinctly different pre-Columbian culture and attitude toward life and the land exist within the United States. This presents both opportunities and challenges for tourism development.

Tourism and the Noble Savage

Indian reservations in particular hold a fascination for both domestic and international tourists (Laxson, 1991). For the non-Indian domestic tourist, the reservations provide an opportunity to see and experience a culture that is distinctly different from their own, yet also deeply ingrained in American history. Many non-Indians make annual pilgrimages to the more traditional reservations in Arizona and New Mexico to experience dances and festivals. This is especially true of the Hopi villages. For international tourists, the American Southwest holds a special allure as it has come to symbolize all that makes the United States different from the Old World. Germans appear to be especially fascinated by the Southwest and its Native American inhabitants. The French and Japanese are also frequent visitors to the Southwest's reservations.

European fascination with Native Americans has a long history, dating back to colonial times. It was not until the nineteenth century, however, that

American Indians became major tourist attractions. The image of the Native American held by the majority of Americans and Europeans in the nineteenth century was that of the "Noble Savage": dignified, stoic, reserved, honorable, hospitable, and truthful. The Noble Savage image, in fact, closely reflected the finer qualities of civilized European high culture (Billington, 1981:105). These images also reflected the idealization of nature in eighteenth and early nineteenth century romanticism. The natural world was viewed as being an "Eden" free of the sins of civilization. To romantics, Native Americans epitomized mankind as they believed it once existed—in the pure state. During the nineteenth century, however, Euro-American culture was entering the industrial revolution and eighteenth century romanticism was giving way to utilitarianism. Images, experiences, and interpretations of travels in American Indian country reflect this conflict between romanticism and utilitarianism, frequently marking the downfall of the Noble Savage from his pedestal.

Charles August Murray wrote about his 1835 travels among the Pawnee in *Travels in North America* (1839, cited in Miner, 1970). Murray found the Native Americans in the U.S. military forts to reflect the nobility that he sought in every way:

"He manifests no surprise at the most wonderful effects of machinery—is not startled if a twenty-four pounder is fired close to him, and does not evince the slightest curiosity regarding a thousand things that are strange and new to him."

But Murray noticed that "he is acting a part the whole time, and acts it admirably." Unlike many of the visitors to the American Indian lands, Murray went beyond the surface to seek out the "real Indian." One of the major goals of cultural tourism, it has been argued, is to penetrate into the "back region" of a tourist attraction (McCannel, 1976). Murray found that it was necessary to leave the fort setting to see the real Indian. What he found was contrary to the Noble Savage stereotype that he originally held: "at home, the same Indian chatters, jokes and laughs among his companions—frequently indulges in the most licentious conversation; and his curiosity is as unbounded and irresistible as that of any man [or] woman...on earth."

Murray complained of the Pawnee constantly begging for food and "ransacking his provisions." He felt that they did not treat their horses with care and believed that they stole his dog and ate it. He ultimately determined that the American Indian, especially the Pawnee, "was a subject unworthy of a traveler's attention" (Miner, 1970:269). With this conclusion, Murray's disillusioned romanticism reflects a more utilitarian attitude toward Native Americans. Miner (1970) argues that the rising popularity of Darwin's evolutionary theory in the nineteenth century supported the interpretation of

Native Americans as an example, not of the pristine and noble, but rather of a lower level of evolution. Murray was a romantic searching for an ideal and finding only reality. Despite his disappointment, Murray continued to believe that the Noble Savage was out there somewhere, just not among the Pawnee. He continued to idealize Native Americans in his novels although he never did find the archetypal model for his generalizations.

Paradoxically, at the same time that American Indians were being deprived of their land and their culture, they were being celebrated for noble character. This became especially true after the Indian wars came to a close in the latter part of the nineteenth century. One of the most highly acclaimed extravaganzas of this era was Buffalo Bill's Wild West Show (Martin, 1998). In 1883, the former "Indian fighter," Buffalo Bill Cody, began touring with "authentic" Indians and cowboys, showing a fanciful characterization of an uncivilized and untamed West that had already almost entirely disappeared. The show attracted large numbers of tourists and spectators throughout the United States and Europe.

The Santa Fe Railroad Company and the Fred Harvey Company (a hotel developer) were instrumental in bringing the image of the American Indian as the Noble Savage into the twentieth century. In the early 1900s, the Santa Fe Railroad began to promote the attractions of the Southwest as a means of creating a distinct identity for itself as well as boosting travel along its railway line. Famous painters and illustrators were brought in to produce posters and calendar art that were widely distributed throughout the country (Jett, 1990). The Santa Fe Railroad Indian was a "prototype of preindustrial society. Simplicity. Freedom. Nobility. This was the life and culture that inhabited Santa Fe's 'friendly' oasis of the desert Southwest" (McLuhan, 1985:19). Today, these images continue to draw large numbers of tourists to the Indian lands of the Southwest.

The desire to see and experience traditional cultures appears to be a characteristic that is closely associated with industrialized societies (Cohen, 1979; 1988). There are things about industrialized life, especially popular culture, that tend to generate a feeling of alienation toward the world around us. All too frequently, popular culture is wasteful of the environment (Blake, 1979; Jakle and Wilson, 1992) and is often seen as creating placelessness (Relph, 1976), a lack of community, and a feeling of being divorced from traditional moral standards. To see and experience a traditional culture, such as that of many Native Americans who still live on reservations in the Southwest, perhaps provides tourists with both a sense of uniqueness of place and a belief that there are still alternative ways of living.

Whether or not individual Native Americans can possibly live up to the expectations and stereotypes forced upon them may be irrelevant. There are some tourists who, upon visiting a reservation, are disappointed to find that the idealized Noble Savage is less primitive and less noble than they had envisioned. Many more tourists, however, will do their best to make sure that their expectations are actually fulfilled and that their time and money are not wasted. Unfortunately, either way, Indians on reservations frequently must bear the brunt of tourists' desires to mold them to fit a stereotype. Little wonder many Native Americans feel ambivalence toward tourist activities.

The Allure of Southwestern Indian Reservations

Today, Americans Indians continue to be romanticized by the tourism industry (Lew, 1998b) and popular culture in general. The release of the movie *Dances with Wolves* in 1990 generated a major increase in tourism to reservation lands and was made part of the marketing campaign of the state of South Dakota (Lew, 1998a). About the same time, a survey of tourists to Indian country in northern Arizona and New Mexico found that motivations for visiting Native Americans have changed little in the last 150 years (Parker and Lew, 1991). In the survey, over 60 percent of visitors stated that the primary purpose of their trip to the American Southwest was to visit Indian country. (This response increases to 75 percent for group tourists.) Tourists tended to be highly educated (53 percent college graduates), young (51 percent between ages 35 and 49), and wealthy (average expenditures of $40/day/person, excluding accommodations.) The most visited reservations in this study were Navajo, Hopi, Taos, Zuni, and Acoma, and the most important experiences sought can be seen in table 14.2. It is interesting to note that two of the reasons given by tourists for visiting reservations are similar to reasons expressed for visits to back-country wilderness areas: (1) to be in a natural setting, and (2) to enhance personal spiritual values. Wilderness areas, like Indians, have qualities attributed to them lacking in today's cities where most of us live. In fact, it is possible that tourists do not clearly distinguish Native Americans from the reservation lands on which they live. If so, this would mean that, in some instances, tourist perceptions and Native American perceptions overlap. The Native American homelands, which include lands found on some reservations, can be seen as critical in defining Native American culture and identity (Wilkinson, 1992; Green, 1995; Kennedy and Lew, 2000). Tourist identification of tribes with the land on which they reside is especially strong in Arizona. Examples include Hopi village mesas, the waterfalls of the Havasupai, the Navajos with Monument Valley and Canyon de Chelly, and the Apaches with the White Mountains. It

Table 14.2. Reasons for Visiting Northern Arizona and New Mexico Indian Reservations

Reason for Visiting Reservation	% responding "Extremely Important"
To see Indians and how they live	75%
To be in natural setting	75%
To have new and different experiences	73%
To develop a deeper understanding of Indian beliefs	72%
To attend Indian ceremonies and dances	63%
To personally communicate with Indians	61%
To enhance personal spiritual values	49%
To buy Indian arts and crafts	46%

N = 464 respondents
Source: Parker and Lew, 1991.

may be argued that any attempt to divorce Native American culture from the natural environments in which it belongs is doomed to be less than successful because it does not fit the larger, popular image of Indians nor, indeed, the image that many Native Americans have of themselves.

The importance of visiting the American Indians in their environment also implies that it is not just Indian culture but the context of that culture as it exists with the land that has true meaning for mainstream culture. To cross onto reservation land is experientially akin to crossing a border into another country. This experience will continue to be meaningful for tourists so long as the Indian reservation continues to maintain a high degree of political sovereignty, cultural integrity, and a lifestyle that emphasizes close ties to the land. As reservations develop in ways taken from mainstream economic models, some of the attraction may be lost.

Like all cultures, Native American cultures are in a continual process of change. It is unrealistic to expect cultures to stand still and become museum displays for "outsiders." The problem with romanticism is that preconceived images cloud reality. This is as true today for tourism in Indian country as it was for Murray in the early nineteenth century. Because of their complex history and relationship to mainstream society, American Indians are perceived in a variety of ways by tourists. Cultural tourism visitors to southwestern reservations tend to fall into three types, based on their orientations and personalities—romantics doomed to disappointment, romantics able to maintain their ideals, and observers of common humanity (see table 14.3).

Table 14.3. Visitor Experiences to American Indian Reservations

1. Romantics doomed to disappointment. These tourists reflect Murray's shattered idealism, where the reality of the American Indian does not confirm their preconceived image.

> "I was actually very disappointed."

> "The Indians we met were sullen and did not seem to be particularly pleased that we were there. Because of that experience and because we had read that the Indians did not always welcome visitors, our initial interest in learning more about Indians turned into a feeling of hesitation, so we left the area much sooner than we had originally planned."

2. Romantics who maintain their romantic ideals. This experience is found among many artists and writers who manage to only see what they want to see. It is typical of the tourist who does not venture "beyond the fort" to actually live with the Indian.

> "I was raised on the Colorado plateau and have always loved Indian country, including its jewelry, spirituality, and way of life."

> "We found the people and the land to be wonderful. It was renewing and revitalizing to be in this area."

3. Observers of common humanity. This type of tourist is able to move beyond the stereotypes that cloud image and reality. They are frequently searching for the common bond of experience that is shared among all people. They are most observant (in their writings) of common and natural behaviors that reflect ways in which American Indians and Euro-American life is the same.

> "I like the fact that the Indians do not change their rules to accommodate tourists. I don't want to be patronized—just allowed to observe their culture."

> "I don't know where we were—small town, gift shop—the Indian lady was very informative, loved to talk about her tribe. Friendly lady, we felt very welcome."

Source: Parker and Lew, 1991.

American Indian Perceptions of Tourists

It should not be surprising that American Indians also hold stereotypes of tourists (Evans-Pritchard, 1989). These stereotypes of Anglo-Americans tend to be similar to those that foreigners hold: outgoing, loud, wealthy, disrespectful, racially prejudiced, always in a hurry, and ignorant of local (in this case American Indian) culture (Kohls, 1979). Sweet (1989) identified several subcategories of tourist stereotypes among the Pueblo Indian tribes of New Mexico. Easterners were seen as the most ignorant and patronizing, holding the most stereotypical Hollywood views of Native Americans and believing that Indians all ride horses, wear buckskins, and hunt buffalo. Texans are considered loud, pushy, boisterous, and wealthy. Hippies (in the 1960s and 1970s) and back-to-the-land environmentalists (in the 1980s and 1990s) are seen as clumsy and a nuisance because they often try to take part in rituals and assume that all Indians eat peyote.

According to Sweet (1989), Indians in the Southwest regard tourists first and foremost as *fools*. The classical fool is someone who is a paradox. He or she is deprecated, despised, ridiculed, and degraded and at the same time valued, tolerated, enjoyed, and privileged. One of the ways that Indians deal with this contradiction, which very much reflects their mixed relationship with the dominant American society, is through play and ridicule. Pueblo dances, which can be major tourist events, sometimes include clowns who make fun of tourists:

> For example, during a 1979 San Juan Pueblo turtle dance, a clown played at being a tourist by borrowing a camera from a tourist and reversing the usual photographic process. The clown became the tourist with the camera while the tourist became the photographed subject. Next, this same clown insisted that a tourist "disco" dance with him in the plaza. After the dance, he convinced another clown to take the role of priest and marry him to his tourist bride. (Sweet, 1989:71)

With time, the tourist can move to the role of "white friend." Pueblo Indians are traditionally very open and cordial to guests and most have developed relationships with white friends who first came as tourists. The tourist must make frequent visits to the pueblo (usually during the dance season) in order to become a friend. Friendship is marked by being invited to one of the all-day feasts that accompany most dances. With additional time, the friend may be allowed and expected to take part in the preparation of food for the ritual feast. The transformation from tourist to friend is accompanied by an erosion of stereotypes. The American Indian's stereotype of the white tourist wanes, as does the tourist's stereotype of the Indian. Both become real people.

Impacts of Tourism on Indian Reservations in Arizona

Like many other rural areas in the United States, where traditional forms of extractive industry have declined in recent decades, tourism has been increasingly looked upon as an option for economic development on many American Indian reservations. Some of the positive impacts that tourism is purported to offer include the following: (1) increased employment opportunities in tourism ventures, (2) development of new businesses to meet tourist needs, (3) preservation of natural environments as tourist attractions and, (4) preservation of cultural traditions as tourist attractions. Among the negative impacts that are often associated with tourism are: (1) tourism jobs tend to be low wage and seasonal, (2) there is a high level of tourist dollar "leakage" out of the local economy, (3) degradation of the natural environment from overuse, and (4) changes in local cultural from external influences (Mathieson and Wall, 1982).

In the following discussion, these issues are discussed and summarized for Arizona under the broad categories of "economic impacts" and "cultural and environmental impacts." Gaming is not included in the discussion.

Economic Impacts

In Arizona, there have been few attempts to estimate the economic impact of reservation tourism. Determining the number of visitors to only one reservation is difficult, let alone to all of the state's twenty-one reservations. A 1993 study claims to have "conservatively" estimated that 1,734,840 tourists visited Arizona's Indian reservations in 1991 (CAR, 1993). It estimated that these visitors spent approximately US$62,500,000 on reservations they visited and an additional $346,968,000 off-reservation. Reportedly, the expenditures generated 1,786 full-time equivalent jobs on the reservations and 9,921 jobs off-reservation in Arizona. As these numbers demonstrate, a persistent complaint of all reservations is that tourists enter the reservation, spend some money on arts and crafts, and then leave. In most instances, visitors are brought in by off-reservation tour companies, stay in off-reservation hotels, and eat in off-reservation restaurants.

Expenditures on reservation arts and crafts can be very high. However, the legal status of Native Americans and, for many, lack of entrepreneurial experience help contribute to a shortage of reservation tourist services— limiting their ability to capture tourists dollars. Only a few tribal members have started businesses that tap the tourism market. Some artisans on the Hopi and other pueblo reservations have been able to make a comfortable living by selling their arts and crafts to tourists. Back-country guides on the Fort Apache and San Carlos reservations make extra income during the hunting and fishing seasons. Some tribal members of the Yavapai-Prescott and Camp Verde reservations make an adequate income in hotel and gaming ventures. Most Arizona Indians, however, are not directly affected by tourism, and for cultural reasons may prefer to keep tourists at arm's length.

Cultural Impacts

Many tribes exhibit a general sense of ambivalence toward tourism on their reservations (Sweet, 1991; Lujan, 1993). They concede that they have attractions that would probably be of great interest to outside visitors, but after a long history of experiencing animosity and disrespect toward their culture and way of life, many prefer to keep these attractions to themselves. As one San Carlos Apache told one of the authors, "Yes we have many potential attractions, but once you let the 'blue-eyes' in they will overrun everything!"

The marketing of American Indian arts to non-Indians is one area of positive contact between the two culture groups. There has long been a strong artisan tradition at the household level in American Indian societies. Many crafts products have lost their primarily utilitarian functions and are today produced for religious and purely artistic purposes (Tschopik, 1940; MacCannell, 1994). These continue to provide an important resource for both individual and group identity. Various tribes promote their artisan tradition to tourists who are interested in high quality Native American products (Deitch, 1977). American Indian culture is also marketed to non-Indians through ceremonial performances and archeological sites. The success of these efforts is evidence of an innate respect for some aspects of American Indian culture by individuals from the dominant American cultural system. The relationship between the two culture groups is probably enhanced by this type of contact. In addition, commercial contacts are often the first, and sometimes only line of person-to-person communication between these two divergent cultural groups. While this communication can help in cross-cultural understanding, the influence of this contact may be overestimated (Mathieson and Wall, 1982:135–7).

On the other hand, tourism is known to have changed traditional arts and crafts of the Southwest, beginning over a century ago when the railroads entered the region (Jett, 1990). Traditional dances and ceremonies have also been commercialized to some extent for off-reservation performances, although those practiced on the reservation are still largely authentic (Hunter, 1994). It is these reservation traditions that Americans Indians are most sensitive about protecting. Sacred places and sacred rituals are increasingly under pressure from tourists who not only wish to see "real" Indian culture but also are increasingly interested in taking part in traditional ceremonies. Pueblo reservations, with their clustered settlements and secretive religious practices, are particularly susceptible to offensive intrusions by tourists (Lew, 1999). Many post signs in an effort to regulate tourist behavior (table 14.4). They are occasionally briefly closed to visitation during religious ceremonies and are sometime closed to tourists for lengthy periods of time because of outsiders who were disrespectful.

Today, some Indians see the New Age "wanna-be" tourists as the latest assault by the white man on their traditional culture (Haederle, 1994). And they are just as likely to put the blame for this assault on those Indians who encourage wanna-bes and allow their entry into sacred places and traditions—typically for a handsome fee. Because of these experiences, there will always be a sense of uneasiness and caution in the way most reservations approach tourism.

The cultural impacts of tourism on reservations should not be overestimated, however. Change is taking place and will always occur and the influences of the mass media, federal government programs, and dominant American social values in general have had a far greater influence on the loss of Indian traditions than has tourism. Nonetheless, tourism plays a significant role because it occurs as a physical invasion of the outside world onto the reservation itself. Tourism can contribute to cultural preservation and

Table 14.4. General Visitor Information for the Hopi Reservation

1. Visitors are welcome but should remember that they are guests of the Hopi, and should act accordingly.

2. Possession of alcohol or drugs anywhere on the reservation is prohibited by Tribal Law.

3. Archeological resources and ruin sites are off-limits to all nontribal members— removal of artifacts is a criminal offense.

4. Photographing, recording, and/or sketching of villages, religious ceremonies, or individuals is strictly prohibited on the reservation unless permission is granted by the village chief or governor.

5. If spending an unusually lengthy period of time in a village, permission must be obtained from the village chief or governor.

6. Drivers are cautioned to obey posted speed limits on the reservation and to watch for livestock on roads and highways, especially at night.

Source: De Mente, Boye, 1988.

economic prosperity, but it can also contribute to the deterioration of cultural traditions and permanent loss of a way of life.

Conclusions

American Indian reservations exhibit many of the characteristics of a frontier border (Ryden, 1993, cited in Timothy, 1995a). They are interfaces between two different "nations" (a terminology commonly used by tribes), where life and livelihood on one side of the reservation border is different from that on the other side. However, because reservations are subterritorial boundaries within the United States, their political boundary only generates secondary interest as a physical entity in and of itself (Timothy, 1995b). In the remote and sparsely populated American West, there is often no indication that one is entering or leaving reservation land except where cultural or physical resources are protected by "no trespassing" and other regulatory signs. The social and cultural differences that exist on the two sides of this boundary, however, are as diverse as those found on either side of any international border and perhaps, in some instances, are even greater. These differences engender distinct cultural landscapes on each reservation, which form the basis for much of their tourism.

Lessons for the study of frontier and boundary tourism on Native American lands center on the role of cultural differentiation more than political separation. That reservations exist at all is due to the mutual incompatibility of American Indian and Euro-American values. Reservations were an interim attempt to deal with the "Indian problem" by allowing the federal government to concentrate Indians and then systematically assimilate them by destroying their traditional culture. This did not work. The vitality of Native American cultures lives on. Despite serious economic hardships and continuing outside pressures, many reservations are able to maintain traditional values while evolving and adjusting to aspects of the contemporary world.

Tourism has become a part of this adjustment as the attraction of traditional Native American values is recognized by increasing numbers of alternative, New Age, and ecotourists. Transition from the world they know into the world of Native Americans is what these tourists seek, and visits to reservations are the best way to experience this. Unfortunately, increased tourism does not relieve the American Indian of the burden of 500 years of stereotyping. When external pressures to fit a stereotype are strong, it becomes especially difficult to define one's own identity (Nilsen, 1999). More than lack of entrepreneurial experience and the constraints the special legal status of reservations place on reservation businesses, this stereotyping may be the single greatest problem of tourism on Native American lands today. Because it is a predominantly one-way process, tourism both continues the acculturation of traditional Indian society (making it more like the dominant society) and stifles the development of Indian culture and self-identity (through ethnic stereotyping). It is no wonder that many American Indians are ambivalent toward tourists and tourism.

When Europeans arrived on the eastern seaboard of North America, they faced a continent-wide frontier that they deemed largely unoccupied and available for settlement. Throughout the nineteenth century, that frontier shrank to the point of virtual nonexistence—at least in popular perception. However, the original continent was *not* unoccupied. The frontier between the dominant American society and indigenous peoples of North America still exists in very real places—on reservations. Tourism is the principal form of contact between these two cultural worlds. It offers opportunities for greater cultural understanding, empathy, and renewal. But the path toward these goals is strewn with a long history of animosity and misunderstanding that needs to be addressed in constructive ways. Most important, this frontier, the reservation system itself, must never be allowed to disappear. As Wilkinson eloquently stated, "Indian societies should be preserved because they are different. This country, with its gray that presses in on us daily, desperately needs differentness. It is the off-shade threads that enrich the fabric of our society and give it richness and beauty" (1992:41).

References

Adair, J. J., and E. Z. Vogt. 1949. Navajo and Zuni veterans: A study of contrasting modes of culture change. *American Anthropologist,* 51:547–561.

Alcoze, T. 1999. Personal conversation, Sept. 16, 1999. Dr. Thom Alcose is an associate professor of forestry at Northern Arizona University.

Blake, P. 1979. *God's Owen Junkyard: The Planned Deterioration of America's Landscape,* 2nd ed. New York: Holt, Rinehart and Winston.

Brophy, W. A., and S. D. Aberle. 1966. *The Indian, America's Unfinished Business.* Norman, OK: University of Oklahoma Press.

Billington, R. A. 1981. *Land of Savagery, Land of Promise: The European Image of the American Frontier in the Nineteenth Century.* New York: W. W. Norton.

Cadwalader, S. L. 1996. Native Americans. *Microsoft Encarta.* Funk Wagnalls Corporation.

The Center for Applied Research (CAR). 1993. The economic and fiscal importance of Indian tribes in Arizona. Prepared for the Arizona Commission of Indian Affairs by CAR, 1738 Wynkoop St., Denver, CO., January 1993.

Churchill, W. 1994. *Indians Are Us? Culture and Genocide in Native North America*. Monroe, Maine: Common Courage Press.

Cohen, E. 1979. A phenomenology of tourist experiences. *Sociology,* 13:179–201.

———. 1988. Authenticity and commoditization in tourism. *Annals of Tourism Research,* 5:371–386.

De Mente, B. 1988. *Visitor's Guide to Arizona's Indian Reservations*. Phoenix, Arizona: Phoenix Books.

Deitch, L. 1989. The impact on tourism on the arts and crafts of the Indians of the southwestern United States. In V. Smith ed., *Hosts and Guests: The Anthropology of Tourism*. Philadelphia PA: University of Pennsylvania Press.

Evans-Pritchard, D. 1989. How "they" see "us": Native American images of tourists. *Annals of Tourism Research,* 16:89–105.

Ezell, P. H. 1961. The Hispanic acculturation of the Gila River Pimas. *American Anthropologist,* 63:1–171.

Findlay, J. M. 1992. An elusive institution: The birth of Indian reservations in Gold Rush California. In G. P. Castille, and R. L. Bee eds., *Perspectives of Federal Indian Policy*. Tuscon: University of Arizona Press..

Haederle, M. 1994. Homage of Hokum?—Wanna-bes are intruding on Native American ritual. *The Arizona Republic,* 14 May 1994, p. B6–B7.

Henderson, M. L. 1992. American Indian reservations: Controlling separate space, creating separate environments. In L. M. Dilsaver, and C. E. Colton eds., *The American Environment: Interpretations of Past Geographies*. Lanham, Md.: Rowman & Littlefield.

Hoxie, F. E. 1984. *A Final Promise: The Campaign to Assimilate the Indians, 1880–1920*. Lincoln, NE: University of Nebraska Press.

———. 1988. The problems of Indian history. *The Social Science Journal,* 25:389–399.

Hunter, G. 1994. What price tourism? In S. Norris ed., *Discovered Country: Tourism and Survival in the American West*. Albuquerque: Stone Ladder Press.

Jakle, J. A., and W. David. 1992. *Derelict Landscapes: The Wasting of America's Built Environment*. Lanham, MD: Rowman & Littlefield.

Jett, S. C. 1990. Culture and tourism in the Navajo country. *Journal of Cultural Geography,* 11:85–107.

Joseph, A., R. B. Spicer, and J. Chesky. 1949. *The Desert People: A Study of the Papago Indians of Arizona.* Chicago: University of Chicago Press.

Kennedy, C. B., and A. A. Lew. 2000. Living on the edge: Defending American Indian reservation lands and culture. In J. R. Gold and G. Revill eds., *Landscapes of Defence.* London: Prentice Hall, pp. 146–167.

Kohls, L. R. 1989. *Survival Kit for Overseas Living.* Chicago: Intercultural Press.

Laxson, Joan. 1991. How "we" see "them": Tourism and Native Americans. *Annals of Tourism Research,* 18:365–391.

Lew, A. A. 1990. Traditional culture and planning culture: Native American reservations in the United States. Paper presented at the Association of Collegiate Schools of Planning, 32nd Annual Meeting, 1–4 November 1990, Austin, Texas.

——. 1998a. American Indian reservation tourism: A survey of resources and practices. In A. A. Lew, and G. Van Otten eds., *Tourism and Gaming on American Indian Lands.* Elmsford, NY: Cognizant Communications Corporation.

——. 1998b. American Indians in state tourism promotional literature. In A. A. Lew, and G. Van Otten eds., *Tourism and Gaming on American Indian Lands.* Elmsford, NY: Cognizant Communications Corporation.

——. Managing tourist space in Pueblo villages of the American southwest. 1999. In T. V. Singh ed., *Tourism Development in Critical Environments.* Elmsford, NY: Cognizant Communications Corporation.

Lujan, C. C. 1998. A sociological view of tourism in an American Indian community: Maintaining cultural integrity at Taos Pueblo. In A. A. Lew, and G. A. Van Otten eds., *Tourism and Gaming on American Indian Lands.* Elmsford, NY: Cognizant Communication Corp. (Republished from *American Indian Culture and Research,* 17:101–120, 1993.)

MacCannell, D. 1976. *The Tourist: A New Theory of the Leisure Class.* New York: Schocken Books.

——. 1994. Tradition's next step. In S. Norris ed., *Discovered Country: Tourism and Survival in the American West.* Albuquerque: University of New Mexico Press.

Martin, B. M. 1998. Return of the native: The big picture for tourism development in Indian country. In A. A. Lew, and G. A. Van Otten eds., *Tourism and Gaming on American Indian Lands.* Elmsford, NY: Cognizant Communication Corp.

Martin, C., ed. 1987. *The American Indian and the Problem of History.* New York: Oxford University Press.

Mathieson, A., and G. Wall. 1982. *Tourism: Economic, Physical and Social Impact.* New York: Longman.

McLuhan, T. C. 1985. *Dream Tracks: The Railroad and the American Indian 1890–1930.* New York: Harry N. Abrams.

Meriam, L. 1928. *The Problem of Indian Administration.* Baltimore: Johns Hopkins Press.

Miner, D. D. 1970. Western travelers in quest of the Indian. In J. F. McDermott ed., *Travelers on the Western Frontier.* Urbana: University of Illinois Press.

Murray, C. A. 1983. *Travels in North America during the years 1834, 1835, and 1836.* London: Bentley and Sons.

Nilsen, R. 1999. Native images. *The Arizona Republic* (14 November): E1, E10.

Parker, T., and A. A. Lew. 1991. Pueblo tourism management. Flagstaff, Arizona: Arizona Hospitality Resource and Research Center, Northern Arizona University.

Paul, A. N., and G. A. Van Otten. 1992. The need for cultural sensitivity in American Indian education. *Excellence in Teaching,* 8:8–11.

Relph, E. 1976. *Place and Placelessness.* London: Pion.

Ryden, K. C. 1993. *Mapping the Invisible Landscape: Folklore, Writing and the Sense of Place.* Iowa City: University of Iowa Press.

Schoepfle, M., M. Burton, and K. Begishe. 1984. Navajo attitudes toward development and change: A unified ethnographic and survey approach to and understanding of their future. *American Anthropologist,* 86:885–904.

Sears, J. F. 1989. *Sacred Places: American Tourist Attractions in the Nineteenth Century.* New York: Oxford University Press.

Smith, K., and D. R. Hardy. 1984. Moving toward self-sufficiency for Indian people, accomplishments 1983–84: An interdepartmental report prepared by the Department of Interior and the Department of Health and Human Services. Washington, D.C.: U.S. Government Printing Office. 1984-421-587-814/15304.

Snipp, M. 1994. The changing political and economic status of the American Indians: From captive nations to internal colonies. In R. Wells Jr. ed., *Native American Resurgence and Renewal: A Reader and Bibliography.* London: Scarecrow Press.

Striner, H. E. 1968. Toward a fundamental program for the training, employment and economic equality of the American Indian. Kalamazoo, MI: Upjohn Institute for Employment Research.

Sweet, J. D. 1989. Burlesquing "the Other" in Pueblo performance. *Journal of Travel Research,* 16:62–75.

——. 1991. "Let 'em loose": Pueblo Indian management of tourism. *American Indian Culture and Research Journal,* 15:59–74.

Thomas, L. 1950. *Culture in Crisis: A Study of the Hopi Indians.* New York: Harper.

Timothy, D. J. 1995a. International boundaries: New frontiers for tourism research. *Progress in Tourism and Hospitality Research,* 1:141–152.

——. 1995b. Political boundaries and tourism: Borders as tourist attractions. *Tourism Management,* 16:525–532.

Trosper, R. 1998. Hunters-gatherers in late modernity: Is survival becoming easier? A paper presented at the Seventh Common Property Conference of the International Association for the Study of Common Property "Crossing Boundaries," June 10–14, 1998, Vancouver, BC.

Tschopik, H. 1940. Navajo basketry: A study of cultural change. *American Anthropologist,* 42:444–462.

Van Otten, G. A. 1985. A geographer's perception of land use planning in Arizona's Native American reservations. *Papers and Proceedings of the Applied Geography Conferences,* 8:307–313.

——. 1992. Economic development on Arizona's Native American reservations. *Journal of Cultural Geography,* 13:1–14.

Van Otten, G. A., A. A. Lew, S. W. Swarts, and M. Swift. 1988. A development feasibility study for San Lucy district. Flagstaff, AZ: Department of Geography and Planning, Northern Arizona University.

Vogt, E. Z. 1951. *Navaho Veterans, A Study of Changing Values.* Papers of the Peabody Museum of American Archeology and Ethnology, Harvard University, Vol. XLI, No. 1; Reports of the Timrock Project Values Series, No. 1.

Waldman, C. 1985. *Atlas of the North American Indian.* New York: Facts on File Publications.

Wilkinson, C. 1992. *The Eagle Bird: Mapping a New West.* New York: Pantheon Books.

Wishart, D. J. 1979. The dispossession of the Pawnee. *Annals of the Association of American Geographers,* 69:382–401.

Chapter 15

The Changing Cultural Geography of the Frontier: National Parks and Wilderness as Frontier Remnant

C. Michael Hall

The notion of frontier is an integral part of the New World cultures of Australia, Canada, New Zealand, and the United States. The frontier was the boundary between wilderness and civilized nature. However, with the "closing of the frontier" in 1890s America and other New World settler societies, the following cultural crisis led to a desire to retain the frontier as a cultural artifact, which became transformed into a recreational and tourism commodity in the form of national parks.

Therefore, this chapter examines the concept of frontier from a cultural perspective and focuses on the manner in which national parks were initially created and have continued to be maintained as a way of saving elements of the frontier for recreational consumption. The chapter first discusses the concept of frontier with reference to the role of the Turner thesis for national cultural identity. The chapter then examines the creation of national parks in New World countries and the role played by tourism and the need to maintain a frontier with nature. The chapter concludes by noting the contemporary cultural symbolism as frontier lands for recreationists and tourists seeking adventure and relationships with commodified nature.

The frontier is the boundary between civilization and wild nature, and in the frontier societies of the New World, the frontier was a moving boundary that symbolized the dominance of mankind over nature. Wilderness is the land beyond the frontier. However, while for much of the history of Western civilization, wilderness has constituted a landscape of fear and loathing, in recent years it has become something not only to be preserved but even an important tourism resource. The national park that conserves wild nature may therefore be interpreted not only as a physical boundary between civilization and wild nature but may also serve as a symbolic reference point to the central role of the frontier in Western society.

To set aside an area of land as wilderness is as representative of cultural values as is the conversion of land to agriculture. Understanding the values of wilderness and its preservation may therefore provide insights into the manner in which national parks constitute representations of the frontier through their use and management. The value of wilderness is not static. The value of a resource alters over time in accordance with changes in the needs and attitudes of society. Ideas of the values of primitive and wild land and the frontier itself have shifted in relation to the changing perceptions of Western culture. Thus, the purpose of this chapter is to examine the role of the frontier as an element in the attractiveness, or otherwise, of wilderness and the role that this may play in contemporary nature-based tourism. The discussion focuses primarily on the American experience of wilderness and the frontier and the contribution this has made to the establishment of national parks and certain outdoor recreation activities, but also relates these developments to other colonial societies' experiences of wilderness.

"The Howling Wilderness"

The early European settlers in North America found themselves confronted by a harsh, forested environment, reminiscent of that of *Beowulf* (Wright, 1957). The forests were regarded as being a haven not for the settlers but for "primitive" Indians, wild animals, and beasts. Michael Wigglesworth (1662 in Adams, 1966:1), a Puritan pioneer of New England, described the New World before him as

A waste and howling wilderness,
Where none inhabited
But hellish fiends, and brutish men
That Devils worshipped

The Puritan attitude toward the forest wilderness set the tone for North American attitudes toward wilderness for the next century, while the biblical notion of a "howling wilderness" is also to be found in early nineteenth century Australian and New Zealand colonist descriptions of their antipodean new worlds (Hall, 1992). To the Puritans and other early settlers, the "howling wilderness" was as much a state of mind as a state of fact. Although the discovery of the New World had initially raised expectations that an earthly paradise did exist, it was soon recognized that any anticipation of a second Eden was unrealistic. The American wilderness was not a paradise. The wilderness was something to be "conquered," "subdued," or "vanquished." If the settlers expected to enjoy an idyllic environment, then it would only be created through their own toil. The pioneers were aware that transforming the wilderness into a pastoral idyll had biblical precedents. To many of the settlers, the conquering of the wilderness was as much a religious as a practical consideration. However, both spiritual and utilitarian attitudes were directed toward similar ends; the creation of a cultivated, well-ordered landscape. As Count Buffon decreed, "wild nature is hideous and dying; it is I, I alone, who can make it agreeable and living" (in Glacken, 1967:663).

Prenineteenth century North Americans perceived the wilderness mainly in terms of two images—the religious and the utilitarian. The religious image of the wilderness was that of a desolate forest inhabited by wild beasts and savages. A wild land that provided a challenge for the religious and a land in which God's kingdom on earth could be created. The utilitarian image of wilderness conveyed the perception of wilderness as wasteland, a land that needed to be cultivated and ordered by civilized man in order to become bountiful and productive. These two images were not mutually exclusive, rather they evolved and blended into a theme still present in contemporary Western perceptions and use of wilderness (e.g., Simmons, 1966; Short, 1991; Hall, 1992) and that laid the foundations for the development of Romantic visions of the land beyond the frontier.

The Romantic Vision

In the intellectual climate created by the romantic movement, wilderness and untamed nature lost much of their repugnance. "It was not that wilderness was any less solitary, mysterious, and chaotic, but rather in the new intellectual context these qualities were coveted" (Nash, 1967:44). Mountains and wilderness that once were landscapes of fear now became panoramas of awe and admiration (Nicholson, 1959; Tuan, 1979; Honour, 1981). As an aesthetic category, the sublime dispelled the notion that beauty in nature was to be found only in the comfortable and well ordered. Although some of the Romantic landscapes, such as the Lake District in England, were actually human modified, they symbolized the spiritual value of wild nature. Nature's roughness and ability to inspire terror and horror came to be seen as a positive value (Pepper, 1984). The association of nature with religion reemerged as an important social and cultural force. The wilderness was prelapsarian, and within the natural theology of this period it was assumed that through the spiritual vision of nature, man could draw closer to God. To the romantics, the New World was perceived as a new Eden in which man could draw close to wild nature. A cult of the primitive developed in which native peoples and the frontiersman, untouched by the civilized hand of European man, became archetypal Romantic heroes. For instance, in the poem *Don Juan,* Lord Byron perceived Daniel Boone as a Romantic hero, not as a conquering pioneer. Contact with wilderness was believed to give man great strength and hardiness and an innate moral superiority over his more civilized counterparts (Honour, 1975), while the wilderness man's erotic prowess allegedly made that of civilized man pale in comparison (Nash, 1967).

The European romantic's perception of nature and of the New World was exported to America where it became adopted by the intelligentsia of the eastern seaboard. A romantic attitude toward the wilderness gradually began to emerge. However, it was a perception held by those who already lived a comfortable urban existence rather than by the pioneer, who only developed an appreciation of the positive virtues of nature and of the wilderness after some of the wild lands were converted into a cultivated or semicultivated landscape. Until this stage was reached, the pioneer was more concerned with survival than with appreciation (Tuan, 1974).

Nature became a manifesto for the transcendental movement and helped to inspire a generation of American artists and men of literature. Emerson's treatise on nature provided a literary counterpart for the paintings of artists such as Thomas Cole, Jasper Francis Cropsey, and Frederic Edwin Church, in which a distinctively American appreciation of nature and wilderness began to develop. As Talbot (1969:14) expressed it, "American landscape painting of the mid-nineteenth century was unique." The virgin frontier that the American wilderness offered the artistic imagination became a subject matter in which the American artist could distinguish himself from his European colleagues. The primeval quality of the landscape was far removed both in space and time from the European landscape in whose vision eighteenth-century American artists had sought to paint. The supposed moral superiority of the frontier primitive and virgin land provided an allegorical setting in which to cast the American landscape, newly set free from the bonds of colonialism. The importance of the early nineteenth century allegorical setting of wilderness cannot be overstated, as it was within this newly emergent set of attitudes that the first desires to preserve wilderness began. Wilderness came to be increasingly recognized as an essential part of the American cultural identity. As the landscape painter Thomas Cole (1836 in Nash, 1970:727, 728) observed, "though American scenery is destitute of many of those circumstances that give value to the European, still it has features, and glorious ones unknown to Europe...the most distinctive, and perhaps the most impressive, characteristic of American scenery is its wildness." It is therefore perhaps of no great surprise that the first callings for the preservation of American nature came from an artist.

In May 1832, George Catlin, a student and painter of the American Indian, arrived at Fort Pierre in what is now South Dakota. Catlin "wanted to capture with brush and pen the grace and beauty of Nature before it was obliterated by the advance of civilization" (Nash, 1970:728). However, at Fort Pierre, he was shocked to discover that only a few days before his arrival, a large party of Sioux Indians had traded fourteen hundred fresh buffalo tongues for a few gallons of whisky. "This profligate waste of lives of these noble and useful animals...fully supports me in the seemingly extravagant predictions that I have made as to their extinction, which I am certain is near at hand" (Catlin, 1968 [1832]:7). Yet Catlin was convinced that "even in the overwhelming march of civilized improvements and refinements do we love to cherish their existence, and laud our efforts to preserve them in their primitive rudeness." The romantic and transcendental influences on Catlin's thought are revealed when he noted: "Such of nature's works are always worthy of our preservation and protection; and the further we become separated... from that pristine wildness and beauty, the more pleasure does the mind of enlightened man feel in recurring to these scenes, when he can have them preserved for his eyes and his mind to dwell upon" (1968 [1832]:7).

Catlin found the waste of animals and humankind to be a "melancholy contemplation," but he found it "splendid" when he imagined that there might be in the future "[by some great protecting policy of government]... a magnificent park," which preserved the animal and the Indian "in their pristine beauty and wildness." "What a beautiful and thrilling specimen for

America to preserve and hold up to the view of her refined citizens and the world, in future ages! A nation's Park, containing man and beast, in all the wild and freshness of their nature's beauty!" Catlin's seminal call for "a nation's park" highlighted the new mood in America toward wilderness. Almost exactly forty years after Catlin's journal entry, President Ulysses S. Grant signed an act establishing Yellowstone Park, creating the institution of which Catlin desired "the reputation of having been the founder" (Catlin, 1968 [1832]:8, 9).

Catlin and the work of other artists helped to change the American perception of the value of wilderness. Indeed, it was in the field of literature that the biggest changes of attitude were occurring—a point of special importance, as the opinions conveyed in the books, journals, and newspapers of the time by writers such as Emerson and Thoreau would have the greatest impact on wilderness appreciation. For example, Emerson was significant in that he influenced American literature and culture to the point whereby the "history of nature" was "speaking through man, not men shaping nature" (Ziff, 1982:12), and therefore helped install wilderness as an integral part of American popular culture. Emerson's *Address Delivered Before the Senior Class in Divinity College, Cambridge* (1838, in Emerson, 1982) was regarded by Oliver Wendell Holmes as the American "intellectual declaration of independence" (in Ziff, 1982:12). Through Emerson and his followers, America developed its own appreciation of primitive frontier lands, distinct from that of Europe, that would result in the creation of an intellectual climate in which wilderness preservation and recreational use could be received with some sympathy by the public.

If Emerson provided the kindling for the establishment of an American wilderness preservation movement, then it was Henry David Thoreau who provided the spark. Inspired by the writings of Emerson, Thoreau continued to expound the transcendental viewpoint of nature in his writings and attracted an even wider audience. Although perhaps better known for his writings in Walden (1968a [1854]), some of the clearest indications of Thoreau's attitude to wilderness and nature are contained in the lecture *Walking*, first composed in 1851. As Nash (1968:10) noted, *Walking* "is crowded with ideas about the significance of the American environment for patriotism, character, and culture." The opening sentence of the address highlighted the new ecological thinking of Thoreau: "I wish to speak a word for nature, for absolute freedom and wildness, as contrasted with a freedom and culture merely civil, to regard man as an inhabitant, or a part and parcel of nature, rather than a member of society" (1968b:10).

In this new intellectual climate, wilderness, the land beyond the frontier, became more and more important. The workings of wild nature, rather than the works of man, came to be seen as perfection. Wilderness, according to Thoreau, provided the spiritual home for the American people, toward which they should draw themselves and away from the gross materialism of the time. Wilderness therefore came to be regarded as much an intellectual experience as a physical entity. The spiritual values of wilderness, identified by Thoreau and the transcendentalists, led to the growth of demands to preserve the wilderness. To Thoreau, "wildness and refinement were not fatal extremes but equally beneficent influences Americans would do well to blend" (Nash, 1967:95). America's future, Thoreau believed, lay in the physical and metaphorical wilderness frontier of the West. "The West of which I speak is but another name for the Wild; and what I have been preparing to say is, that in Wildness is the preservation of the World" (Thoreau, 1968b:11, 12). This was a dictum that provided the inspiration over the next 150 years for the legislative preservation of wilderness.

Romantic Monuments

The transcendentalists provided the intellectual legacy that laid the foundations for the preservation of wilderness in Western society. Americans gradually began to regard wilderness as being worthy of preservation because it was something that was held to be distinctly American and superior to anything that the Old World had to offer. Indeed, the relationship of settler to wilderness was seen as crucial to the formation of national identity.

Both Thoreau and Catlin, two of the main influences in the development of American artistic nationalism, had called for the preservation of natural areas. However, one of the main influences on wilderness preservation was George Perkins Marsh's book *Man and Nature; or, Physical Geography as Modified by Human Action* in 1864 (Marsh, 1965)). Marsh's book contained two main theses. First, when nature is left alone, it is in harmony. Second, mankind impoverishes nature. In an alternative interpretation of Genesis 1:28, Marsh (1965:36) argued that "the earth was given to him for usufruct alone, not for consumption, still less for profligate waste." The intention of Marsh was to demonstrate the need to balance man's use of the natural world. Influenced heavily by his observations in Europe, especially by the example of flooding caused by the clearing of forests in the Alps, Marsh identified major economic as well as romantic arguments for the preservation of nature. In the second edition of *Man and Nature*, which was produced in the same year as the establishment of Yellowstone National Park (1872), Marsh recorded: "It is desirable that some large and easily accessible region of American soil should remain, as far as possible, in its primitive condition, at once a museum for the instruction of the student, a garden for the recreation of the lover of nature, and an asylum where indigenous tree, and humble plant ... and fish and fowl and four-footed beast, may dwell and perpetuate their kind" (in Nash, 1963:7).

Marsh identified America's long-term economic well-being as depending upon the maintenance of her renewable natural resources. However, recognition of the aesthetic or economic conservation dimensions of wilderness preservation were not of themselves sufficient to establish reserves. The first natural area national reservation to be set aside in the United States was the Arkansas Hot Springs in 1832. "It was not scenically important, and was reserved to the government" because the springs "were thought to be valuable in the treatment of certain ailments" (Ise, 1961:13). However, the reservation was not a "park" nor was it a wilderness area, yet like so many of the national parks that would be established, it did have tourism potential. Satisfaction of preservationist ideas would have to wait until 1864, with the creation of a park in the then remote Yosemite Valley in California. The reasons for the creation of Yosemite as a park are relatively obscure. On June 30, 1864, President Lincoln signed a bill granting Yosemite to the state of California as a state park "for public use, resort, and recreation" (Nash, 1963:7).

Yosemite Valley is a spectacular glaciated valley with wild scenery that was compared more than favorably with the European Alps (Jones, 1965). The surrounding Cascade Range was described in 1857 as "mountain scenery in quantity and quality sufficient to make half a dozen Switzerlands," while William Brewer, a member of the California Geological Society described Yosemite Falls as the "crowning glory" of the valley (in Runte, 1979:19). Such views helped to reinforce the notion of American nature and wilderness as a source of national pride. It is therefore no coincidence that, on introducing congressional legislation in 1864 to grant Mariposa Big Trees and Yosemite Valley to the state of California for conservation, Senator John Connes of California assured his colleagues that the lands were "for all public purposes worthless, but ... [they] constitute, perhaps, some of the greatest wonders of the world" (in Runte, 1977:71). Two streams of thought can be identified in Connes's statement. First, that lands would only be reserved if they had no monetary value in terms of timber, mining, grazing, or agriculture. Second, that as nature's monuments, they are part of American culture and contribute substantially to national identity and deserve some form of protection.

Thoreau's metaphor of lumbermen murdering trees was frequently alluded to in response to the desecration of nature's monuments. However, the American democratic ideal also played a prominent part in attempts to prevent further desecration. Thoreau observed that the private game and forest parks of the European aristocracy were unsuited to the needs and ideals of America. "Why should not we, who have renounced the king's authority, have our national preserves, where no villages need be destroyed, in which the bear and the panther ... may still exist ... our forests, not to hold the king's game merely, but to hold and preserve the king himself" (Thoreau 1858:316–317). Similarly. Frederick Law Olmsted (1952 [1865]:21) opposed the "monopoly ... proposed that parks should be established to ensure that natural scenery was available to all the people. One early visitor to the region, Samuel Bowles, recognized that Yosemite might serve as a model for a national system of nature and wilderness reserves (Nash, 1967:107). Indeed, it was with the establishment of what is generally recognized as the world's first national park, Yellowstone in 1872, that the political duty of government to preserve wilderness areas was established not only in the United States but elsewhere in the world as well.

The End of the Frontier:
The Rise of Progressive Conservation

The year 1890 was notable not only for the creation of Yosemite National Park but also for an event that would have far greater impact on the popular consciousness of the United States—the closing of the frontier. The results of the census of 1890 indicated that for the first time, centers of population stretched out across the continental United States. This did not mean that vast, empty spaces did not exist rather it indicated America was becoming increasingly characterized by industrialization and urbanization instead of by the pioneer. For two and a half centuries, "the frontier had been synonymous with the abundance, opportunity, and distinctiveness of the New World" (Nash, 1968:37). With the closing of the frontier, a form of cultural anxiety developed that focused on the need to retain links with the wilderness out of which the American nation had been created. The most eloquent expression of this occurred in the writings of the historian Frederick Jackson Turner (Turner, 1920, 1966).

In Turner's eyes, it was the wilderness that led to the creation of an American people distinct in customs, traditions, and values from the Old World whence they or their ancestors originally came. Wilderness provided for the "perennial rebirth" of the American character. According to Turner writing in 1893, the frontier, "the meeting point between savagery and civilization," was "the line of most rapid and effective Americanization," while the advance of the frontier "meant a steady movement away from the influence of Europe, a steady growth of independence on American lines" (Turner, 1966:2,3,4). The loss of the frontier therefore meant the close of the "first period of American history" and the possibility of losing the "striking characteristics" that American intellect owed to the frontier (Turner, 1966:29, 28).

Turner's frontier thesis struck a receptive chord in American popular culture as well as other "frontier" societies, such as Australia, Canada, and New Zealand. The thesis united traditions of American nationalism noted above with respect to the transcendentalists such as Thoreau and Emerson with popular, almost imperialist, perceptions of the need to conquer the landscape (Cross, 1970; Kearns, 1981). Reaction to the loss of the frontier manifested itself in two ways. First, the rise of progressive conservation, in which the finite nature of America's natural resources was recognized (Hays, 1957, 1959). Second, the reinforcement of the perception of wilderness having cultural and spiritual values for the American people and the consequent rise of what Nash (1966) described as "the wilderness cult," elements of which, it may be argued, are still with us with respect to contemporary nature-based tourism.

The progressive conservation movement represented a "wise use" approach to the management of natural resources, and its conservation motives were economic rather than aesthetic in intent. Hays (1959) saw three agencies as being the product of the movement: the Bureau of Reclamation, the National Park Service, and the United States forest service. However, as Clarke and McCool (1985:35) argued, "of the three, the forest service stands out as the most complete representation of the several concerns and issues that fueled the early conservation movement" in the United States.

Though the forest service was not founded until 1905, momentum for its creation had been building up in the two prior decades. Several bills relating to timber on public land had been introduced from the 1870s onwards, but in 1891 the President was given the power to set aside vast acreages in the public domain as forest reserves (Clarke and McCool, 1985). Both preservationists and progressive conservationists saw the Forests Reserves Act of 1891 as a means to protect wilderness areas. Preservationists, led by John Muir, wanted wilderness to contain no human activity that would be unsympathetic to the primitive nature of a wilderness area. However, progressive conservationists, led by the noted forester Gifford Pinchot and Theodore Roosevelt, wanted forest lands managed on a sustained yield basis and were therefore in favor of timber harvesting, the building of dams for water supplies, and selective mining and grazing, all in the name of conservation.

The first great fact about conservation is that it stands for development. There has been a fundamental misconception that conservation means nothing but the husbanding of resources for future generations. There could be no more serious mistake. Conservation does mean provision for the future, but it means first of all, "the recognition of the right of the present generation to the fullest necessary use of all the resources with which this country is so abundantly blessed. Conservation demands the welfare of the country first, and afterward the welfare of the generations to follow" (Pinchot, 1968 [1910]:9).

Pinchot and the progressive conservationists advocated the "wise" use of natural resources, while the preservationists continued to focus on the aesthetic and spiritual qualities of forest wilderness. As Fernow (1896 in Nash, 1967:137) wrote in *The Forester*, "the main service, the principal object of the forest has nothing to do with beauty or pleasure. It is not, except incidentally, an object of esthetics, but an object of economics." Such a viewpoint was anathema to the preservationists. Muir believed that "government protection should be thrown around every wild grove and forest on the mountains" in order to preserve the "higher" uses of wilderness (in Nash, 1963:9). The problem that faced Muir and that exists to this day is that the existence of high-quality wilderness is incompatible with productive forest management. However, Muir was but one influence on the "discovery" of wilderness in American popular culture. As Nash (1966) recorded, the period around the turn of the century was, par excellence, the time of the "cult of the wilderness."

With the closing of the frontier, many Americans searched for their national identity in the primitive. The romantic and transcendentalist perception of nature was appreciated with renewed vigor, especially by those who lived in the cities of the eastern seaboard. In a reversal of attitudes, the city gradually came to be seen as having a degrading affect on the virtues of American civilization, while wilderness and contact with nature was held as having a regenerative influence on the moral fiber of the American people. The sense of fear and terror, once only associated with nature's wilderness, increasingly came to be associated with the urban wilderness of the sprawling cities and their accompanying alienation (Hays, 1957). As Tuan (1974:111) noted, "the growing appreciation of wilderness, like that of the countryside, was a response to the real and imagined failings of city life."

Turner's frontier hypothesis received much support from Roosevelt, who believed that wilderness promoted "that vigorous manliness for the lack of which in a nation, as in an individual, the possession of no other qualities can possibly atone" (in Nash, 1967:150). The importance of the frontier values was also supported by the creation of hunting clubs such as the Boone and Crockett Club and mountaineering and walking clubs such as the Appalachian Mountain Club and the Sierra Club in the 1880s and 1890s (Jones, 1965; Sax, 1980; Manning, 1984). The wilderness cult represented a nostalgic attempt to regain America's lost past in the wilderness. However, the acclamation of the primitive was also matched by a desire to preserve monuments that had a national historical significance.

With an increased appreciation of the position of wilderness in American culture the Grand Canyon and Yellowstone assumed the mantle of national symbols. At the turn of the century, wilderness and natural landscape preservation became important as many Americans felt the need to retain cherished parts of former environments. Wild scenery enthralled Americans. Elaborate albums and books on wilderness were extremely popular. The success that had eluded Thoreau during his lifetime was reaped by his intellectual inheritor, John Muir, because it was "the context rather than the content of the respective philosophies [that] determined their popularity" (Nash, 1967:160), with the frontier as an essential element in the cultural context of conservation and appreciation of wilderness.

The Frontier in Contemporary Context

The above discussion has highlighted the manner in which ideas of and relations to "the frontier" influenced the overall human-environment relationship in American society and, more particularly, the establishment of national parks and other forms of conservation. In the early twenty first century, the cultural history of the frontier is still extremely important in relation to contemporary tourism activity. Ideas of sustainability and nature-based tourism are extremely influential in terms of tourism policy and development, yet their historical antecedents and the cultural framework within which they occur had already been well established by the turn of the nineteenth century (Hall, 1998). However, the significance of the cultural basis for tourist visitation to frontier and wilderness areas is given relatively little attention in the tourism literature.

A number of themes emerge in the analysis of the values associated with wilderness: experiental, mental and moral restorational, scientific, and economic (e.g., Hendee, Stankey, and Lucas, 1978; Hall and Page, 1999). Experiential values highlight the importance of the "wilderness experience." Given its essentially personal nature, the wilderness experience is extremely difficult to define (Scott, 1974). Nevertheless, aesthetic, spiritual, and escapist values, are related to the cultural geography of the frontier and to strong elements of the "experience" that is commodified for the benefit of wilderness tourists. Indeed, no less a writer than the ecologist Aldo Leopold argued that the opportunity to relive or imagine the experiences of pioneers or the "frontier" that formed national culture—a point reiterated in the Australian context by Hamilton-Smith (1980) and Johnston (1985) among others (also see Hendee et al., 1978; Hall and Page, 1999)—was an essential component of the value of wilderness and wilderness recreation.

Associated with the values of the wilderness experience is the idea that wilderness and contact with the frontier can provide mental and moral restoration for the individual in the face of modern civilization (e.g., Carhart, 1920). This theme values wilderness as a "reservoir for renewal of mind and spirit" and in some cases offers "an important sanctuary into which one can withdraw, either temporarily or permanently, to find respite" (Hendee et al., 1978:12). This theme harks back to the biblical role of wilderness as a place of spiritual renewal (Funk, 1959) and the simple life of Thoreau's *Walden* (Thoreau, 1968a). The encounter with wilderness is regarded in the context of adventure-based activities forcing the individual to rise to the physical challenge of wilderness with corresponding improvements in feelings of self-reliance and self-worth. In this context, one might note the current phenomenon of the popularity of such television series as *Survivor*. As Ovington and Fox (1980:3) wrote: "In the extreme," wilderness

> generates a feeling of absolute aloneness, a feeling of sole dependence on one's own capacities as new sights, smells and tastes are encountered...The challenge and the refreshing and recreating power of the unknown are provided by unadulterated natural wilderness large enough in space for us to get "lost" in. Here it is possible once again to depend upon our own personal faculties and to hone our bodies and spirits. (Ovington and Fox, 1980:3)

In contemporary society, the preservation of wilderness is regarded as an essential component in the scientific study of the environment and mankind's impact on the environment. Furthermore, wilderness has increasingly come to assume tremendous economic importance because of the value of the genetic material that it contains. However, the multidimensional nature of the wilderness resource may lead to value conflicts over the use of wilderness areas. In particular, wilderness has importance as a tourist attraction for frontier communities. Yet while the overt tourism dimensions of frontier and wilderness tourism in relation to such issues as regional development are highlighted in the literature, the cultural underlay has been lost or ignored.

This chapter has sought to emphasize the notion of the frontier as culturally based. National parks and wilderness areas are therefore part of the changing cultural geography of the frontier, without which any discussion of frontier tourism must surely remain incomplete. Importantly for tourism in frontier regions, this chapter has also noted that the intellectual and spatial representation of the frontier is constantly changing. Therefore, any notion as to the future direction of frontier tourism development needs to be related to ideas of cultural change as much as to notions of the economic periphery.

References

Adams, R. L. A. 1966. The demand for wilderness recreation in Algonquin Provincial Park. Unpublished Thesis, Department of Geography, Clark University.

Carhart, A. H. 1920. Recreation in the forests. *American Forests,* 26:268–272.

Catlin, G. 1968. An artist proposes a national park. In R. Nash ed., *The American Environment: Readings in the History of Conservation.* Reading: Addison-Wesley Publishing.

Clarke, J. N., and D. McCool. 1985. *Staking Out the Terrain: Power Differentials among Natural Resource Management Agencies.* Albany: State University of New York Press.

Cross, M. S. 1970. *The Frontier Thesis and the Canadas: The Debate on the Impact of the Canadian Environment.* Toronto: Capp Clark.

Emerson, R. W. 1982. *Ralph Waldo Emerson Selected Essays.* L. Ziff ed. Harmondsworth: Penguin.

Funk, R. W. 1959. The wilderness. *Journal of Biblical Literature,* 78:205–214.

Glacken, C. 1967. *Traces on the Rhodian Shore, Nature and Culture in Western Thought from Ancient Times to the End of the Eighteenth Century.* Berkeley: University of California Press.

Hall, C. M. 1992. *Wasteland to World Heritage: Preserving Australia's Wilderness.* Carlton: Melbourne University Press.

———. 1998. Historical antecedents of sustainable development and ecotourism: New labels on old bottles? In C. M. Hall and A. Lew eds., *Sustainable Tourism Development: Geographical Perspectives.* Harlow: Addison-Wesley Longman.

Hall, C. M., and S. Page. 1999. *The Geography of Tourism and Recreation.* London: Routledge.

Hamilton-Smith, E. 1980. Wilderness: Experience or Land Use. In R. W. Robertson, P. Helman, and A. Davey eds., *Wilderness Management in Australia*. Canberra: School of Applied Science, Canberra College of Advanced Education.

Hays, S. P. 195. *The Response to Industrialism, 1885–1914*. Chicago: University of Chicago Press.

———. 1959. *Conservation and the Gospel of Efficiency: The Progressive Conservation Movement 1890–1920*. Cambridge: Harvard University Press.

Hendee, J. C., G. H. Stankey, and R. C. Lucas. 1978. *Wilderness Management*. Washington, D.C.: U.S. Department of Agriculture, Forest Service.

Honour, H. 1975. *The New Golden Land: European Images of America from the Discoverers to the Present Times*. New York: Pantheon Books.

———. 1981 *Romanticism*. Harmondsworth: Pelican Books.

Ise, J. 1961. *Our National Park Policy A Critical History*. Baltimore: Johns Hopkins Press.

Johnston, S. 1985. The beauty and significance of wild places. *Habitat*, 13:27–28.

Jones, H. R. 1965. *John Muir and the Sierra Club: The Battle for Yosemite*. San Francisco: Sierra Club.

Kearns, G. 1981. Closed space and political practice: Frederick Jackson Turner and Halford Mackinder. Working Paper No. 5. Liverpool: Department of Geography, University of Liverpool.

Leopold, A. 1925. Wilderness as a form of land use. *Journal of Land and Public Utility Economics*, 1:398–404.

Manning, R. E. 1984. Man and mountains meet: *Journal of the Appalachian Mountains Club*, 1876–1984. *Journal of Forest History*, 28: 24–33.

Marsh, G. P. 1965. *Man and Nature; or, Physical Geography as Modified by Human Action*. D. Lowenthal ed. Cambridge: Belknap Press of Harvard University Press.

Nash, R. 1963. The American wilderness in historical perspective. *Journal of Forest History*, 6:2–13.

———. 1966. The American cult of the primitive. *American Quarterly*, 18:517–537.

———. 1967. *Wilderness and the American Mind*. New Haven: Yale University Press.

———. ed., 1968. *The American Environment: Readings in the History of Conservation*. Reading: Addison-Wesley Publishing.

———. 1970. The American invention of national parks. *American Quarterly*, 22:726–735.

Nicholson, M. H. 1962. *Mountain Gloom and Mountain Glory.* New York: Norton.

Olmsted, F. L. 1952, orig. 1865. The Yosemite Valley and the Mariposa Big Tree Grove. *Landscape Architecture,* 43:13–25.

Ovington, J. D., and A. M. Fox 1980. Wilderness—A natural asset. *Parks,* 5:1–4.

Pepper, D. 1984. *The Roots of Modern Environmentalism.* London: Croom Helm.

Pinchot, G. 1968. Ends and means. In R. Nash ed., *The American Environment: Readings in the History of Conservation.* Reading: Addison-Wesley.

Runte, A. 1977. The national park idea: Origins and paradox of the American experience. *Journal of Forest History,* 21:64–75.

——. 1979. *National Parks: The American Experience.* Lincoln: University of Nebraska Press.

Sax, J. L. 1980. *Mountains without Handrails: Reflections on the National Parks.* Ann Arbor: The University of Michigan Press.

Scott, N. R. 1974. Towards a psychology of the wilderness experience. *Natural Resource Journal,* 14:231–237.

Short, J. R. 1991. *Imagined Country: Society, Culture and Environment.* London: Routledge.

Simmons, I. G. 1966. Wilderness in the mid-twentieth century U.S.A. *Town Planning Review,* 36:249–56.

Talbot, W. S. 1969. American visions of wilderness. *The Living Wilderness,* 33:14–25.

Thoreau, H. D. 1858. Chesuncook. *Atlantic Monthly,* 2(August).

——. 1968a. *Walden.* London: Dent.

——. 1968b. The transcendental view. In R. Nash ed., *The American Environment: Readings in the History of Conservation.* Reading: Addison-Wesley Publishing.

Tuan, Y. 1974. *Topophilia: A Study of Environmental Perception, Attitudes, and Values.* Englewood Cliffs: Prentice Hall.

——. 1979. *Landscapes of Fear.* New York: Pantheon.

Turner, F. J. 1920. *The Frontier in American History.* New York: Henry Holt.

——. 1966, orig. 1893. *The Significance of the Frontier in American History.* El Paso: Academic Reprints.

Wright, D. (trans.) 1957. *Beowulf.* Harmondsworth: Penguin.

Ziff, L. 1982. Introduction. In E. Ziff ed., *Ralph Waldo Emerson Selected Essays.* Harmondsworth: The Penguin American Library.

About the Authors

Richard W. Butler is presently Professor of Tourism and deputy head of the School of Management Studies for the Service Sector at the University of Surrey, UK. He previously was affiliated with the University of Western Ontario, where he taught and conducted research on tourism since 1967. He is a past president of the International Academy for the Study of Tourism, and coeditor of *Tourism and Hospitality Research: The Surrey Quarterly Review*. He has published and edited several books on tourism including most recently *Tourism and National Parks* and *Tourism and Recreation in Rural Areas* and has authored and coauthored many articles and chapters on tourism studies and related topics. R.Butler@surrey.ac.uk (March 22, 2001)

Daniel Felsenstein is a senior lecturer in the Department of Geography, the Hebrew University of Jerusalem, Jerusalem, Israel. He specializes in local economic development and impact analysis. His recent research has focused on regional employment impacts of small firms, the local growth effects associated with casino gambling, and estimating local externalities arising from public subsidies. msdfels@mscc.huji.ac.il (August 27, 2001)

Aliza Fleischer is lecturer in the Department of Agricultural Economics and Management at the Hebrew University of Jerusalem, Rehovot, Israel. Her research interests involve the economics of tourism, rural tourism, economic evaluation of open space and landscape, and regional and rural development. fleische@agri.huji.ac.il (September 2, 2001)

Daniel Freeman is a private consultant with Computerized Economic Models, Rehovot, Israel. He specializes in developing regional economic models and conducting economic evaluations. His recent work has dealt with multi-regional input-output analysis of the Israeli tourism sector and with developing an I-O based model for estimating environmental impacts. dfreeman@ netvision.net.il (September 12, 2001)

Tomer Goodovitch is a senior lecturer at the Department of Geography, Tel Aviv University, Tel Aviv, Israel. He serves as an advisor to the mayor of Tel Aviv on urban and transportation policies. Among his interests are land use and location of public facilities and national or regional development policy issues, such as casinos, airports, and public transit. tomer@post.tau.ac.il (May 7, 2001)

Yehuda Gradus is Harry M. Levy Professor of geography and regional planning and the former dean of the Faculty of Humanities and Social Sciences at Ben-Gurion University of the Negev (BGU), Beer Sheva, Israel. He is past president of the Association of Israeli Geographers and served as chairman of the Department of Geography at BGU. Currently Professor Gradus is a member of the city of Beer Sheva Municipal Council and Director of the Negev Center for Regional Development. He has published many journal articles and coauthored or coedited several books, among them: *The Atlas of the Negev, The Land of the Negev, Desert Development, The Industrial Geography of Israel, The Mosaic of Israeli Geographers,* and *Frontiers in Regional Development.* ncrd@bgumail.bgu.ac.il (September 12, 2001)

Sigal Haber is a Ph.D. student in the School of Management, Ben-Gurion University of the Negev, Beer Sheva, Israel. Her thesis focuses on success measures of small tourism ventures, mainly in the rural areas of Israel, as well as on the success factors of these ventures. Her articles were published in the *Journal of Business Venturing* and in the *Annals of Tourism Research.* Until 1996 she served as the head of the marketing research and information unit at the Negev Tourism Development Adminsitration, Israel. m_haber@ inter.net.il (September 12, 2001)

C. Michael Hall is currently based at the Centre for Tourism, University of Otago, Dunedin, New Zealand, as well as being Visiting Professor in Tourism Management at Sheffield Hallam University, School of Leisure and Food Management, in the United Kingdom. He has wide-ranging interests in the geography, public policy, and environmental history of tourism. cmhall@commerce.otago.ac.nz (March 22, 2001)

Christina B. Kennedy is an associate professor of geography and public planning at Northern Arizona University. She teaches cultural geography, rural spatial patterns, and courses dealing with the U.S. landscape. Her research foci and publications range from studies on aesthetics in geography, and use of landscape in film to resource management and Native American issues. tina.kennedy@nau.edu (May 1, 2001)

Shaul Krakover is associate professor at the Department of Geography and Environmental Development, Ben-Gurion University of the Negev, Beer Sheva, Israel. He has been the chairman of the department and currently serves as the president of the Association of Israeli Geographers. He has published many articles in the areas of urban spatial dynamics, urban and regional development, and tourism studies. He coauthored the *Atlas of the Negev* and the *Industrial Geography of Israel*. shaul@bgumail.bgu.ac.il (September 12, 2001)

Elsa Kruger-Cloete of the Development Bank of Southern Africa has a keen interest in sustainable development, particularly in the social, cultural, community and environmental dimensions of development, as well as in knowledge for development. She chaired the Tourism Sector Working Group of the National Research and Technology Foresight. elsak@dbsa.org (September 6, 2001)

Miri Lerner is an assistant professor at the Faculty of Management, The Leon Recanati Graduate School of Business Administration at Tel Aviv University, Tel Aviv, Israel. She has published many papers in the area of entrepreneurship. Her articles appeared in the *Journal of Business Venturing, Journal of Business Research, Social Policy Research, Journal of Small Business Management, Annals of Tourism Research,* and others. She is the head of the Israeli team of researchers of Global Entrepreneurship Monitoring (GEM). lernerm@post.tau.ac.il (September 12, 2001)

Alan A. Lew is a professor of geography and public planning at Northern Arizona University where he teaches urban planning, geography of the United States, and courses in tourism that contribute to a WWW-based Certificate in International Tourism Management. He is the editor of the journal, *Tourism Geographies*, and has edited books on tourism in China, on American Indian lands, and on the geography of sustainable tourism. alan.lew@nau.edu Additional information is available at <www.geog.nau.edu/~alew>. (August 3, 2001)

Naomi Moreno obtained her B.A. in Behavioral Sciences, M.A. in Mass Communications, and Ph.D. in Communications and Politics. She has served as head of the city of Beer-Sheva's Community Service Department and the city's Tourism and Public Information Department. She is currently director of the Business Development Division—WIZO, Israel. dmoreno@ netvision. net.il (March 25, 2001)

Abraham Pizam is interim dean and professor of tourism management in the Rosen School of Hospitality Management, and director of the Dick Pope Sr. Institute for Tourism Studies at the University of Central Florida, Orlando, Florida. Professor Pizam has served as a consultant in more than thirty countries in the field of hospitality and tourism management and has held various academic positions in the United States, United Kingdom, France, Austria, Australia, New Zealand, Singapore, Israel, and Switzerland. He is the author of 135 scientific publications and four books, and is on the editorial staff of twelve academic journals. apizam@mail.ucf.edu (September 4, 2001)

Arie Reichel is professor of management and chairman of the Department of Hotel and Tourism Management in Ben-Gurion University of the Negev, Beer Sheva, Israel. In addition, he is associate dean of the School of Management. He earned his Ph.D. at the University of Massachusetts in Amherst. He also taught at New York University and the New School for Social Research. Professor Reichel serves on the board of advisors to the Israel Ministry of Tourism. arier@nihul.bgu.ac.il (September 2, 2001)

R. B. Singh is a research scientist and professor in the Department of Geography, Delhi School of Economics, University of Delhi, Delhi, India and a full member of IGU Study Group on Land Use and Cover Change; South Asian Representative in Commonwealth Geographical Bureau (1992–2000); Member, ICAR Programme on Indo-Gangetic Plains—Landuse/Cover Change and Comprehensive Food Security. Dr. R. B. Singh has specialized in environmental studies, tourism and environment, remote sensing, GIS technology, and urban and regional development. He has to his credit twenty research volumes and more than 100 research papers. He is founder president of the Environmental Monitoring Society, India, and joint secretary of the National Association of Geographers, India. singhrb@ndf.vsnl.net.in / rbsgeo@hotmail.com (September 12, 2201)

Esther Sultan is director of the Statistics and Database Division, Ministry of Tourism, Jerusalem, Israel.

Dallen J. Timothy is assistant professor at the Department of Recreation Management and Tourism, Arizona State University, Tempe, Arizona. Previously he was an associate professor at Bowling Green State University, Bowling Green, Ohio. He earned his Ph.D. in tourism studies at the University of Waterloo, Canada. Dallen.Timothy@asu.edu (September 2, 2001)

Randall S. Upchurch is an associate professor in the School of Hospitality Management at the University of Central Florida, Orlando, Florida. Dr. Upchurch has twenty-one years of experience in the lodging industry, working for a variety of hotel companies including Hilton, Holiday Inns, and Ramada Inn. As part of his industry tenure, he was responsible for operation management, training and development, marketing, sales, strategic planning, and quality control. In his present position, Dr. Upchurch is actively working with the American Resort Development Association. rupchurc@mail.ucf.edu (September 12, 2001)

Natan Uriely earned his Ph.D. in sociology at the University of Illinois at Chicago. He is currently a lecturer in the Department of Hotel and Tourism Management at Ben-Gurion University of the Negev in Israel. Dr. Uriely specializes in the sociology of tourism and leisure. His articles have appeared in *Annals of Tourism Research, Tourism Management, Sociology of Sport, International Sociology,* and other leading journals. urielyn@bgumail.bgu.ac.il (September 2, 2001)

Index